James Oswald Dykes

From Jerusalem to Antioch

Sketches of the Primitive Church

James Oswald Dykes

From Jerusalem to Antioch
Sketches of the Primitive Church

ISBN/EAN: 9783743370654

Manufactured in Europe, USA, Canada, Australia, Japa

Cover: Foto ©Lupo / pixelio.de

Manufactured and distributed by brebook publishing software (www.brebook.com)

James Oswald Dykes

From Jerusalem to Antioch

FROM

JERUSALEM TO ANTIOCH:

SKETCHES OF THE PRIMITIVE CHURCH.

BY

J. OSWALD DYKES, M.A., D.D.

AUTHOR OF
"THE BEATITUDES OF THE KINGDOM,"
"THE RELATIONS OF THE KINGDOM TO THE WORLD,"
"THE LAWS OF THE KINGDOM."

Ἰουδαίῳ τε πρῶτον καὶ Ἕλληνι.

London:
HODDER AND STOUGHTON,
PATERNOSTER ROW.
1874.

UNWIN BROTHERS, PRINTERS BY WATER POWER.

Preface.

THE first half of this volume has already appeared in the pages of the "Preacher's Lantern." Nor was it quite out of place there, since these chapters had been originally spoken from the pulpit, substantially as they now stand, in the ordinary course of the writer's ministry. It is only right to add that, in preparing them for publication, an effort has been made to remove the traces of spoken address, in order that the flow of an historical narrative may be as little as possible impeded. But of course the standpoint is still that of Christian faith, the end hoped for is still Christian instruction. Therefore it has not been deemed necessary to defend against objectors those miraculous incidents which stud Luke's pages, any more than it is possible for the candid historian to get rid of them. The battle for miracle, however, is not to be fought out over the Book of Acts. He who has been led to accept such stupendous evangelical miracles as the Incarnation and the Resurrection, will hardly find much in the records of the primitive

Church to try his faith. It is not strange if the sweep through human history of the Very God in His own person should have left in its wake a whirl of supranatural commotion, felt even by remote actors, or in ways that look at first sight trivial.

In venturing to prefix to each chapter a "revised version" of the sacred text which is nearly our sole authority, it may be as well to say that I have not presumed to aim at idiomatic elegance (such as any revision of the Authorised Version must retain which is designed to supersede it in popular use), but simply at such a measure of literal accuracy as may enable the English reader to see what support the original affords for the view I take of the events related.

Contents.

		PAGE
I.	Ascension Day	1
II.	Waiting for the Promise	19
III.	Pentecost	39
IV.	The First Gospel Sermon	59
V.	The First Christian Baptism	77
VI.	The Infant Church	95
VII.	St. Peter's Second Apology	115
VIII.	In Collision with the Sanhedrim	137
IX.	Ananias and Sapphira	161
X.	A Second Collision with the Sanhedrim	181
XI.	Hellenist and Hebrew	203
XII.	The Proto-Martyr	223

CONTENTS.

		PAGE
XIII.	SIMON MAGUS	247
XIV.	THE ETHIOPIAN COURTIER	267
XV.	SAUL'S CONVERSION	287
XVI.	AFTER CONVERSION	305
XVII.	AN APOSTOLIC TOUR OF INSPECTION	325
XVIII.	CORNELIUS	345
XIX.	PETER REPORTS TO THE CHURCH	383
XX.	THE CHURCH OF ANTIOCH	399
XXI.	FRUIT FROM THE GENTILES	417
XXII.	PETER AND AGRIPPA	435
XXIII.	CONCLUSIONS	455

I.
Ascension Day.

SIC ITUR AD ASTRA.

Acts i. 1–11 ; cf. Luke xxiv. 45–53.

Revised Version.

The first history I made, O Theophilus, about all things which Jesus began both to do and teach, until the day when, having given commandments through the Holy Ghost to the apostles whom He had chosen, He was taken up: to whom also He showed Himself alive after His passion by many proofs, during forty days, being seen by them and speaking the things concerning the kingdom of God. And being assembled with them, He charged them not to depart from Jerusalem, but to await the promise of the Father, "which ye heard of Me. For John indeed baptized with water, but ye shall be baptized in the Holy Ghost after not many days."

They therefore, when they were come together, asked Him, saying—

"Lord, is it at this time Thou dost restore the kingdom to Israel?"

But He said to them: "It is not yours to know times or periods which the Father fixed by His own authority, but ye shall receive power when the Holy Ghost is come upon you, and shall be My witnesses both in Jerusalem and in all Judæa and Samaria, and unto the furthest part of the earth."

And having said these things, while they were looking, He was taken up, and a cloud received Him from their eyes. And while they were gazing into heaven as He went, behold, two men were standing beside them in white garments, who also said:

"Men of Galilee, why do ye stand looking into heaven? This Jesus, who has been taken up from you into heaven, shall so come in the same manner as ye have seen Him go into heaven."

Then they returned to Jerusalem from the hill called "Hill of an Olive-yard," which is near Jerusalem, a Sabbath journey. And when they entered, they went up to the Upper Room where they usually resorted: both Peter and John, and James and Andrew, Philip and Thomas, Bartholomew and Matthew, James of Alphæus and Simon the Zealòt, and Judas of James: these all were continuing with one accord in prayer with the women, and Mary the mother of Jesus, and His brothers.

I.

NOTHING can appear more natural than that St. Luke, who was himself a Gentile Christian, a cultured Greek, and a fruit of that great missionary movement to the westward which it was the work of his master and friend St. Paul to lead, should have been prompted by the Spirit of God to tell the story how the new Christian Church sprang out of the bosom of Judaism, and how, under the propulsion of its Divine Head, it moved forward till it had traversed the Greek-speaking provinces on either side the Ægean, and reached at length the mistress city of Rome. From Jerusalem "unto the uttermost parts of the earth," is the thread which gives unity to his narrative. The oldest title given by the Church to that narrative—"Acts of Apostles"—scarcely expresses its design. What this earliest of Church historians has really done is, first, to show by what successive stages there were formed out of the purely Hebrew Church, of which the nucleus had been gathered by our Lord's personal labours, first, a mixed Hebrew-Hellenistic Church in Judæa, next, a Samaritan, and lastly, a purely Gentile one; and then to trace the westward spread of Christian missions from that Gentile mother-church at Antioch, till its chief missionary had reached the centre of the heathen world. This precisely describes the actual contents of the book: and no other treatment of primitive Church history could have possessed equal interest for its first reader, a Greek convert of rank, residing, probably, in the imperial capital. "From Jerusalem to Rome" marks the extreme points embraced in the eight and twenty chapters of the volume sent to Theophilus. "From Jerusalem to Antioch" defines the earlier half of it, with which alone we propose to deal. Antioch, where the battle of Gentile freedom from Mosaic law was first waged, and where the followers of Jesus were first termed Christians, constitutes the middle point or halfway house of the whole narrative.

The book of Acts, however, as every one knows, does not form an independent work. It is, speaking strictly, the Second Part of a larger history, of which Part First is our third Gospel. In its opening sentence, the author expressly links it on to his "former treatise" (or *first history*[1]), and by dedicating it more briefly to the same person, he makes it plain that it is a mere continuation of the Gospel. I apprehend, too, that this second part is marked by the same historical thoroughness of research and careful reference to the best authorities to which Luke in the preface to his first volume lays such express claim.[2] It is of course impossible for us to be sure where or from whom this writer got those minute particulars regarding the earliest days of the Church, which he has recorded in the first twelve chapters; but if he resided at Cæsarea during St. Paul's long imprisonment there, and came into such close intercourse with the Judæan apostles and other eyewitnesses as to verify at their lips all the facts which his Gospel contains respecting Jesus' ministry and passion,

[1] Τὸν πρῶτον λόγον, Acts i. 1. [2] Luke i. 1–4.

it is easy to see how he may have gathered from St. Peter himself, or equally competent authorities, the course of events which immediately followed our Lord's departure.

This continuity in St. Luke's double history is more than a literary accident. It expresses a deeper fact. The events which precede Jesus' Ascension, and those which follow it, are themselves continuous. The history of our Lord's own earthly life, and the history of our Lord's Church, are, in a very real and deep sense, not two, but one; two parts of one whole. I am not quite sure that St. Luke meant us to find all this in his peculiar expression, "All that Jesus *began* both to do and teach;" but it is certainly most true, and it is a truth which underlies the whole "acts of apostles." Jesus' personal work on earth was not His whole work. It was properly no more than preliminary, initiating, or fundamental work. By His own obedience unto death, satisfying justice, reversing the curse and redeeming the world, He laid first a firm platform on which He could rear the true spiritual kingdom of God among men. By choosing and training twelve apostles to head a band of less eminent disciples round them, He prepared receptive and fit agents, through whom He could continue to work forward by the Holy Ghost, after He Himself was gone. By withdrawing then His personal presence in the body, He made way for the advent of that spiritual Agent through Whom alone a spiritual kingdom could be built. But all this was only "beginning to do and teach." The transference of His local seat from earth to heaven put no arrest upon His own activity. It did not relegate Him to a place of sublime inaction, from which He could thenceforth only see the work done here by others, but could not co-operate.

No—the agents here are His agents; the Church is His body; the Spirit His messenger. He continues to be as much as ever, one might even say, more than ever, the Head and Heart of the whole movement; the Originator of life, Determiner of action, Guide of progress, Lord of influence, and Controller of events within the Christian Church and each Christian soul. He is the Worker and the Teacher still; though He has withdrawn His corporeal presence behind the veil, and must carry on His work and teaching through lips and hands that are moved by a far-reaching spiritual influence "sent down from heaven."

It is quite necessary to seize firmly and hold fast by this thought that the "acts of apostles," and all subsequent "acts" of their true successors, are (as Bengel says) a "continuation of Christ's own history," if we would understand either St. Luke's opening section of Church history, or any after section of it from Luke's day till now. The one event in which St. Luke finds the meeting point of these two great eras is the Ascension. It finds a place at the end of his Gospel, and at the beginning of his Church history, because it is really common to both. It was needful, first, as the crown and end of His earthly life, Who came down from heaven that He might return thither. That ambiguous, mysterious state of life in which our risen Lord spent forty days, could not possibly be His abiding state. To be neither of the earth nor of the heaven; to pass at uncertain intervals from invisibility out into visibility, and back again; to eat, yet not live by food; to frequent the society of mortals without being mortal; to wear a glorified body, and in it haunt the abodes of our present humiliation: this, indeed, became very well an interval of transition, in which temporary ends were to be served, and which was to break to the disciples the abruptness of the change from constant material intercourse with Him to no such intercourse at all. But it could not be the permanent condition of the glorified Redeemer. Back to the Father's bosom the Son must fly[1] when His work is done, to receive the assurance of approval and the earnest of reward. Up to that brighter land He must carry with Him the humanity which, though fashioned once in Mary's womb, has been made anew in Joseph's grave, and made now unfit for the limitations, and the strenuous, sorrowful toils of earth. Our Lord's gospel life will halt lamely to its close if it be not crowned by the peaceful exodus of an Ascension. On the other hand, the Ascension is a starting-point as well as a conclusion. It is not less urgently demanded by the history to follow than by the history past. In order to the coming of the Holy Ghost, and that work which by the Spirit Jesus had still to prosecute upon earth, it was needful that He should mount His throne at the seat of divine empire, and gather (as one says[2]) into His pierced hands the reins of providential government. He must receive from the Father the promise of the Spirit, and be installed as both Lord and Christ, and exchange the service of obedience for the service of command. Only thus could there open for the development of the divine kingdom a new era—that of the Christian Church. This era, in

---

[1] Compare Watts's spirited lines:—

"See how the Conqueror mounts aloft,
    And, to His Father flies."

[2] See Lange, *in loc.*

which we also live, opened when the Supreme Citizen of the Jewish commonwealth " went into a far country," as He said once in parable, " to receive for Himself a kingdom ;"[1] and it shall take end at His return. The Christian Church was an impossibility till its Head had been taken up to the right hand of power. It dates, in a sense, from the Ascension.

It is from this latter point of view that we have now to consider the recapitulation which Luke has given us (by way of preface to the second portion of his history) of what happened on " the day in which He was taken up."

We have reached the last of the forty days. It is the Thursday (as we reckon) of the sixth week since that first Day of the Lord on which He rose again with gladness from the grave.[2] It is a day in early summer, when the heavens are clear with sunlight. There is a solemn preconcerted meeting in the city of Jerusalem of the full apostolic band, of the eleven, that is ; for none can avoid noticing the vacant place from which one has fallen. For the last time the apostolic college meets in session, with its Divine President at its head ; a day to be remembered; *His* last on earth—*their* first of loneliness. The forty days, with their many appearances[3] and " infallible proofs ;" the proof of touching and eating, which showed He was no spirit, but had flesh and bones ; and the still better proof of " speaking the things of the kingdom" with His old grace and truth, which showed He was nowise changed in thought or heart, but in-

---

[1] Luke xix. 12, ff.   [2] 18th May, A.D. 30, according to Wieseler.
[3] Nine or ten at least can be counted up.

ASCENSION DAY.

wardly, as well as outwardly, the same Man He ever was; these forty days, I say, had done their work. Not a misgiving lurked in a single apostle. No Thomas doubted now. The glad fact that He was alive had become real to every one of them, indubitable, a thing to die for. So for the last time, yet (like many of us when our treasures are about to leave us) not knowing that it was the last time, they clustered round Him—Him Whose fitful transient visits, by the Galilean lake or in the city chamber, had become their chief joy of life.

Their meeting this time was neither by lonely lake nor in close-shut chamber. In some disguise, I suppose, which hid Him from the street crowd, He led them forth by the city-gate, and down the well-known path that still crosses Kedron by a narrow arch, and past Gethsemane,[1] and up the hill which breathed all over with memories of the last three years, and over its summit, where the tradition of three centuries later has fixed the Ascension scene.[2] On the summit He did not stay. Tradition loves the conspicuous; Jesus loved the retired. The crest of Olivet is a Sabbath-walk from the city, as Luke says;[3] but it was nearly twice as far as that He led them forth, "as far as to Bethany." There He paused. It had often been a sore stiff walk for His weariness to climb that hill after a day's work in the city; His long earthly walk is ended now. Often it had been like going home, to reach at evening the quiet hamlet where Martha lived with Lazarus and Mary; now He was going home indeed.

[1] If the traditional "Gethsemane" may at all be trusted, which I doubt.
[2] Tradition grew up round the memorial church which the Empress Helena erected on the top of the hill.
[3] Acts i. 12.

It was not at the village itself, as I take it,[1] that He halted, but at a point equally remote from Jerusalem, and beside the village. It seems difficult when one is at the spot not to identify it. Close by the tiny hamlet, yet not within sight of it, there lie at this day such sweet secluded little hollows, softly scooped out in the mountain's eastern slope, shut in so by neighbouring ridges from the prying of curious eyes, and set still with fig and olive and almond—that when on a fair Easter morning I first set eyes on them, I could not choose but think it a place to go to heaven from. "It is very secluded indeed; out of sight of Bethany and of the high road to Jericho, with the mountain between you and the city behind, shut in by its spurs on both hands, but looking down the wilderness of bare rocky knolls towards the deep valley of the Dead Sea, and the lonely far-off walls of Moab. A deliciously rural, quiet, exquisite little spot, snugly embosomed in the mountain-side, gay with anemones when I saw it in the sprightliness and coolness of that spring morning."[2]

The farewell words which, after they had gained this solitude, Jesus addressed to the eleven men on whom, so far as agents went, the whole results of His earthly work rested, are very notable words. They mix command and rebuke with the strong wine of hope. When I try to realise the position of the apostles—so confident in their Lord's restored presence, so unsuspicious of His impending departure—I feel that they stood on the brink of a very grave danger. A few weeks before they had been disbanded, scattered, smitten into hopelessness by His

---

[1] The words of Luke xxiv. 50, ἔξω ἕως εἰς βηθανίαν, do not necessarily imply this, and the occasion was one which evidently called for more privacy and quiet.

[2] From the writer's note-book, written at the time.

ASCENSION DAY. 13

death, even though He had expressly foretold to them His rising again, and the very day of it. May not this second departure work similar mischief? Let them see Him go away before their eyes, and vanish into the distant sky—let them feel afresh their loneliness and feebleness just when they expected, as they plainly did, that the Risen One was going to crown His work by setting up Israel's kingdom in visible glory: what was to keep them from being plunged from dreams of fancied royalty into the depths of disappointment and disheartenment? A second shock, a second panic, a second scattering like the first, might have proved fatal. So Jesus, with consummate skill as well as kindness, held out before their eyes, to kindle their imagination and stimulate expectation, a splendid though undefined hope. He brought it very near, "not many days hence." He magnified it as the very thing which, before all other things, God had always held out as the hope of men —foretold, not only in express texts of Isaiah, Joel, Ezekiel, and Zechariah,[1] but by he whole tenour of Hebrew revelation—"the promise of the Father." He reminded them how, on the memorable night of betrayal, at the supper table, He had Himself foretold them of it as the advent of a second Comforter, in words which, not St. Luke, but St. John, has preserved to us.[2] He threw them back even on their own past hopes, so many of them as had been scholars of the Baptist, when years before they left one, who only baptized with water to repentance, for the service of a mightier Man, Whose more excellent mission it was to baptize with the Holy Ghost

---

[1] *E.g.*, Isa. xliv. 3; Joel ii. 28; Ezek. xxxvi. 25-27; Zech. xii. 10.
[2] John xiv. 16, 26; xv. 26; xvi. 7-14; cf. vii. 38.

and with fire.¹ In the hope of that better baptism, numbers of them had abandoned John for Jesus—in the hope of it had clung to Jesus to that hour. Let them wait yet "not many days," and the long-deferred promise shall be fulfilled, and the better baptism will come. But, as if hope alone might prove too weak a motive, He reinforced it by authority. He straitly charged them on their allegiance not to separate, nor go home, nor on any pretext be drawn or driven from the Holy City, till this promise of the Father should have come.

What this "promise" precisely meant, it will be our duty by-and-by to inquire. How the near prospect of it did bind in one the waiting disciples through the ten days of suspense which followed, and kept hope alive in their hearts, we shall see in next chapter. At the time, however, their preoccupied minds seem hardly to have taken it in. We read between the lines of God's word as our own wishes or preconceptions prompt us: and so did they. For I think that, when they put that question about "restoring at this time the kingdom to Israel," they had some idea that such a restoration of their oppressed countrymen to ancient independence and prosperity might turn out to be the "promise of the Father," or, at least, might coincide with it. Their patriotic interest in a national restoration met with no rebuke from Jesus. Their mistaken interpretation of Messianic prophecy (if it was mistaken) found no correction. One thing only the Master censured, and He censured it that He might enforce practical duty. As when, long before, some one had asked, "Are they few that be saved?" He somewhat sternly answered, "Strive to

¹ See Luke iii. 16, with synoptic parallels.

enter in ;" or as, a few weeks before, on the other slope of this same hill, He had said, "Of that day and hour knoweth no man :" " Watch, therefore, because ye know not the hour ;"[1] so here again He called them from an idle, meddling curiosity about future "times and seasons," to the duty of the present. It is a weakness which has not died out of the Church to this day. For some persons it seems a hard lesson to learn that periods of time during which divine dispensations run on unchanged, as well as such epochs or crises of change as do come at last—both the duration of the one and the date of the other—are things which the Father has "settled in the exercise of His own authority,"[2] and of which He has given account to no man.

"But," added the Master, recalling His apostles from vain questioning to hard prosaic duty, "but ye shall receive power, after that the Holy Ghost is come upon you, and ye shall be My witnesses."[3] Thus He brought them back to His own former point, and renewed to them His unapprehended promise. But He did so in such a way as virtually to answer their question. There can be no such restoration of the kingdom as they are dreaming of, for a long time to come, if first they are to be "witnesses" in Judæa, in Samaria, and to the ends of the earth. Did they dream of "power"—the power of coregents with a regnant Messiah? Yes, power they shall receive, but only to "witness a good confession," as Jesus had done "before Pontius Pilate,"[4] but as they had not done; such power as would lately have saved

[1] Cf. Luke xiii. 23, 24; and Matt. xxiv. 36-44.
[2] Acts i. 7 : Χρόνους ἢ καιροὺς οὓς 'ο πατὴρ ἔθετο ἐν τῇ ἰδίᾳ 'εξουσίᾳ.
[3] Μου μάρτυρες, not μοι, is the better reading.
[4] Cf. 1 Tim. vi. 12-14.

Peter, had he possessed it, from denial, and all of them from desertion; such power as we shall see they did get in splendid measure after the Holy Ghost had descended upon them. It is the power to be faithful, to be sure of the truth, to speak it boldly, to suffer for it gladly —the power that wraps up all the graces of the missionary and the martyr. Or did they dream of royalty in such a restored kingdom of Israel? of sitting on thrones with the King of the Jews? Ah, but they had first to learn, as we all have to do, what means that deep answer given by the King of the Jews to Pontius Pilate's question—"Art Thou a king, then?" "Thou sayest that I am a King. To this end was I born, and for this cause came I into the world, that I should bear witness unto the truth. Every one that is of the truth heareth My voice."[1] Are not these eleven apostles become true kings in history? What realm so wide as the realm of souls over which their words are law? What dynasty has stood so long as the authority of apostolic men? Before what monarch in his apotheosis did subjects ever pay such homage as Christendom has paid to the names of Peter, Paul, and John? They won it, as Jesus won His own crown, by bearing witness to the truth. In their case, as in His, it was a witness-bearing which rose into martyrdom. But it is the secret of strength. Out of such weakness comes forth power. To be His witnesses, to speak and live His truth, to show men the Father as He showed Him, to proclaim the Son in His passion to be a Prince and Saviour, to confess Him by the Holy Ghost as our living Lord, our very life, when men jeer, or curl learned lips, or pity our credulity, or

[1] John xviii. 37.

are deaf to our voice: this is the Christian's royalty, his true successorship to apostolic witnesses.

After these weighty, yet heartening words were spoken, while the eleven were dimly divining in their souls of what sort their apostolic task was likely to prove, but with what divine aid they were to be furnished for it, Jesus added one more word of supreme and unspeakable consolation. In order to wipe from their hearts the last trace of disappointment or regret or cowardice, "He lifted up His hands" in solemn gesture, "and blessed them."[1] Last parting blessing, as of one who dies and leaves an orphaned family; full of clinging love, and tender with the grief of a farewell! Yet, unlike the feebleness of good wishes on men's dying lips, this strong benediction of the Prince of Life commands and confers the blessing, while from His radiant face and form, and down from His uplifted hands, there rains into the souls of the eleven a rain of gracious influence, of hope and courage and content and gladness. Then came a wonder. There, as He stood, His hands still raised, raimented as He was, without a hint or voice, His blessed feet ceased to touch the soil. Like a thing of rarer quality, which by its own upward virtue ascends through the grosser atmosphere below, His blessed body rose with a still and slow and stately movement into the pure bright upper air. Nor stayed; but, followed by the fixed gaze of the amazed men, rose on, until, still raining blessings down, He reached the region where white clouds rest. Then suddenly there swept beneath His feet a cloud that shut Him from their envious eyes. Oh, who of us would not strain a wistful gaze into the sky, if back from its

[1] Cf. Luke xxiv. 50.

blue depths we might but see Him come and grow upon the sight, or if perchance some cloud like that which swallowed Him would open to let Him through? Do not our hearts, when new-robbed only of some most dear but mortal friend, whom the other world has snatched too soon from our embrace, yearn towards that other world and long to follow, and hope almost against hope, by might of love's desire, to draw even yet from the place beyond one more word or look or token of remembrance? How much more these men who on the Hill of Olives had lost Jesus Christ, who came out from Jerusalem with Him, but must go back without Him!

Yet the two shining ones were right.——" Why seek ye the living among the dead?" "Why stand ye gazing up into heaven?"[1]

This is no time for idle, melancholy despondencies, that root themselves in the past: for profitless longings after that which is not. Gazing into heaven will not fetch Christ back, nor any other departed. Let us return to Jerusalem. Earth has its calls to duty, and heaven will chide us if we do not heed them. Let us go; to watch and pray in the upper room—to receive power from on high—to be His witnesses in the earth—to work for Him, speak for Him, die for Him; and let this be the spur which quickens labour and the hope which cheers exhaustion, that "this same Jesus Who is taken up from us into heaven, shall so come in like manner as they saw Him go into heaven."

[1] With Acts i. 11, compare Luke xxiv. 5. The (same?) two men in white had appeared forty days earlier, with a very similar message.

II.
Waiting for the Promise.

DUM EXPECTAT ORAT.

Acts i. 12–26.

REVISED VERSION.

And in those days, Peter standing up in midst of the brethren said (the crowd of names [i.e., of persons] in one place was about a hundred and twenty):
"*Men and brethren, it behoved that the scripture be fulfilled which the Holy Spirit spake before through the mouth of David concerning Judas, who became guide to those that arrested Jesus; because he was numbered among us and received the lot of this ministry. This man, then, purchased a field out of the wages of the iniquity, and falling headlong, burst in the middle, and all his bowels gushed out. And it became known to all the inhabitants of Jerusalem, so that that field is called in their own dialect, 'Akeldamach,' that is, 'field of blood.' For it has been written in the Book of Psalms:* 'Let his habitation become a desert, and let the inhabitant of it be no more;' *and,* 'His office let another take.' *It behoves therefore, that of the men who companied with us at every time when the Lord Jesus came in to us and came out, beginning from the baptism of John until the day in which He was taken up from us, that of these one should become a witness of His resurrection along with us.*"

And they put forward two, Joseph called Bar-Sabbas who was surnamed "*Justus,*" *and Matthias; and praying, said:*

" *Thou, Lord, Who knowest the hearts of all, appoint whom Thou hast chosen, one of these two, to take the place of this ministry and apostolate from which Judas turned aside [transgressed] to go to his own place.*"

And they cast lots for them: and the lot fell on Matthias, and he was numbered along with the eleven apostles.

II.

OUR Lord went back to heaven on the fortieth day after His resurrection; on the fiftieth day, the Holy Ghost came down from heaven. The ten days between, of which we have the history in this section, formed an interval of silent suspense, a pause during which the outward march of events seemed to be arrested. God never works in haste. Here, at the last moment, when, after so long time spent in preparation, the gospel is at length complete, and its heralds stand together, ready in act to fly abroad with the message on their tongues which is to bring life to countless souls and hope as from the dead to all men,—here, in the supreme moment of the world's fate, when our impatience would have rushed forward, God holds back. For ten weary days of inaction were these men kept waiting in the chamber of prayer, prisoners of hope, kept there dumb witnesses to the truth which saves, while outside their chamber door a world lay dying.

It was not merely to show the absolute dependence of the Church on God the Holy Ghost, that it was made to wait so long for His advent; nor only to check that restless temper which will have the kingdom to appear at once, chafes at the long delays of providence, and is for ever antedating the turning-points of history; nor was it just to postpone the birthday of the Church till another festival should have filled Jerusalem again with strangers, that the *éclat* and success of its first appearance might be the greater. I think that, in fact, all was not ready for the coming of the Holy Ghost when these ten days began. Outwardly, no doubt, everything seemed to be ready. There, in heaven, was the Christ gone up : here, in Jerusalem, were the disciples assembled. What wait we for ? But the true preparation for each onward step in God's kingdom is within us, not without. It is to hearts that are gathered well into themselves, exercised upon the past sayings of God, roused to wait on Him for new blessings, and quick with patient, resolute desire, and the calm strength of faith, that the Spirit comes. Christ came, indeed, in the night-time, when busy Bethlehem had other things to think of; He will come again as a robber by night, and shall not find faith, perhaps, on the earth. But when the Holy Ghost comes, He comes to expectant, prayerful, and prepared men. Our Father gives this gift, Jesus tells us, to those who ask Him. Ten days, or ten times ten days, if need be, He will wait and withhold Himself till we feel we need Him, and have learnt to ask for Him, and are disciplined into faith by the long silence of the heavens, and can say, as we continue daily in unwavering petition, "We have waited for Thy salvation, O Lord." This interval before Pentecost is the model for all seasons of united and special prayer which are wont to precede a revival of the Church.

When the Eleven returned from the " Hill of the Oliveyard "[1] and entered the city again, they went straight to their well-known place of meeting in that large hall immediately under the roof of a disciple's dwelling-house,

---

[1] Ver. 12: ἐλαιῶνος only here in New Testament; but see Josephus, *Antiq.* vii. 9. 2.

of which we read so much under the name of "the upper chamber."[1] Very probably, I think, it was in this same room that Jesus had held the Last Supper, and had again and again appeared to them on successive Lord's Days after His rising. Probably it was from this very room He and they had gone forth together but an hour or two before on their last walk to Olivet. Here they seem to have found the company of disciples awaiting their return, into whose greedy ears they poured the joyful news that He had actually gone bodily up into heaven, with words of blessing on His lips, and an angelic promise of His coming back again. No troubled or despondent party was this, although they were the few partisans of a Leader Whose cause seemed to the public to have been defeated: although they were the slender orphaned relict of a Guardian just vanished from their sight. Their Leader lived; their vanished Guardian was gone up to be the Lord of all; all that they had expected from this Man was true; their Jesus was Christ, and King, and God's eternal Son. So their souls were nerved by the strength of assured conviction, and made buoyant with the joy of hope. True, they had lost Him from their midst, yet not for ever; true, they were alone and weak, but the Spirit was to come. To lose Him thus, Jesus had said, was to be a gainer. The magic of His last words worked potently within them, infusing comfort; and the radiance of that recent glimpse into the heavens lay still upon their faces.

The infection of this joy of the apostles wrought effectually on all the rest. Day by day they went regularly as pious Jews to the Temple services, and

[1] Note the article in εἰς τὸ ὑπερῷον (ver. 13). Such rooms were usual under the flat roof, reached by an outer stair from the court.

while their fellow-worshippers thought bitterly of one more pretender exposed, and the true Christ as far off as ever, those hundred and twenty were in their secret souls singing songs of rejoicing to Jehovah over His Messiah's advent and the glory which had crowned His passion.[1] The more this joyful faith of theirs contrasted with the blindness and the blunders of their incredulous fellow-citizens, so much the more must the disciples—warm-hearted and impetuous as some of them were—have burned to bear witness to their faith; and the more they must have been driven back, under the recollection of their former disgraceful failure and cowardly dispersion, upon that mysterious word which barred their way—"Ye shall receive power when the Holy Ghost is come;" "Wait for the promise of the Father." It was not enough as Jews to praise Jehovah in public; as Jesus' destined witnesses, they must in secret learn to seek from Him that gift which was to be the condition of their strength. United prayer-meetings in the upper room were thus the natural out-come of their situation. To this, circumstances shut them up. Statedly and habitually they spent their time together in this exercise of special prayer; not the Eleven only, but all those who trusted in Jesus and were at that time to be found in Jerusalem. The little company included His own now believing "brethren,"[2] His mother herself, who here for the last time appears in the story ere she passes back

[1] See Luke xxiv. 52, 53.

[2] The mention of His "brethren" here, separate from the apostles, is thought by some to exclude them all from the number of the apostles (see John vii. 5). Like Jacob's sons, they now knew their Joseph (Gen. xlv. 15). Tradition makes St. John take Mary, somewhat later, to Ephesus, where she died.

into the obscurity of private life, and the other faithful and loving women, who had either come up (like the Magdalen) from Galilee, or resided (like the Bethany sisters) in the vicinity of the capital. All these, fused in one by a common hope, kept together as helpers of one another's faith. Through daily fellowship in prayer, they nourished the new-born grace of brotherly love. With supplications which were not wavering, and though earnest, were not impatient; perchance with tears too, which sprang out of tender memories of the Departed, and were full of happy love; all these, who had ever clung about our blessed Jesus in the days of His flesh, and never proffered a neglected request, clung now to the footstool of His grace, and, where He had so lately knelt and prayed with them, they knelt now and prayed to Him.[1] Ah, such prayers, how could they fail to be like silken cords thrown about the heart of that new-departed Friend, drawing back His thoughts to the friends He had left. When mother and brothers, John the beloved, and Peter, and she who loved much, and all that was dearest and most familiar to His human heart, pleaded before Him those sweet words He had spoken only six weeks before—"Hitherto have ye asked nothing in My name: ask and ye shall receive, that your joy may be full,"—why, oh, why were the heavens so shut and deaf for ten lingering days?

It was expedient for them, as the like delays are for us. It taught them to pray. It educated them to think of their well-known One as God their Saviour. It gave them time to realise their own helplessness and dependence on spiritual aid. It drew out their confidence in

[1] Yet He was praying with them still. See John xiv. 16.

His power to hear and to help, in spite of the interval which now stretched between. Be sure their prayers grew deeper, purer, and more trustful, as day passed after day; less alloyed with earthly feeling, as though they were favourites of heaven, privileged to be impatient; more full of such humble confidence as becomes devout, forgiven men, who only echo back the strong sure words of God. It could not but be for good reasons that Jesus refrained Himself while they prayed; for who could think that delay meant refusal? Had He not Himself bidden men pray always and not faint? When their hearts are purged through this trial, and their faith is sure of its ground, and their hope has ripened into patient expectation, and their waiting longing souls are ready for Him—then, and not till then, the Holy Ghost will come, and come abundantly. Let us pray and wait, as they did. Surely we, too, shall have our Pentecost.

To this general preparation of the whole body of disciples for the Spirit's advent, there was added during those ten days a special preparation of the apostolic body, by the election of a successor to Judas. I do not know that there is anything in the sacred text to make it quite certain that this step was taken in compliance with the mind of Christ. But I cannot imagine that in such a matter the whole body of disciples should have been left to blunder on their very first attempt at co-operation with their ascended Head. Besides, Jesus had expressly foretold [1] that the twelve apostles should be at last enthroned as twelve judges, one over each of the tribes of the chosen people. This promise, which is

[1] Matt. xix. 28; Luke xxii. 30.

in entire harmony with the whole relation of the first-chosen apostolic band to their Jewish countrymen, is specially restricted to apostles who "followed" Jesus, and "endured His temptations" with Him. It therefore excludes that noblest of all apostles,[1] whose name is apt to occur to one's mind as the true Christ-elected successor of the apostate. St. Paul was not a personal companion of Jesus' footsteps; and he seems even to distinguish himself from the complete body of the Twelve, not only as "one born out of due time," but also as the one apostle of the Gentiles, to whose single hand that mighty ministry had been entrusted.[2]

I cannot but think, therefore, that St. Peter was rightly led in this matter. He seems to have felt that, as the approaching advent of the Comforter was designed to fit the apostles for their peculiar work as witnesses, the normal number should be first made up, so that there might be no blank when on them all the heavenly Might descended. Only it must strike every one as remarkable that it should be Peter, of all men, who called his brethren's attention to the lapse of the unhappy Iscariot, and the seat his fall had emptied. On Peter, no doubt, the leadership very naturally devolved, since even during the presence of Jesus he had uniformly acted as their foremost spokesman. Natural disposition, recognised publicly by Christ Himself, fitted this man for the post of chief among his fellows, which we shall see him henceforth hold. Still, of all the Eleven, Peter's own conduct at the trial of his Master had been the worst, and had in its external features come the nearest to that of Judas.

[1] This is Rudolph Stier's view. See his *Reden d. Ap.* 2nd edition.
[2] Cf. his words in 1 Cor. xv. 8; Gal. ii. 7-9; Eph. iii. 8.

If Judas betrayed Christ in His security, Peter abjured Him at His need. Although between the two cases there was all the difference betwixt a deliberate crime which tops a career of conscious imposture and unconfessed hypocrisy, and a solitary fall, under sudden provocation, due to the weakness of self-deception—a difference this so vast, that while the one stands as the New Testament type of an honest man's infirmity and repentance, the other is the whole world's example of that dark remorse which precedes suicide—yet between the two cases there was also enough of superficial resemblance to make us watch narrowly how Peter the saved will have the heart to speak of Judas the lost. It says a good deal for the purity of Peter's penitence that he speaks as he does. He handles the sad facts of his brother apostle's sin and ruin with unaffected frankness and simplicity. He neither conceals nor palliates them. Yet he is as far as possible from either vulgar abuse or unctuous lamentation. Judas' sin is simply this—"He was guide to them that took Jesus." Judas' fate is veiled in the words of the prayer under this soft phrase (but more, and not less, awful because it is soft)—"He went to his own place." It must have cost Peter something to speak on this subject at all; but his words are, in their spirit, a model to all Christian men whose duty it is to deal with the scandal or with the punishment of a sinning brother.

It is further worthy of notice in the same connection how St. Peter lifts this whole matter as much as possible from the level of a wicked man's free and guilty will to its place in the higher purposes of Providence. The traitor's act was indeed an "iniquity," a "transgression," by which he wilfully threw away the "portion" Jesus had given him,[1] in the highest rank of spiritual service, for sixty shekels' worth of land on earth, and the lot which was justly his own in the next world. That is not concealed. Yet that aspect of it, now that the wretched man had gone into God's presence, was a thing betwixt him and God. Peter was not his judge, nor are we. What he had to do with was the divine predestination which permitted such a gap to be made in the most select number of Christ's servants, and the divine will which prescribed how the gap should be filled. Both these points, therefore — the vacancy, caused not by Judas' death, but by Judas' sin, and the filling up of the vacancy —Peter finds divinely foreshadowed in the experience of Jesus' great ancestor and type, King David. In going back upon the psalms of David's exile for a prophetic parallel, Peter closely copied his Master; for a few words from the 41st Psalm had been once quoted by Jesus with reference to this very case of Judas;[2] and the betrayal He had repeatedly spoken of as necessary to fulfil old predictions. From two other psalms of the same class as the 41st, Peter accordingly selects texts, which, though written anciently of the foes of David, were, by the consent of Hebrew expositors and the sanction of Christ's own example, applicable in a higher degree to David's Anointed Successor. From the 69th Psalm,[3] first, he deduces the inevitable vacating of Judas' apostolic seat in consequence of his crime; since the expulsion of the rightful king's rebel foes out of their places and inheritances in the kingdom is a principle applicable both to

---

[1] Or "lot" (tr. "part") = κληρος. s. v. 17. cf. "clergy."
[2] In John xiii. 18; cf. xvii. 12; Matt. xxvi. 24.
[3] Psa. lxix. 25 is quoted from LXX., not literally : αὐτοῦ for αὐτῶν.

King David and King Christ. This psalm is one cited repeatedly elsewhere, even by our Lord, and is full of messianic allusions.[1] Next, from another psalm, which used in the ancient Church to be called "Iscariot's,"— the 109th [2]—he deduces that it is God's will the vacant office should not be left vacant. The psalm is one full of imprecations against Ahithophel, imprecations which, whatever may be thought of the royal sufferer's right to utter them, or the spirit in which he did it, are plainly understood here as prophetic references by the Spirit of God to one who with more than Ahithophel's malice sold over to death One Who was better than David.

It is this wonderful foreshadowing of the events of our Lord's history in antecedent type which makes it plain how every part of that history (including even men's freest and worst acts) was foreseen and prearranged of God. Though we might not have been able, like Peter, to deduce the need for a new election from a verse of the 109th Psalm, yet we see enough to feel how pregnant the old Scripture must have become to apostolic readers, after it had pleased the Lord Christ to open their eyes to it, and expound to them the things concerning Himself.[3]

There is even in form a curious parallel between the fate of Absalom's adviser, who, when he found his treason against his sovereign on the point of being baffled, went home and hanged himself, and the very similar end of Christ's betrayer. In deeper fact, Judas is the archtype of all treason within the kingdom of God; of all men, before or since his day, who, not being in their

[1] Cf. Psa. lxix. 4 c. John xv. 25; v. 9 c. John ii. 17 and Rom. xv. 3; v. 21 c. Matt. xxvii. 34, 48, &c.

[2] Psa. cix. 8 is from LXX., literally.

[3] Luke xxiv. 27, 32, 45. Cf. 1 Pet. i. 10–12.

hearts content with the spiritual privileges to which God has called them in His spiritual realm, betray the interests of God's cause for some selfish worldly gain. The honour of being an elect apostle of Messiah, the moral advantages such a position offered, loyalty and gratitude to his Master, the very life of Him on Whom man's hope depended;—all these seemed to the covetous heart of the man, hardened by years of secret peculation and embittered by detection, of less value than thirty silver coins. For the lowest market price of a slave, he sold the Son of God, sold his apostolate, sold himself. Satan drives hard bargains with men when evil passion blinds them, but never a bargain harder than this. The chance of doing such a crime came only once in this world's history; and the unhappy man who, tempted by circumstances and impelled of the devil, chose to do it, reaped so little from it, that the hatefulness of his deed is almost equalled by the pitifulness of his fate. About the particulars of that fate of his, indeed, there hangs a mist of uncertainty. The two accounts we have present differences which it is not easy to harmonize. According to St. Matthew,[1] Judas, in a fit of passionate remorse, flung back the "blood-money" into the hands of those who had hired him, and "went and hanged himself." The scrupulous councillors, who thought their own bribe would pollute God's treasury, invested it in a bit of land, to be used as a cemetery for foreign Jews dying at Jerusalem; and the name of the place was changed from the "Potter's Field" to the "Field of Blood."[2] But in the

[1] Matt. xxvii. 3-10.
[2] Matthew's quotation is not from our present text of Jeremiah. Zech. xi. 13 is not very closely related to it, but may be the one meant. Tradition showed a field on the south slope of Zion, near

book of Acts, St. Peter or St. Luke (for I cannot feel sure whether verses 18 and 19 are or are not an explanation by the reporter, or how much of them is so) tells us that Judas himself bought the field, and met his death, in that very field, apparently, by falling on his head with such violence as to produce rupture of the body. Of course, conjectures in reconciliation of these narratives have been often hazarded. That Judas is only said to have done what the Sanhedrim did with his money; that he hanged himself first, but afterwards fell in the way described, through the breaking of the rope or otherwise; and that the spot on which his suicide occurred was the spot purchased for that very reason by the priests: these guesses are possible, and may serve, therefore, to repel a captious objector. But if they silence, they hardly satisfy, and we shall do best, I think, to say that without the knowledge of some more particulars it is not possible now to be sure how the apostolic traitor met his end. While the details remain thus doubtful, the horrid fact remains to appal us, as it has appalled eighteen centuries. The intolerable remorse of guilt; the dark despair of life; the rash dismissal by his own hand into the presence of his Judge; the going away to his own place: this is what Judas made by his sin. Let the fearfulness of such a typical example solemnize and terrify all of us, especially if ever we are tempted to make gain out of our godliness, to thrive through the advantages of our religious position, or to sacrifice spiritual concerns entrusted to us to some personal end. No sin a man can do ever pays in the long run—this sort of sin least of all. He who tries to traffic

Tophet, where Williams says there is a bed of white potter's clay (?), and Baumgarten makes much use of this connection with Tophet.

WAITING FOR THE PROMISE.

for a portion in this world, with the portion to which God has called him in the next, shall forfeit both. There is a "place"[1] which may be called "his own;" but it is neither the "potter's field" on earth, nor a throne in heaven.

Peter's speech being ended, the brethren proceeded to fill up the vacant office. The way in which this appointment was gone about is very instructive. It was done at the suggestion of the leading apostle; yet it was done not by the apostles, but by the whole hundred and twenty;[2] nor because an apostle proposed it, but because he supported his proposal with Scripture. The body of disciples took action up to a certain point; they defined the qualifications of the office, sought out such men as possessed these qualifications, and possibly selected from among them the two best qualified. But this was as far as they dared to go. It was the prerogative of an apostle to be expressly designated by Jesus: the others had been so, and the new one must be so, too. At this point, therefore, the brethren pause, stand aside, and invoke the direct personal decision of their departed Lord. Both the candidates—the unsuccessful Joseph, son of Sabbas, with his Latin cognomen "Justus," and Matthias the successful—are said by tradition to have been of the Seventy, but are previously unknown to history. Both must have been early converts of Jesus, His companions from the opening of His ministry, and witnesses of His risen life; for this was the condition of their selection.[3] Probably, too, they were in all outward signs of character alike unexceptionable;

---

[1] Cf. τόπον in v. 25, bis.

[2] "Together," v. 15 = "in one place," ἐπὶ τὸ αὐτὸ (χωρίον sc.).

[3] The *conditions* are:—1. Knowledge of His ministry (*a*) in its whole duration (St. John xv. 27): (*b*) minute and constant (St. Luke xxii. 28). 2. Personal evidence of His resurrection.

since the appeal is made to Jesus as the Divine Searcher of hearts, and on this heart-knowledge, unattainable by the brethren, the choice is at last made to turn. But in their prayer to Jesus (which seems to have been offered by Peter in the name of all) the brethren take for granted that the " Lord " has already made His choice. With an allusion perhaps to His own words, " Have not I chosen you twelve ?"—" Ye have not chosen Me, but I have chosen you;" they beg the Lord Jesus to show[1] them " whether of these two Thou *hast chosen.*" And, having prayed, they remit the matter to the decision of the lot. These men, let it be remembered, stood still on the platform of Mosaic Judaism. They had not yet received the Spirit Who confers the gift of " discerning of spirits." In this special election, as never again, their object was to leave the choice immediately in God's hands. Lot-casting was not only in heathendom (in Greek classic times, for example) a mode of divination; it was also among the ancient Hebrews a recognised means of ascertaining the divine will, resorted to in the partition of territory, the detection of criminals, the election of rulers, and the conduct of war.[2] But this solitary and extraordinary example of it before Pentecost is no precedent for its use in the appointment of Church office-bearers; and it never has been imitated in the Church, save once in Spain, about the seventh century, and by the modern Moravians. Still less can its solemn and prayerful application here, to decide what man could not decide, be any apology for the frivolous or irreverent employment of

[1] " Show," rather " appoint," v. 24.

[2] Cf., *e.g.*, the partition of Palestine (Josh. xiv. 2); the detection of Achan (Josh. vii. 16, &c.) (?); the election of Saul (1 Sam. x. 20). See examples, heathen and Hebrew, in Smith's Dict. Cf. Prov. xvi. 33.

the lot, either to relieve men from the responsibility of decision, or to afford them the excitement of gambling. The rightness or wrongness of all such applications of it must be judged of on other grounds.

Thus, then, at length the framework of the Christian Church stood complete, a prepared body of Hebrew believers in an attitude of devout and joyful expectation. Boldly closing their ranks and perfecting their broken organisation, in the energy of a faith which counts that what God promises is already as good as done, this noble band stood and waited, ten days long, praying in their upper room. What is this but the last result of all the long Hebrew ages, the product from millenniums of Hebrew piety? A body of saints whom the last "Minister of the circumcision"[1] has Himself trained, and who, full of the ripe faith which expects and desires, the grand old waiting faith of patriarch and prophet, are ready to be transformed at a stroke into the Church of Christ? What is lacking save the Transformer? the life, the energy, which shall knit, and fuse, and kindle, and turn the mere framework into a body, and be the soul of that body, and dwell in it, and work through it for ever; the life, the energy, of the Holy Ghost? *The next step is Pentecost.*

[1] Rom. xv. 8.

III.
Pentecost.

ἐν ἑνὶ πνεύματι ἡμεῖς πάντες εἰς ἓν σῶμα 'εβαπτίσθημεν.

Acts ii. 1–13.

Revised Version.

And while the day of Pentecost was being accomplished, they were all together at the same place; and suddenly there came out of heaven a sound as of a rushing mighty blast, and filled the whole house where they were sitting; and there appeared to them cloven tongues as of fire, and sat upon each one of them, and they were all filled with the Holy Spirit, and began to speak with different tongues, according as the Spirit gave them to utter.

Now there were dwelling in Jerusalem Jews, devout men, from every nation of those that are under the heaven. And when that voice occurred, the crowd came together and was confounded because they heard them speaking each one in his own dialect. So they were all amazed and wondered, saying:

"Behold, are not all these who are speaking Galileans? And how do we hear, each in our own dialect in which we were born? Parthians, and Medes, and Elamites, and the inhabitants of Mesopotamia, of both Judæa and Cappadocia, Pontus and Asia, Phrygia and also Pamphylia, Egypt and the parts of Lybia which lie towards Cyrene, and the Roman sojourners, both Jews and proselytes, Cretes and Arabians, we hear them speaking in our own tongues the great things of God."

So they were all amazed, and were disputing one with another, saying, "What may this be?" But others mocking said, "They are full of sweet wine!"

III.

AT last the birthday of Christ's Church had come. The tenth morning after His return to heaven brought round to the disciples the second great national festival of the year;[1] and whether or not they felt that indefinite presentiment which now and then betokens some impending change in one's life, at least they could hardly escape a tenser stretch of expectation than on any of the nine days already spent in waiting prayer. Pentecost, or the Fiftieth, was the Greek name for what in the books of Moses is called, variously, the Feast of Harvest, or of Weeks, or of First-Fruits.[2] It marked the lapse of seven times seven days from the one which succeeded to Passover Sabbath, and seemed to round off the final close of the great Paschal solemnities. Its usual name at the time of our Lord denoted this: "The Concluding Assembly."[3] It was, in its primary design, an agricultural festival of thanksgiving. As Passover was supposed to coincide with the opening of harvest operations, when the earliest crop, the barley, was ripe, so that its first cut sheaf could be waved before Jehovah on the morning

[1] Whether this fell on a Saturday or Sunday, depends on the day when our Lord held His last supper. Wieseler says Saturday; Meyer, Sunday.

[2] See Exod. xxiii. 16; xxxiv. 22; Num. xxviii. 26 c. Lev. xxiii. 17; Deut. xvi. 10.   [3] "*Atsereth.*"

after the Paschal Sabbath, so the intervening seven weeks were presumed to have brought the staple cereal, wheat, also to maturity. Grain harvest was now about to become general, in fact; and the characteristic ceremony of Pentecost consisted in the sacrifice by fire of a couple of leavened loaves, baked from the new wheat of the season, "a new meat-offering" of the land's first-fruits in the form of prepared human food. Who can tell whether it dawned that day on any of the more thoughtful disciples, such as John, that whereas Jesus had been offered up at Passover, like the first sheaf of God's great spiritual harvest of men, so perchance at Pentecost there might be consecrated to the Lord the first-fruits of a wider ingathering? At all events we can now see how scrupulously it pleased the wise Builder of the Church to respect the memorials of the old whilst laying the foundations of the new; how He honoured the festivals of an economy which was about to vanish away, by making them the initial points of a larger history; and how gently He slid into His scholars' hearts the vaster thoughts of His spiritual kingdom through the all but worn-out and effete machinery of Mosaic ritual.

Modern Jews are now accustomed to find in the Pentecostal service another significance.[1] As Passover was the anniversary of the Exodus, so Pentecost was the anniversary of the legislation on Sinai; for that great moral birthday of the Hebrew polity followed fifty days after the Red Sea was crossed. Remembering this, it may be permitted to detect a special propriety in the coming of the Spirit at Pentecost, to rewrite in men's

---

[1] Cf. Meuschen's "Nov. Test. e Talmude Illustratum," p. 740. Also Smith's Dict., Art. *Pentecost*.

hearts what under the legal covenant had been on that day written only on tables of stone. From the earthly mount which, when God's finger touched it, burned with fire, Moses, the cloud-concealed, received for the redeemed from Egypt a law, hard as the granite it was written on, a law which only caused offences to abound, and ministered to the offender condemnation.[1] But now the law has led the world to Christ; and He from His celestial mount, His holy hill of Zion into which the cloud received Him, sends down to His redeemed no code of impossible precepts, but the Spirit of law, the Spirit of that love which fulfils law and makes obedience for the first time possible. Beautiful as this parallelism unquestionably is, it is not biblical, nor have we any reason to think that it had occurred to the Jews of our Lord's age. The Hebrew literature even of the next generation knows nothing of it.[2] It is an after thought, for which we have to thank some later Rabbi; but to the patristic Church, some three or four centuries later, it became a familiar idea, and lent its own charm to the Whitsuntide festival.[3]

Men who live through any marked epoch in history rarely if ever see its meaning as those do who come after. I dare say the minds of the hundred and twenty (or as many more of Jesus' followers as had joined them for the feast) were full that morning only of a dim vague longing for something, a blind going forward of the soul to meet they hardly knew what. At least, they were early at the

[1] Cf. 2 Cor. iii, 7 ff.; Heb. xii. 18–24; Rom. v. 20; viii, 2–15; Gal. iii. 19–iv. 7.
[2] It is not named in Philo or Josephus. See Hofmann's *Schriftbeweis*.
[3] Cf., for example, Jerome and Augustine, quoted in Smith, l. c.; and Severian and Theophylact, referred to by Wordsworth, *in loc.*

place of meeting, in an attitude of expectation. Before the sun was three hours up, before the morning time of prayer had brought worshippers to the temple, these were in their places at their upper room. Probably they had already prayed, and now they sat¹ to wait. Yet that which we wait for most intently comes on us at the last as a surprise. Suddenly, with a shock that struck through every soul, there rushed down upon the house roof, as if it fell out of the clear sky, a sound, which was like nothing so much as the impetuous, furious blast of a gale;² a sound which in a moment filled the house. With the sound came a brightness, as of a fiery stream, which parted itself to each, so that each brother or sister saw on every other's head a flame-like tongue-shaped thing, which seemed to alight there and to rest. These were material signs, audible to the ear or visible to the eye, which expressed in a language of nature the advent and the presence of God.³ The elements are the servants of the Eternal. They herald His coming. They proclaim His presence. He Who cannot be seen robes Himself in them as in a garment, and men trace in thunder His voice, His marching in the light. "The winds He makes His messengers; His ministers are the flaming fire."⁴ When the storm-blast leaps down with a roar from the upper currents, or the forked tongues of

---

¹ See ver. 2. Why does the earlier Christian art represent them as *standing*? See this still retained, *e.g.*, in the frescoes in the Spagnuoli Chapel at Santa Maria Novella, at Florence.

² ὥσπερ φερομένης πνοῆς βιαίας, v. 2.

³ See examples of *wind* as a symbol of God, in Song of Sol. iv. 16; Ezek. xxxvii. 9 (i. 4?); Isa. xl. 7; John iii. 8; xx. 22. And of *fire*: Isa. iv. 4 (Gen. xv. 17?); Mal. iii. 2; Matt. iii. 11 c. Luke iii. 16; Rev. iv. 5. ⁴ See Psa. civ. 4, quoted in Heb. i. 7.

flame play with fierce dartings through the air, we see, as Elijah did at Horeb, forerunners of the Divine Majesty, trumpeters of His strength. Yet it is not in the wind nor in the fire that the Lord is. Behind the material portents of Pentecost, which were like dramatic accessories to startle and pierce the stupid hearts of men into apprehension of the divine, we must look for the Divine Comer Himself. Invisible as the breath from which He borrows His human name, penetrating as the flame to which He likens His working, the Holy Spirit comes into the human spirit of each waiting believer in the crowd; quickens with His breath the slumbering fire of spiritual life; pours light and heat, insight and holy passion, into the soul; fills up the vessel of the heart with unheard-of certainty, courage, gratitude, and exultation in God: till the over-brimming tide of celestial emotion almost drowns consciousness or self-restraint, and flows out in rapt ecstatic passionate utterance of jubilant praise. Here is the true inner wonder of the day. Here lay the heart of the event—in this simultaneous elevation of the whole company who had prayed so long to such a level of divine emotion that they could not choose but praise, could not choose but utter their praise aloud, testifying to God, in the hearing of whoever might hear, what magnificent mercies God had granted them. A feebler presence of God the Spirit within men quickens that desire of the heart which is prayer; but to be full of the Spirit is to praise. Before Pentecost, the Holy Ghost had enabled these disciples to believe, to hope, to wait, to ask. Hitherto He had been with them in the measure of the old economy. It was an economy which expected, but had not attained; which reached out towards the assurance and the adoption and the liberty and the fellowship of sons in God's Son Jesus. But when He came to them to make them Christians by baptising them into the new economy of the Church, He lifted them as by a sudden flood-tide up to another level— to Jesus' own level. He broke the barrier, now grown very thin, which held them back at their legal standpoint, and floated them in to a new world of privilege, in to closer nearness to God, in to confidence, to freedom, to the joy of possession. In a word, He made them in full and conscious standing sons of God, and, like other sons of God, they shouted aloud for gladness.

We are not permitted—no man is—to set eyes on the exact point at which God the Spirit touches man the spirit, nor to catch the manner of His work. But the effects of the divine coming reveal its nature. The noise as of a storm-blast which smote the house had been loud enough to spread over the adjacent part of the city at least, and to arrest the attention of many of the citizens. Its apparent direction guided the astonished neighbours to the spot. Crowding in, they found something stranger even than the rushing blast. A hundred and twenty persons of both sexes talking simultaneously, in an excited manner, not to each other, but— as if unaware of each other's presence—addressing all of them some invisible Hearer; their many discordant voices mingling and confounding one another till nothing could be understood: this scene was certainly extraordinary enough. But among the crowd which gathered, many, both of the born Jews and of the heathen proselytes, were natives of foreign lands, who had either come up to the feast, or were from motives of religion settled in the

Holy City, as so many pious Jews are to this day, that they might spend their remaining years beside the sacred temple, and lay their bones at last in sacred soil. By degrees, these foreigners began to distinguish, amidst the medley of sounds, familiar words of their mother-tongue from one or other of the disciples; and listening more carefully, they discovered, to their still greater perplexity, that each dialect of every land of the Dispersion had its representative among the speakers. The utter amazement which Luke labours to depict in the audience at this discovery,[1] has not to this day ceased among the expositors and commentators of his history. But however wonderful this gift of tongues may have been, it is hardly open to doubt what its nature was. A veritable speech in languages or dialects which the speakers had never learned, is what Luke means us to understand, if words have meaning. That the number of such languages spoken was considerable, is plain both from his rhetorical phrase, "every nation under heaven," and from the list he gives of fifteen territories. Beginning with four oriental races which then inhabited the lands about the Caspian and the Euphrates, over which Babylon and Persia of old held sway, and linking these to western Asia by the link of Palestine itself,[2] Luke names next five provinces of Asia Minor, crosses to the two leading political divisions of North Africa, and closes with the imperial city itself, as representing the whole Latin West. Or rather, meant to close with it; but, recollecting himself, adds as a supplement the important

[1] Cf. the expressions, συνεχύθη, ver. 6; ἐξίσταντο, ἐθαύμαζον, ver. 7; ἐξίσταντο, διηπορῦντο, ver. 12.

[2] It seems impossible to explain the occurrence of Ἰουδαίαν in ver. 9.

island of Crete (now Candia) and the great Arab family.

The power of speaking the six or eight distinct languages used in all these lands, to say nothing of their local dialectic varieties, was no permanent gift bestowed on these disciples for the purpose of preaching the gospel. It is next to certain that the apostles availed themselves of no such power. The gift here was given to every one, but it was not used for preaching. It was not used for speaking to men at all. The crowd of outsiders found these brethren speaking to God—not, for edification, to one another; still less, for conversion, to unbelievers.[1] The effect on the hearers of such a Babel of tongues could only be to excite wonder, or, as in the Corinthian Church at a later date, to make ignorant persons think the Christians were mad or drunk. When it became needful to preach the gospel to the multitude, Peter used no foreign tongue, but spoke to all in the language of every-day life. Hence it appears that these mysterious utterances (which probably the utterer did not understand, or would not have understood had he heard another utter them) were what St. Paul himself calls them, "a sign." I take the matter thus. The soul and spirit of the believer being full of the Holy Ghost, and uplifted thereby into a state of extraordinary spiritual elation, intent on God and rapt in His praise, must utter what it feels. Naturally, it would do this in its own most familiar mother-tongue. But, supernaturally, the laws of mental association which govern utterance have been

---

[1] Cf. Acts x. 44–47 (c. xi. 15); xix. 6; 1 Cor. xiv., for the relation of the "tongues" to (1) praise and (2) "prophecy." See in Neander (*Pflanz. u. Leit.*) passages from Irenæus and Tertullian, which he thinks prove the continued existence of such a gift.

in certain cases overborne, and the organs of speech used by God the Holy Ghost to utter sounds which expressed the same emotions in a foreign tongue. The man himself may or may not be aware with his understanding of what he is actually saying; he may not know what his words in themselves mean. He is absorbed in spiritual emotion. He feels rather than thinks. His spirit praises or prays, his understanding being unfruitful. He means praise, and praise only; but over the form in which his praise is uttered, he exerts no intelligent volition, but is the instrument of God, and speaks, literally, as the Spirit gives him utterance. Now, wherever such a miracle as this was wrought,—whether in Jerusalem, or Cæsarea,[1] or Corinth—it was, in Paul's words, "a sign to them that believe not;" a proof, as any other miracle would have been, of the special presence and favour of the Almighty. Further, such a miracle, done, not on nature, but on men; nor on man's body only, but on his intellectual powers and habits; a miracle wholly interior, subjective, controlling the *nexus* betwixt the willing emotional soul of a man and his bodily organs, was (I venture to think) specially in its place under the dispensation of the Spirit. Such work as the Holy Ghost does on the very soul itself, when He kindles the life of faith and love to God, can be made directly visible or audible to no man: but when the first hot living utterance of this new life is plainly seen to be divinely guided on its way from the soul to the tongue, seen to be seized, as it were, by God's own hand, liquid from the heart, and turned past the wonted channel of speech into another unknown channel; when, I say, God thus breaks

[1] See Acts x. 46.

open a path for the tide of spiritual life through words never before heard by the ear or uttered by the voice of His servant; does He not proclaim to all how intimately He has made Himself Lord of the inner being, the Master and the Quickener of the very soul? What is this but a counterpart in saved men to that last worst instance of diabolic domination over lost men?[1] Where a legion of unclean spirits had forced the tongue to talk blasphemies, there God the Holy Ghost inspires and guides the utterance of praise. A glorious exchange; a sweet miracle of mercy, where sin had wrought its miracles of blasting!

Nor is this all. There is a notable propriety about the use which it pleased God to make of the gift of tongues on the first day of the Christian Church. These believers in the messiahship of Jesus are to be turned into His witnesses. The truth which, held hitherto in their hearts, has made new men of them, is to be carried to the hearts of their countrymen, and thence beyond to the far-off world, by means of spoken testimony. Hitherto Jesus alone has borne witness to the truth, and on that witness-bearing of His, His royalty as a spiritual Sovereign reposes. Now, each subject of His is to have a tongue to speak for Him. Now, through fiery speech fresh from a soul on flame and charged with the enthusiasm of personal conviction—in a word, through preaching—is the glad message to fly abroad, and run from lip to heart, and from heart back again to lip, till all men shall have heard and all men have believed. The new-born Church takes therefore, as by instinct, to her proper work—she preaches. But her preaching is based on her praises. It

[1] Cf. Luke viii. 27-35.

is because the disciples believe, they speak. And before they testify of God to men, they must testify their own faith to God. A Church that shall first praise, then preach, and shall do both with spontaneous impulse and a tongue of fire, is an apostolic Church.

The congregation in that upper room was thus the representative, or, as it were, the seed-germ, of the whole catholic Church of all the centuries and of every land. First of all, indeed, it met there as the ripe and ready "first-fruits" of Israel's twelve tribes scattered abroad, made ready, through so tedious a ripening time, to be offered now at last on this Pentecostal festival. But it was more than a first-fruit of Israel: it was in eminent measure what Israel was always looked upon as being, the world's first-fruit.[1] For a symbol of this, its world-wide significance, the little new-made Church rehearsed the praises of redemption in all the tongues of all the lands over which God had scattered the tribes of Israel. This polyglot praise was the consecration of heathen speech to the service of Israel's Jehovah. It foreshadowed the catholic grace of God which has turned common and unclean tongues to holy use. It meant, though they knew it not, the gathering in of Gentile races to the God of Jacob. One thinks naturally enough of the ancient sundering of our race into mutually repellent tribes through another "gift of tongues" on the plains of Babylon. But I cannot conceive how some can find here [2] the reversal of that ancient curse, or any type of the reduction of mankind to unity through the abolition of

---

[1] Cf. what St. James, the apostle of the Hebrew Church, says in his letter to the Diaspora, James i. 18.

[2] As Stier does, for example. See his *Reden d. Apostel, in loc.*

national distinctions. There *is* a reduction of mankind to unity foreshadowed here, but it is to a unity in faith and worship by one Spirit—not surely to a denationalised cosmopolitanism such as should obliterate ethnic and tribal peculiarities by reducing all to one type of life or one mode of speech. Had a hundred and twenty persons, whose mother-tongues were diverse, been made to talk the same language, then one might have seen in it an emblem of that formal mechanical union which the so-called catholic Church of Rome aims at when, over all the lands of the globe, she demands a rigid compliance with one ritual, and serves God in the unvarying monotony of one dead tongue. Pentecost reads me a different lesson from that. The Holy Spirit of God brings a spiritual coincidence out of various life.[1] Frankly accepting the diversities which obtain among men, He only penetrates them all alike with the spirit of one Master, adapts them to the worship of one Father; and so out of superficial discordance He fetches forth a heavenly harmony. Let us not be too fond of uniformity: that is false catholicism. Let us seek the higher unity which rests on freedom and variety. In the true catholic Church which stands in our creed and is dear to our hearts, there are many tongues and forms of utterance—tongues so diverse that, alas! we often fail quite to recognise one another; yet is there only one Spirit, Who inspires, and, having inspired, interprets; Who is above all, and through all, and in us all!

We are the heirs of Pentecost. Then first the waiting Church below was linked tight in uttermost unity of life

---

[1] See Wordsworth *in loc.* on συνεχύθη (ver. 6). c. בָּבֶל, in Gen. xi. 9 (cf. LXX.).

to its reigning Lord above. One Spirit embraces the throne in heaven and the upper room on earth. Down from the King-Priest, Who ministers and prays and rules in the true sanctuary on high, there falls the precious purchase of His passion, a Divine Person, to animate and unite His still mortal members; then from their mortal tongues there goes up to their Priest-King on high one various consenting song of confident, thankful praise. The blessed link has never since been broken. "From that day," said Pope Leo the Great in the fifth century, "the trumpet of gospel preaching has sounded; from that day showers of gifts, rivers of blessings, have watered every desert and the whole parched earth."[1] It is true. Hard as it is to recognise the identity of Christ's visible Church, during much of her sorely-corrupted annals, with the Church of Pentecost, yet it is true that the gift of that day has never been recalled; the fire of divine life has never gone quite out; the tongues of the saints have never wholly ceased to echo back heaven's praises and preach to men the mercy of God. To each Christian man in every Christian age, there has stood, and still stands open, the unrevoked grant of the fulness of the Spirit —such fulness as will fill him, if he be willing to take it in, up to his capacity. To each of us it is, and has been, according to our faith. If we are carnal, cold, timid, desponding, servile-hearted, fearful; it is not because we live under the law, nor because God has set bounds to His grace, nor because the Holy Ghost is not yet, as if Christ were not yet glorified. It is because we have either no heart to desire, or no faith to expect. We have not, now, because we ask not. "Ask and ye

[1] Quoted by Dr. Wordsworth *in loc.*

shall receive," said Jesus. It is true that the ecstasy which marked the first full bestowal of the Spirit, when for the first time in this world sinful men knew themselves to be the redeemed sons of God, is not a normal effect of the Holy Ghost. Entire absorption and forgetfulness in devotional rapture is exceptional in the kingdom of Christ. But it is not unknown. It has been seen since. It has occurred, and is at any time possible, that some Christian heart, long purged by trial and kept waiting for its joy, may be of a sudden so filled with the new wine from the Vine of God,[1] as to seem, like the first disciples, beside itself with joy. The fervours of Christian life, the holy excitement of one who lives in another element than common men know, and sees what is hidden from them, may be mistaken by outsiders for the intoxication of fanaticism or of wine, the excess of incipient delirium. Yet it never passes beyond self control, unless other elements than the divine one mingle in the case. From ecstatic praise, Peter could pass on the instant to cool and temperate reasoning. The spirits of the prophets, in Paul's experience, were subject to the prophets. In all His ordinary working, at any rate, God the Holy Ghost still retains those characters which He displayed at Pentecost. He is still wind-like, to go abroad with untraced feet; fire-like, to penetrate, reduce, and inflame the soul. He is still the Spirit of confidence, of courage, of praise, of gladness. To such as mourn and fast and pray in Zion, He still gives " beauty for ashes, the oil of joy for mourning, the garment of praise for the spirit of

---

[1] This reference to vessels (or bottles) full of new wine is found in many patristic writers, as, *e.g.*, in Augustine, Cyril, Tertullian, &c. Cf. Eph. v. 18, "Be not drunk with wine, wherein is excess; but be filled with the Spirit."

heaviness."[1] What need have we for a baptism in the Spirit![2] It is to us the need of needs. We languish and are half asleep; we falter and hold our hand for trifles; we are slothful and cowardly; we expect little good, and do less; we find all duty hard and much of it impossible; we sigh, we grumble, with shaking knees and eyes that seek the ground; without praise, or with such as is heartless; without testimony to Jesus, or with such as is timid — what un-Pentecostal Christians are we! Down, if down we must be, on our knees! If we are to grovel, let it be in penitence and shame! Dumb are we? Then let us weep! If we can do no more, at least let us lie, and cry, and wait: it may be that even to us a Pentecost will come, which shall set us on our feet again, and put a new song within our mouth, and make new the spirit within our breast!

[1] Isaiah lxi. 3.
[2] "In the Spirit;" for it is always 'ἐνΠνεύματι, just as it is 'ὕδατι. See the passages in Bruder, sub voce βαπτίζειν.

IV.

The First Gospel Sermon.

FAITH COMETH BY HEARING.

Acts ii. 14-36.

Revised Version.

But Peter, standing with the Eleven, lifted up his voice and cried to them:

"*Men of Judæa, and all the inhabitants of Jerusalem, be this known to you, and give ear to my words! For these are not, as you suppose, drunk, for it is the third hour of the day; but this is what was spoken of through the prophet: 'It shall be in the last days, saith God, I will pour out of My Spirit upon all flesh, and your sons and your daughters shall prophesy, and your young men shall see visions, and your elders shall dream dreams, and even upon My bondmen and upon My bondwomen will I pour out of My Spirit, and they shall prophesy. And I will give wonders in the heaven above, and signs on the earth below, blood and fire and vapour of smoke. The sun shall be turned to darkness, and the moon to blood, before the coming of the great and manifest day of the Lord. And it shall be, every one whosoever shall call on the name of the Lord shall be saved.'*

"*Men of Israel, hear these words: Jesus the Nazarene, a man certified to you by God with mighty works and wonders and signs, which God did through Him in the midst of you, as yourselves know—this Man, betrayed in the fixed counsel and foreknowledge of God, you through the hands of lawless men nailed up and despatched, Whom God raised again, having loosed the* pangs of death, since it was not possible for Him to be held by it. For David says with reference to Him :

" ' I foresaw the Lord before me at every moment,
    For on my right hand is He, in order that I be not moved.
    For this was my heart glad,
    And my tongue exulted,
    Nay, even my flesh shall tabernacle in hope ;
    For Thou wilt not leave my soul to Hades,
    Nor give Thy holy one to see corruption.
    Thou wilt make me know paths of life,
    Thou wilt fill me with gladness with Thy countenance.'

" Men and brethren, it is permitted to say to you with boldness of the patriarch David, that he both died and was buried, and his tomb is among us to this very day. Being therefore a prophet, and knowing that with an oath God swore to him to seat of the fruit of his loin upon his throne, he foreseeing this, spoke about the resurrection of the Christ, that neither was He ' left to Hades,' nor did His ' flesh see corruption.' This Jesus God raised again, of which all we are witnesses. Being therefore by the right hand of God exalted and having received the promise of the Holy Ghost from the Father, He poured out this which ye [both] see and hear. For David did not go up to the heavens, but says himself :

" ' The Lord said to my Lord :
    Sit on My right hand
    Till I make Thine enemies a stool for Thy feet.'

" Assuredly therefore let the whole House of Israel know that God made Him both Lord and Christ — that same Jesus Whom ye crucified !"

IV.

ST. PETER made a fit reply to those Jews who, "mocking, said, 'These men are full of new wine,'" when he quietly reminded them that the sun was still barely three hours up and the morning sacrifice not yet slain, an hour before which no reputable Jew was accustomed either to eat or drink, nor any one, Jew or Gentile, to be found the worse for wine. For, as St. Paul says, "they that be drunken are drunken in the night." All suspicion even of overexcitement through the influence of the Holy Ghost, or such intoxication of the feelings as for the time obscures the judgment, is still more fully laid to rest by the tone of his speech. Anything more quiet, or better considered, or freer from every trace of agitation, it is difficult to conceive. Fresh from that first burst of divine enthusiasm which, following the rushing noise, had set each disciple's heart on fire, with the confused sounds of many-tongued exultation still in his ear, this man, who was wont to be so hot and easily moved, delivered his first address, as the Christian spokesman, with greater composure of manner and closeness of thinking, than, before Christ's death, his words had ever exhibited. His sermon is a chain of argument buttressed by texts of Scripture and by appeals to fact, unfolded with admirable tact, as of a man who had all his wits about him, and leading up to his desired conclusion by rigorous force of logic. It is plain that the spirit of this prophet is "subject to the prophet." It is plain that the Spirit Whom Jesus has sent is of another sort from that wild breath of demoniac inspiration which pervaded heathen religion, which flung the foaming priestess of Apollo to the ground in nervous convulsions, or drove the worshippers of Thammuz in frantic dances over the mountains of Phrygia. The superstitions of those tribes in Western Asia, with which the Hebrews were ethnologically allied, were full of such delirious and frenzied worship. It is in notable contrast to these, that this sober rational enthusiasm of Christianity, as a quite new thing in religious experience, claims special admiration. Peter, speaking here under circumstances which might have quickened the pulses even of a cooler man, is full of the Spirit; yet the Spirit by Whom he is filled only constrains him to calmer, wiser, and more cogent speech.

A brief analysis of the sermon will help us to realise this. It consists of two parts. The handle which the occasion offered led him first to explain what had so astonished the bystanders — I mean that simultaneous praising of God in many languages by the whole crowd of believers. The explanation of this is, therefore, the first part; but it leads on to the second, which establishes the messiahship of Jesus.

Speaking as he did, a Jew to Jews, at the moment when one of the last great predicted crises in Hebrew history was occurring, Peter needed few words of his own to explain the event. As soon as he had refuted the intoxication theory, he turned for a better explanation to those prophetic writings in which, under God's teaching, the forefathers of his audience had anticipated, centuries before, what had now occurred. Out of the short book of Joel, an early prophet of Judah, he cited by memory from the Septuagint [1] (whence it may be gathered that he spoke in Hellenistic Greek) five verses in which God had foretold a great outpouring of His Spirit. In the original text, the date at which this prediction was to be fulfilled had been left purposely vague. "It shall come to pass *afterward*," said Joel; and his words have had many a fulfilment. This "afterward," however, St. Peter exchanged for another phrase, elsewhere used in prophetic Scripture. "In the last days" is more definite than "afterward;" for "the last days" cover the whole indeterminate extent of that final economy of God toward men which began with the first coming of Christ, and shall end probably at His second. How soon the close of this period should follow on its opening, St. Peter here, and generally the apostolic writers, did not know. We know now that its duration has already been vastly longer than any of them expected, and the end of it is hidden from our forecasting no less than from theirs. Alike to them and to us, all that lies betwixt the two fixed points which bound this vast section of human history is comprehended in the prophetic phrase "the last days." Whatever has happened or shall happen between the two advents, happens in the "last time." In the verses which Peter quotes, events from the beginning and events from the end of this long era are brought into one line of vision so as to appear together.

[1] See Joel ii. 28–31, in LXX.

The effusion of the Spirit marked its opening, and is continued or renewed all along its course; it is probable that the portents in earth and heaven, the blood and the fire, are to be more immediate heralds of its close. Such convulsions in nature, or in the civil polity of nations, or in both, are foretold as harbingers of the end in our Lord's prophecies and in His revelation which He sent to His servant John.[1] Repeatedly during the past history of Christendom has Europe traversed such zones of disaster, when prodigies in the sky, with war and flame and pestilence on earth, have affrighted the souls of men and shaken the timorous or superstitious with apprehension of approaching judgment. In fact, they are become the stock-in-trade of professional alarmists, whose cry of "wolf" excites now only incredulous contempt. The true moral or lesson from this and the like Scriptures is not that our hearts should be set a-quaking by every epidemic or breach of public peace, as if it were a trumpet of doom; but that at all times, even the serenest, we should recollect, with reverent and sober awe, that our lot is to live in "last days," with Pentecost behind us, bequeathing to us the final gift of the Holy Ghost, and judgment ahead of us, as the next chief incident in the divine economy. To the spiritual eye, the time already past, which we know to have been long, and the time to come, which for aught we know may be also long, are equally drawn near. The great event at Pentecost and the great event at Judgment are each of them to us the next or nearest act of God in history. The grace of Pentecost which brought the gospel close to us that we

---

[1] See Matt. xxiv. 29; Rev. vi. 12, ff. (Cf. similar imagery in Isa. xiii. 10; Ezek. xxxii. 7, 8.)

might be saved, and the reckoning of the end which shall avenge all disobedience and unbelief, are both of them impending facts, between which, and under the spiritual shadow and power of both of which, it is ours to live.[1] We expect no other or greater revelation of mercy: we do expect now the final revelation of judgment. To us, therefore, as to Peter's hearers, the strong plain lesson from the time we live in, still is, to "call on the name of the Lord," that in this "great and notable day of the Lord," we may be "saved."

To those pious and instructed Jews whom Peter addressed, this mere citation served all his purpose. To them, God's outpouring of His Spirit on "all flesh," on young as well as old, women as well as men, slaves as well as free, and that in such a measure as to make the humblest of the Lord's people not less privileged in the knowledge of His truth than had been the few favoured patriarchs and prophets to whom truth came of old, through vision or dream:—this outpouring, I say, meant to them the advent of Messiah's reign. Only when He should come Who is called the Christ, the Anointed of the Lord, could this supreme hope of Israel be realised. Then only was the entire people to become (what Moses wished them to be) a people of prophets, or (as Isaiah foretold) a nation of priests; then only (in Zechariah's words) should the feeble among them be as David, and the house of David as the Angel of the Lord for strength

---

[1] Besides many other passages in the apostolic epistles, compare especially Peter's own words in 1 Pet. i. 17-21. The "fear" in which our present life is to be spent results from those two great events, between which it lies, and by which it is, so to speak, overshadowed, the Father's judgment according to works and our redemption "in these last times" by Christ's precious blood.

and wisdom.[1] Yet this, and nothing less, was what Peter declared had come to pass. The sum of all ancient promise and of all patient hope lay here. The whole company of souls within the inner circle of belief had received, without one exception, an inspiration from on high, which made every tongue prophesy and set the seal of a divine consecration upon every forehead. Old limitations, inequalities, and short-comings were swept for ever away. God had come down to all, and the times of Messiah had at length appeared.

Where then was the Messiah? Peter felt that this question was seething up in every heart, and that he must answer it in the second and harder portion of his speech.

Not one there but knew how, only a few weeks before, One, Who for years had been calling Himself Messiah, had been formally found guilty of imposture by the court of judges and handed over for execution to the Roman magistrate. Few there perhaps who had not swelled the mob's cry of "Crucify Him." These very men were to be told now to their face, not only that their national Deliverer had come and gone, unrecognised and unhonoured, but that their deliberate judgment on Him had been to reject Him, and that their national response to His call had been to murder Him. They were to be told, yet so that they should not arise and smite the speaker, that the hope and pride of their fathers for more than a thousand years, the One to look for Whom, and wait for Whom, and pray for Whom, had become wrought into the national heart like an hereditary passion; He for Whose sake they would all to a man have called it a

[1] Cf. Num. xi. 29; Isa. lxi. 6; and Zech. xii. 8.

glad thing to die, was the very Nazarene Whose blood last Passover they imprecated on their heads! So to tell them this as to convince them of the fact, convict them of the crime, and persuade them to repent, tasked Peter's courage much, and his skill even more. But now had come the first occasion on which his Master's words were to come true: "It is not ye that speak, but the Spirit of your Father Which speaketh in you."[1] Heightened and guided by his Father's Spirit, the intellect of Peter felt its way by an instinct to the fittest choice, arrangement, and statement of his subject; so that he spoke such words as in the same Spirit's hand were to cleave their way like a sword to the soul and conscience of a thousand sinners. It was the inauguration of the gospel ministry: the first example of gospel preaching. Pray that ministers may preach, and congregations hear, in the Holy Ghost!

Postponing to the end any statement of his grand doctrine that Jesus is Lord and Christ, St. Peter leads up towards it through a series of more and more conclusive historical proofs. Starting afresh in this new section of his address by a solemn call to attention, and setting then in the forefront the well-known historic name of the Man Whom they had slain, he sketches in brief the biography of "Jesus of Nazareth," from His first public appearance down to that very hour, with a view to trace at each step God's dealings with the Man Jesus, and to gather up from these cumulative evidence of His messiahship. There are four links in this chain of evidence. The first two, lying within the knowledge of his hearers, are briefly handled; the last two, being facts lying outside

[1] Matt. x. 20.

their observation, are confirmed at length by Scripture and living testimony.

(1) God's hand first appeared in the public ministry of Jesus by the miracles which He had wrought. The number and variety and notoriousness of such works are hinted at in the accumulation of names which Peter heaps up: "miracles," for the power they revealed; "wonders," for the startling effect they produced; "signs," for the spiritual significance they conveyed. On these proofs the preacher had no need to dwell. They were known to all. They had been done "in the midst of" the public. They had been acknowledged even by the authorities. They had been constantly appealed to by Jesus Himself. The miraculous in the ministry of this Man, was, in those days, a recognised fact to start with, however much it may of late have lost its weight with modern sceptics. It was the earliest public token of divine approval; and such a token as, at the very outset, made the Jews' after treatment of Jesus inexcusable.

(2) But now came the stumbling point with the audience. This Man of Nazareth, the fame of Whose works had filled Palestine, had been by the national rulers solemnly adjudged a cheat and a blasphemer; and they, the people, in a fickle hour, had turned upon their former favourite, and cried out for His blood. If it was needless to enlarge on His miracles, to dwell on this fact was still less desirable. Yet, two things must be done. Their criminal share in the memorable paschal tragedy must be plainly charged home; justice demanded that: and the consistency of such a death with the Sufferer's messiahship must be explained; for the course of his argument required that. In one short sentence Peter does both.

Jesus' crucifixion was not out of keeping with His Christhood; since it was by God's "deliberate counsel and foreknowledge," that He—He Who could raise the dead to life—was Himself "delivered" up to die. Who could have taken away that life, if God had not been pleased to give it up? It was part of the prearranged, predicted history of the Christ (as Peter by this time had learned), that He should "suffer many things and be killed." Suffering and dying were proofs of Christhood; not objections to it. Yet, not for a moment did this divine prelestination of Messiah's sacrifice lighten his guilt, who "delivered" Him up in the garden with a kiss,[1] or theirs, who, by the hands of lawless Roman soldiers, nailed Him up and slew Him.[2] Nakedly Peter recalls the harsh and horrid deeds of seven weeks before, and bluntly charges them on the crowd before him, so that each man's share in that Friday's work might rise up out of memory before his soul and tear his conscience with remorse and shame. Only his proof of the messiahship of the Crucified is still far too incomplete to justify his dwelling on so irritating a theme; and therefore, without giving time for pause, or even breaking off his sentence, he goes on to announce (3) that novel and astounding fact of resurrection, by which God had set His seal for ever beyond all cavil to the innocence, the claims and the sonship of the Lord Jesus: "Whom God raised up."

It was well enough known in Jerusalem[3] that the temporary tomb of Jesus had been found empty on the Sunday morning: but the "public ear" had been "abused"

---

[1] ἔκδοτον in verse 23 refers to Judas probably.
[2] The text is: διὰ χειρὸς ἀνόμων προσπήξαντες ἀνείλατε.
[3] See Matt. xxviii. 11–15.

with a forged tale about the abstraction of the body by His friends; and this was the first time that the true explanation of that vacant, but not rifled, grave, had been given to the world. In proof of the fact that Jesus had come to life, Peter had more than a hundred witnesses at his back, witnesses by eye and ear and finger-touch, each one of them ready to stake his life upon the fact. But Peter knew very well how hard it is for any amount of testimony to win credence for an unwelcome as well as unlikely fact. Before men believe in a miracle, they must be willing to recognize the miraculous. The spiritual probability of divine intervention, or the religious and moral value of the wonder, must be recognised in order to prepare the way for evidence of the fact. Now, it was antecedently probable that, if Messiah ever should come and die, God would restore Him again to life. Nay, it was certain. For, first, it lay in the nature of the case that a dead Saviour could not save; that He Who died for others' sins should not be holden of death, as they are who die for their own; but that the Prince and Captain of life would find the grave to be like a new womb,[1] out of which he should rise to newness of life. Besides this inherent spiritual necessity, of which any one could judge for himself, Jews, who believed their own Scriptures, had an additional reason to expect it. Ancient prophecy had pointed expressly to a resurrection of Messiah. This Peter proved by an elaborate exposition of the last four verses of the sixteenth Psalm, quoted from the Septuagint. The steps of his reasoning are these:—(*a*) The words cannot apply to King David (who is assumed to have been

---

[1] See v. 24, ᾠδῖνες (חֶבְלֵי מָוֶת, Psa. xviii. 5) = "birth-throes;" but the Hebrew has the double meaning of "bands" as well, which the Hellenistic Greek word never has (see Meyer *in loc.*).

the author of this Psalm); for, although the current Rabbinical interpretation might not look beyond the Psalmist, yet it was notorious, and might be affirmed without disrespect to the head of the royal line,[1] that he still slept in his family monument on mount Zion, within a few hundred yards of the spot where Peter stood. (*b*) David knew enough to enable him to speak thus in the name of his descendant, the Christ; both because he was generally a "prophet,"[2] and also because God had in words which it was felt Solomon could not exhaust, sworn to him that He would raise up One of his seed to sit, and sit for ever, on his throne. Was not this indeed the very hope of Israel? But (*c*) what was thus true nevermore of David, but only of One greater than David, of the Christ, had been now, in point of fact, fulfilled in Jesus: and here, with clenching effect, St. Peter could turn and appeal to the unanimous evidence of the whole disciplehood. What any devout and thoughtful Jew ought to have been looking for, as the chief mark of Messiah when He came, as God's crowning attestation to David's Son, could not be a thing incredible, when at last affirmed of a Man Who declared to the death that He was Messiah. If Jesus should be after all what He said He was, God must

---

[1] This is the force of μετὰ παρρησίας. For the unusual title of "Patriarch," in v. 29, s. 1 Chron. xxiv. 31, LXX., where it is applied to David along with other public men of his realm. It is used of Abraham in Heb. vii. 4, and of the twelve sons of Jacob by Stephen in Acts vii. 8, 9.

[2] In the general sense, that is, of a man inspired to teach; for king David did not belong to the order described by the technical title of "prophet," although it seems to have existed from the time of Samuel's prime, nor is the title ever applied to him in the Old Testament.

[3] See 2 Sam. vii. 12-16. (Cf. Psa. lxxxix. 3, 4, and cxxxii. 11.)

have raised Him up : but God had raised Him up, "whereof," adds the preacher, "we all are witnesses."

(4) One more proof, and only one, remained. Resurrection from the dead was neither the only nor the latest test of Christhood offered by ancient prophecy. For in another passage which Peter quotes (as Jesus had Himself quoted it with the same application [1]), the same royal prophet had spoken of the anointed King's exaltation to the right hand of divine rule and power, in terms which could never apply to himself. David had not ascended into heaven to sit there in the seat of supreme celestial monarchy and thence subdue all earthly foes; but Peter was prepared to say that Jesus had. This last token of Jesus' messiahship was one on which Peter himself and ten others with him could have given partial witness, on the evidence of their own senses. They had seen Him rise from the hill-side of Olivet and go up till, behind the veil of cloud, they watched Him disappear into the heavens. But it was not to this St. Peter made appeal. Neither he nor any other mortal had witnessed those stupendous events which followed on the disappearance of the Lord Jesus, and were the real fulfilment of ancient promises. No eye had pursued His retreating figure till it was received into the congratulations of impatient troops of angels, who waited, out of sight of men, that, circling round and heralding before with jubilant trumpet and the waving of celestial palms, they might escort His conquering feet into the heavenly Jerusalem. None saw what august inauguration followed His reception by the Father, and crowned His toil and passion with the joy which had been set before Him,

[1] In Matt. xxii. 44, quoting Psa. cx.

when in His still marred flesh He sat down upon the throne which is at God's right hand, gathered to His hands that were pierced the sceptres which sway creation, and received for the first time, in mediatorial right, the homage of assembled spirits. In the secresy of heaven had been transacted that fulfilment of the Father's promise which conveyed to His Son, man's obedient accepted Substitute, the right and power to pour out upon His waiting Church this oil of gladness—the abundance of the Holy Ghost. Yet, though neither apostles nor we were suffered to witness the effusion of the Spirit on the crowned and priestly head of Jesus in the day of His coronation and enthronement, yet from that Christ, Anointed One, there have come down to earth droppings of the sacred oil. At Pentecost, the chrism touched each disciple's brow, and set each disciple apart for praise, a glad priest, prophet, and king thenceforth.[1] In the change which that anointing Holy Ghost had wrought, in their joyful worship as new-made priests to God, in the prophetic insight with which they preached the Word to men, in the more than kingly power by which their words swayed, and bent, and captured the hearts and souls of thousands—these men at Pentecost were living proofs that their Master, though refused, baffled, slain on earth, had been exalted and enthroned in heaven, and had "received of the Father," what He had now sent down to them, "the promise of the Holy Ghost." Pentecost itself—"what ye now see and hear"—is the supreme demonstration of Peter's thesis that Jesus is the Christ:

[1] Compare St. John's words: "Ye have an unction"—a chrism, χρῖσμα—"from the Holy One;" "The anointing"—the chrism, τὸ χρῖσμα—which ye received from Him abideth in you." 1 John ii. 20, 27.

for on Jesus' friends, and on none else, has come what prophets promised and the just have waited for. He is the Lord on Whom, if one call, one shall be saved. Peter's explanation of the wonder, his apology for his brethren's enthusiasm, his demonstration of his Master's claims, his conviction of the hearers as rejecters of the Messiah, are all now complete; and the preacher sweeps grandly, with rising boldness and the majesty of an ambassador for God, to the conclusion he has been driving at all through:—" Therefore, let the whole house of Israel know assuredly, that God did make that same Jesus, Whom ye crucified, both Lord and Christ."

Peter's message has come down to us through the lips of ten thousand preachers. We are of the "all flesh," on whom God has not only promised to pour His Spirit but is doing it; and calling on the Lord Jesus for salvation, we may plead on our own behalf His ancient "whosoever." The merciful and gracious Man of Nazareth, Who spread out His hands for us on Pilate's cross, has been now for eighteen hundred years King of the spiritual universe and Lord of divine influence, with all hearts beneath His finger, and the keys of heaven and hell at His girdle. The message is: For salvation He is reigning still; not for destruction. Call now, and He will save. In this first gospel sermon there lay the gist of all gospel preaching till the end of time.

V.
The First Christian Baptism.

Ὃ καὶ ἡμᾶς ἀντίτυπον νῦν σώζει βάπτισμα.

Acts ii. 37–41.

Revised Version.

Now, when they had heard, they were pricked in the heart, and said to Peter and the rest of the apostles: " What shall we do, men and brethren?"

Then Peter to them: " Repent, and be baptized each of you upon the name of Jesus Christ for remission of sins, and ye shall receive the free-gift of the Holy Ghost. For to you is the promise, and to your children, and to all who are far off, as many as the Lord our God may call to Him." With many other words, too, did he continue to witness, and exhorted them, saying: " Be saved from this generation of perverseness."

Those, therefore, who did receive His word were baptized; and there were added in the same day about three thousand souls.

V.

"WHEN He is come," said Jesus, speaking of the Holy Ghost, "He will 'convict' the world of sin, because they believe not on Me."[1] Of this prophecy Pentecost saw the first fulfilment. It was not simply that the word of Peter went to the hearts of his Master's murderers like a sword, as it well might; for had that been all, it would have stung them into rage, as did the words of Stephen to the Sanhedrim a little later. Along with the word there struck home, on that first day of grace, the Spirit of God, Whose blessed work it is to arouse within a self-satisfied sinner, not the resentment of impenitent remorse, sorrow twined with hatred and working death,[2] but the gracious relentings of a humble and devout repentance. Already that morning the Holy Ghost had come to those who believed and were waiting for Him; now He came—a second wonder—to men who believed not, and looked for nothing less. If the Spirit of comfort and might has flame for His symbol, the Spirit of conviction is like a goad to "prick" or a hammer to break. He brings not peace to earth, but a sword.

Peter's sermon, like all true gospel preaching, was fitted to stir in the soul, when God's saving power went with it, a tumult of contending emotions. For, first, he had pro-

---

[1] John xvi. 8, 9. [2] Cf. 2 Cor. vii. 10.

claimed that the last days were begun, those days the end of which is judgment, and that he who would escape from that impending doom had need (like Jonah in the ship) to arise and call upon his God. This "terror of the Lord," as St. Paul calls it,[1] heard behind a man, and the hope of salvation set before his face, are two strong persuasions to awake, bestir himself, and flee. Had Peter preached nothing else, fear and hope would have concurred to breed within his hearers a hot and vehement desire to be saved. But he had charged them, on the other hand, with refusing and killing that very Lord and Christ through Whom alone salvation could be had. After heaping proof on proof to convince their understanding that the crucified pretender of Nazareth (as they deemed Him) had after all been God's Anointed, the preacher's closing words had gone into their conscience like red-hot shot, agonising them[2] with their own tremendous, and, as it seemed, fatal guilt. They were crucifiers of their Saviour. Did not this mean that they had thrown their last chance away? What hope of mercy could remain to men who had blundered so frightfully as to murder their Redeemer? As powerfully as the prospect of judgment and the promise of a Saviour combined to impel them forward, so powerfully did the reproaches of their own consciences, starting into life at Peter's voice, thrust them back from deliverance. Men who, when the Deliverer came, had given Him a cross for answer, might well imagine that they had barred against themselves the gates of hope. Thus flung to and fro by conflicting passions in a dilemma out of which

---

[1] Τὸ φόβον τοῦ κυρίου. 2 Cor. v. 11.

[2] The word κατανύσσειν (v. 37) = "compunction" (Alford); only in LXX. and Apocrypha; used of any sharp emotion. See Meyer *in loc.*

THE FIRST CHRISTIAN BAPTISM. 83

they could see no escape, softened, too, by sorrow and desire, many of the Jews cried out in their distress, or, clinging to him who had spoken and to his fellows, assailed them with impatient, eager, and affectionate questionings:[1] "Men and brethren, what shall we do?" Now, in this sudden access of spiritual earnestness seizing a multitude at once, flashing new light along their past life to discover its guilt, and so powerfully affecting them with the apprehension of near judgment and of possible mercy still nearer, as to throw them into a paroxysm of alarm and regret and longing—in this, as in many a similar scene since then, may be seen, not less plainly than in the gift of tongues, that force above nature, for which so many tell us they search human experience in vain. It is God's finger[2] stretched forth to touch men's hearts. Nor ought we to be greatly startled if religious emotion, not less sudden or vivid, should at any time burst forth, as it did at Pentecost, in outcries which transgress the decorous propriety of a modern audience. When a strong wind is wrestling with the forest trees, you expect some crackling of the branches. Only the same power may be traced equally at work, when, alone in his chamber, with no help from the sympathy of numbers, one single sinner is bowed down upon his knees under the same novel sense of guilt; when, horror-struck at the discovery of his real position as a lost, wandered, godless soul, under condemnation, a man cries out bitter cries, with sobs of strong desire, which reach no ear save His Who always listens to catch such sounds amid the uprising din of earthly labour, strife, and grief.

[1] The address: ἀδελφοί (v. 37) shows the relenting of their minds towards the disciples.
[2] Cf. ἐν δακτύλῳ Θεοῦ. Luke xi. 20.

7 *

Challenged to allay, if they could, terror and distress which their own words had occasioned, the apostles again put Peter to the front. He and they together, with I dare say all the unofficial brethren as well, wore that long day away in what may be termed the second function of the Christian ministry, pointing penitents to the Lord Jesus. The gist, however, of the "many words," which, spoken with a loud voice to the crowd, or pressed home to here a little group and there a single listener, did that day, ere the sun went down, turn a Bochim into a Salem, weeping of thousands into peace; the gist of all is found in those few words of Peter, which have been preserved for us by the historian. His own history explains best how St. Peter was led to use them.

Some three years before that day, or rather more, a very strong voice, sounding through Palestine from the waste land along the farther bank of Jordan, had called these same Jews out into the wilderness. Peter himself, and most of the eleven at his side, as well as many among the crowd before him, had heard and followed it. In the heat of a spiritual awakening, of which this scene at Pentecost seems to have reminded him, Peter, and multitudes besides, had obeyed the voice which spoke then in God's name and bade them "repent and be baptised." But John had done more than baptise with water: he had foretold a second baptism and a greater Baptist. Not all the thousands who, in the fervour of a popular movement, went down into the river under the hands of the rude prophet, laid to heart that blessed sequel to his message, or learned to look for the mightier One Who, coming after, should baptise with the Holy Ghost and with fire. Peter, indeed, did: and his long waiting and his patient faith in Jesus as "Him Who should come," have been this very day rewarded. The fire, the Holy Ghost, have been poured upon the heads of Jesus' followers, as John foretold; theirs is the second baptism. But how shall these men before him, who would not believe that Jesus was the predicted Christ to baptise with the Spirit, would not believe, but, on the contrary, very loudly denied, and put denial into deeds, since they refused and sold and slew "the Son of the living God,"—how shall they receive the Holy Ghost? Peter did not falter. No touch of self-righteous jealousy dimmed his frank admission of his Master's murderers to a place as privileged as his own. "Let them become at last even as we are:" this was what his words meant. "Let them now at last repent in very deed, since that show of penitence in John's days has been put to mockery by the crime done seven weeks ago. Let them repent of having refused God's Anointed, and believe now, as we have believed for long, that the Crucified is the Christ. Let them testify their new faith (as Jesus has bidden) by a rebaptism. Then shall they be even as we were this morning, who needed not to prove by any baptism, but had by years of patient devotion proved our discipleship. On them, too, there shall surely come, just as it came an hour ago on us, as free, as full, as blessed, this gift of the Holy Ghost. For Joel's promise is wider than to compass our little band. It is 'to all flesh;' to you, therefore, and to your 'little ones' with you,[1] to the far off, to whomsoever 'the Lord our God shall call,' that they may 'call' on Him. Out therefore from this evil generation of Jews—a generation 'perverse and crooked,'

[1] Cf. Joel ii. 28 with ver. 39. Τέκνοις, not = "descendants" here, but "children."

whose spot is not the spot of God's children,[1]—'be ye saved' whose hearts He hath pricked. Suffer yourselves to be also saved, like us, by Jesus the Christ."

Thus, for the second time, the old cry is repeated, here in the city as by John in the desert: "Repent and be baptised." Yet it is easy to see, even from its first administration, how much more Christian baptism involved than John's, and how much more it conferred. It involved two conditions, of which only one was presupposed in John's, and that one only partially; it conferred two blessings, of which John's conferred neither, but merely promised them.

I. The double condition of Christian baptism is repentance and faith in Jesus Christ.

(*a*) Repentance, or the resolute turning and changing of the life, to face right round, away from old sin, towards new holiness, was the one demand of John, the first baptiser. His was a baptism eminently "of repentance."[2] Yet even this change of mind, as he preached it, and as the people performed it at his bidding, was a much less thorough thing than the repentance which Peter preached. It was more like a reformation of manners then a renewal of the heart. He bade the greedy people learn to be liberal; the farmers of taxes he rebuked for extortion; the soldiers for violence and discontent; and he warned the sanctimonious that for the fruits of good living only, not for a godly lineage, would God spare the tree at whose root the axe lay.[3] Whereas,

---

[1] There is a reference in ver. 40 to Deut. xxxii. 5. Note, too, that σώθητε is not = "save yourselves;" for which cf. Matt. xxvii. 40 (σῶσον σεαυτόν).   [2] It is so called in Mark i. 4.

[3] The fullest record of what sort of repentance John insisted on is found in Luke's own Gospel, iii. 7–17.

now, what the Jews of Pentecost needed was nothing short of a moral and spiritual revolution, equivalent to a second birth. Their whole attitude towards Jesus, as haters of His truth and slayers of His life, had proved them to be (in His own words) children of the devil, who is a murderer and a liar.[1] Because He came a light into the world, they, being sons of darkness, refused Him. His good works rebuked them, and they stoned Him. He came from God, and because God they hated, Him they slew. No mere sweeping of the life as clean as might be (such as John's brief ministry had effected), could turn into saints men whose hands were red with the blood of Christ, whose hearts were filled with hatred to Christ. They must be born again: and the repentance which goes with that means nothing short of a reversal of the innermost springs and sources of moral action; the slaying of one nature, or one set of ruling tendencies, that another may come to life. Since now their hearts were so far touched, and the Holy Ghost had already begun to turn them, Peter urges instant, prompt decision;[2] a yielding at once of their will and entire nature to that tide of sacred influence which had just set in, and was able to swing them round into a new life.

(*b*) A second condition Peter asked, which John had not asked—faith in Jesus as the Messiah. John, indeed, had foretold in general terms that the Christ was at hand, and had used that fact as a motive for repentance; but he

---

[1] In John viii. 31–59. This whole passage, with others from our Lord's teaching, such as John iii. 3–8, v. 21 ff.; vi. 32 ff.; Luke xi. 24–26, &c., shows how He insisted upon a deeper and more vital change than the reformation advocated and partly effected by His precursor.

[2] Cf. the force of the aorist in μετανοήσατε, ver. 38.

did not hinge his baptism on any profession of faith in this impending advent; still less could he ask his hearers to identify as the Messiah a Man Who was still unknown. Now, however, the most central and characteristic thing about the new baptism is that it rests "on the name of Jesus Christ;"[1] that is to say, on the identification of the Man of Nazareth, Whom Pilate crucified, with the promised anointed Son of God, Whom Israel looked for as its King. In this one fact, the fact which Peter's previous discourse had been devoted to proving, lies the centre of gravity of the whole apostolic testimony; and, though the word "faith" is not once named, yet such a cordial acceptance of this fact, as implies reliance upon Jesus Christ for salvation, is plainly the chief *differentia* distinguishing apostolic from Johannine baptism. It was, indeed, a very brief confession of faith on which these primitive converts were received. Yet it is possible to trace the essential Christian verities back into this solitary article of the Church's creed. In it lay undeveloped whatever is most precious in the confessions of Christendom.[2] First, it implied to Jewish hearers, and on Jewish lips, all that Old Testament revelation had led men to expect the Christ either to be or to do. Whatever lay in Israel's messianic hope, of a suffering Victim bearing sin, of an expiating Priest more effectual than Aaron, of a diviner Legislator than Moses, of a Ruler more just and noble than David, more splendid and peaceful than Solomon; nay, of One Who was the eternal Wisdom of the Godhead, the Fellow of Jehovah,

---

[1] Observe, the preferable reading in ver. 38 is $\grave{\epsilon}\pi\acute{\iota}$, not $\grave{\epsilon}\nu$.

[2] It would be instructive, and to our age very helpful, to have this worked out in detail, which cannot here be done. The sentences that follow in the text are meant for suggestions.

before Whom divine, not civil, homage must be paid, and that, not by men only, but by angels—all this is here, at one stroke, swept over to the lowly Son of Mary, Nazareth's carpenter, Who was nailed to Pilate's cross. For next, there is here assumed, as a matter of course, all those facts about the earthly life of Jesus as an historical personage, which, to the first speaker and first hearers of this creed, were so notorious; as well as all such supernatural events connected with His advent, ministry, or departure, as served to substantiate His mission. The miracle of a non-natural entrance into human life, and of a non-natural resumption of it after death, with whatever else lay in His special character as the Sent of God, must plainly be accepted if we call Him Christ. More even than that. The words which He Himself spoke about Himself are all true, if He be Christ; words so strongly and so plainly asserting an unique relation to the Father, that for them, when men thought them false, they sought to kill Him. This Teacher left men no standing-ground betwixt two extremes: either to worship Him as God, or to stone Him as the most impious and daring blasphemer the world had ever seen. As a blasphemer He died. Did they err in His death? then they slew the very God. For He called Himself the Son of God, Whom to see was to see God, Who only knew God, Who had been before Abraham with God. He bade us trust Him as we trust God, honour Him as we honour God; our life He said He was, our light, our door to heaven, our meat and drink, our sole Shepherd, our future Judge. Confess Him, and you confess the everlasting Father, Whom He reveals. Confess Him, and you confess the Holy Ghost, Whom He promised to bestow. His central Name, in the thrice-holy baptismal formula, involves the other Two.

II. So far of the conditions of Christian baptism, by which it widely differed from its predecessor, the Johannine baptism. The difference is not less wide in that which it expressed and sealed to the faithful. Two blessings are named by St. Peter: remission of sins, and the gift of the Holy Ghost.

(a) John's baptism is indeed called, by two of the Evangelists, "a baptism of repentance for the remission of sins."[1] But this could only be because it pointed to the Lamb on Whom every confessed sin was to be laid, and promised forgiveness through His blood, precisely as the sprinkling with hyssop had done under the Mosaic ritual. Peter's converts, on the other hand, accepted an actual, not a prospective, expiation for sin. For the sin of putting Jesus to death, they accepted that very death itself as God's expiatory sacrifice. They looked, as all converts have since done, to the blessed Sufferer on Calvary as the true Lamb, foreshadowed by every sacrificial victim; and they received, through His shed blood, the pardon of their sins. This pardon was expressed to their faith by the rite of baptism, not merely as a washing clean from old stains, which might need frequent renewal all their life long; but rather as a union once for all with the Victim in His death to sin, in order that, emerging with Him again, they might live thenceforth the consecrated and purged lives of men who are one with Christ. Christian baptism, as afterwards explained by the most theological of the apostles,[2] is burial with

---

[1] See Mark i. 4 and Luke iii. 3. The preposition in both cases is $εἰς =$ "with a view to," as the ultimate result.

[2] See Rom. vi. 3–7, and Col. ii. 12.

THE FIRST CHRISTIAN BAPTISM. 91

Christ. It means such acceptance of the sacrifice as identifies with the Victim. It seals for ever, without need of renewal, a sinner's incorporation with the sinner's representative Head, when He bore the sins of His mystical body "in His own body on the tree."

(*b*) But the crowning glory of Christian baptism was that it preceded or followed,[1] and always expressed, the Pentecostal gift of the Holy Ghost. It must have become sufficiently plain to such readers as have followed the history down to this point, that the characteristic effusion of divine influence which dates from Pentecost does not just mean any action of God in impelling to pious or holy activity the souls of men. God has always drawn men to Himself. God the Spirit has always been at work in this world, not only checking evil or suggesting good, enabling wise men to be wise, and true men to be true, but also changing, cleansing, and hallowing sinful hearts. Again and again under Hebrew ordinances (as many as twenty separate times at least), do we read of men into whom the Spirit or Breath of God breathed whatever noble or excellent gift they possessed; as, for example, political sagacity to Joseph, artistic skill to Bezaleel, bodily strength to Samson, insight to the prophets, patriotic valour to Othniel or Gideon, loyalty to the chief of David's captains; and the like.[2] It was the same Spirit

[1] Preceded here, ver. 38; cf. viii. 15–17; but followed in x. 47.
[2] Those who care to study the Old Testament references to the Holy Ghost may compare the following passages:—Gen. xli. 38; Ex. xxxi. 3; Num. xxiv. 2, xi. 25, xxvii. 18; Deut. xxxiv. 9; Judg. iii. 10, vi. 34, xi. 29, xiii. 25, xiv. 6, 19, xv. 14; 1 Sam. x. 10, xi. 6, xvi. 13, xix. 20, 23; 2 Sam. xxiii. 2 (c. Mark xii. 36 and Acts i. 16); 1 Kings xviii. 12; 2 Kings ii. 9; 1 Chron. xii. 18; 2 Chron. xv. 1, xx. 14, xxiv. 20; Ezek. ii. 2, iii. 24, xi. 5, xxxvii. 1, *et alibi*; Mic. iii. 8; &c. (Cf. 2 Pet. i. 21.)

Who alone could sustain the faith of patriarchs, the courage of pre-Christian martyrs, and, in fact, the spiritual life of all the elder saints. Whilst Peter was yet speaking, the same Spirit was working contrition and godly relentings within his hearers, as He had long before wrought them in Peter himself. But the peculiar character of the Holy Ghost's presence, as now sent down by the ascended Christ upon the baptised members of His Church, lies in this, that He is the Spirit of intimate, personal, and conscious union to the Lord Jesus Christ. The Holy Ghost comes specially to us, to dwell in us as the Spirit of Christ; to assure us of acceptance in the Beloved; to fill us all alike, if we choose, with the full life of Christ; to witness to our sonship unto the Father; to seal us against the day of our redemption. He is the Anointing Which teaches; He makes us free; He gives strength; He enables us for all things; He keeps our mind in peace; He knits us all into one body; He fills us with all joy; He is the Spirit of adoption, the Spirit of liberty, the Spirit of unity, the Spirit of glory.[1] It is more than personal conversion He works, or occasional and official qualification. He works that large, bold, joyful liberty, as of an accepted child of God, which distinguishes the Christian saint at his best, and that organised catholic community of interests in one body which ought to mark the Christian Church. There are Christians, indeed, who live to-day as if the Holy Ghost were not yet given. They believe, as men used to believe, who only hoped for mercy to come. They have no more than half thrown off

---

[1] By way of contrast to the list from the Old Testament in the foregoing note, let the following New Testament texts be noted:—Rom. viii. 9–11 and 14–17; 1 Cor. vi. 19; Gal. iv. 6; Eph. i. 13, iv. 30; 1 John ii. 27; 2 Cor. iii. 17; Eph. iii. 16; 1 Pet. iv. 14.

the shackles of a legal spirit, and are as joyless as though Christ were not risen. They have neither courage in their Father's presence, nor any liberty to tell others of His love. They are like owls, that mope and mourn in the twilight; under the open eye of the gospel day, abroad through the free air of heaven, they cannot sweep like doves on gladsome wing. But this is their own fault—not the fault of their time. We are gospel saints; baptised into, not John's, but Christ's own baptism. Let us arise and claim our heritage. Let us invoke the Spirit Who came at Pentecost to come to us; for "where that Spirit of the Lord is, there is liberty," there is life, there is joy in the Lord.

It was a mighty draught which Peter, the fisherman, drew to land that day. Three thousand converts were swept at once into the infant Church; not swamping the modest company of older believers, yet not in any wise inferior to them. How many of these new converts turned out ill on trial, no record survives. It was no time for suspicious inquiry or probation. On a high tide of spiritual feeling the crowd was borne into the bosom of the prepared Church, to be nurtured there on apostolic doctrine, and kept by the more trusty arms of men and women who had followed Christ in His sorrows. Well for them that they were thus kept and nurtured, and well for the Church on the whole — even though Ananias and Sapphira should prove false, and the Hellenists and the Hebrews should by-and-by contend. Tides of grace, as of opportunity, are to be taken at the flood. The Pentecost sun went down on a large Church of tender happy souls, new-washed in the blood their own hands had shed—a Church born in a day. It was a blessed day of hard, yet manageable work, to guide to peace in Christ (in round numbers) some three thousand anxious souls. Divide them among the hundred and twenty (and there were more than a hundred and twenty to start with), and you have but five-and-twenty apiece to be pointed to the Saviour, and baptised in His name, within nine hours, from nine o'clock in the forenoon till sunset. Not here lies the wonder, but in this rather that we think it wonderful; that we see so few times of rapid ingathering and large godward movements of men which can at all compare with it. Some, thank God, have been seen. Would we have more? Then let these two things be noted: That ten days of steadfast, expectant prayer, in which every believing soul took part, preceded Pentecost; and that it was when the Church had first been filled with heavenly assurance, joy, and praise, that the testimony of her first preacher won the hearts of thousands. Lessons! these are lessons. The Spirit works when we beg Him to work; and the ingathering to the Church holds ever a strict proportion to the life of the Church. Christians are the fountain, fed from Christ, out of which dead souls around are to be quickened; but *not till they run over!* As we would have the world converted, let us seek for the Church overrunning life!

VI.
The Infant Church.

HEAVEN LIES ABOUT US IN OUR INFANCY.

Acts ii. 42-47; cf. iii. 32-35.

Revised Version.

And they were continuing in the instruction of the apostles and the common-life, the breaking of the bread, and the [stated] prayers. But on every soul came fear, and many wonders and signs took place by means of the apostles. And all the believers were of the one company, and had all things common, and kept selling their lands and goods, and dividing them to all as each had need. Daily, too, continuing with one accord in the Temple, and breaking bread at home, they did eat food in gladness and simplicity of heart, praising God and having favour with the whole people. And the Lord added those who were being saved daily to the one company.

VI.

A VERY few verses furnish the only record extant of what one would like to know in much fuller detail— I mean the state of the primitive Church in those earliest days which immediately followed Pentecost. During the subsequent wide departures of the Church from its first simplicity, it has happened every now and then that a few earnest and reforming spirits have sought to fall back on primitive Christianity, by reconstructing the Christian community on the lines of its old foundation. The conception is more beautiful than wise; it is only to a certain extent either desirable or realisable. That the Church of Christ should always remain in spirit what God the Spirit first made it, is indeed an aim very earnestly to be striven after. That it should never substitute ceremonial for faith, or worldly ambition for spiritual influence, or the autocratic sway of a hierarchy and the pretensions of a priesthood for the simplicity of a brotherhood made one in Christ—this is an end, not desirable only, but imperative. In doing this, it does keep to the original lines of its constitution, in the best sense, for it keeps to the very idea of its existence. But those who would perpetuate, not the spiritual characteristics, but the details of the primitive Church, or construct a society which in this century should mimic precisely the arrangements of the first, attempt a thing which is impossible, and, if possible, would be inexpedient. The apostolic period covered about seventy years; and there is in truth no single date, from Pentecost to the close of the canon, at which one can say that the apostolic Church is known to have reached its finished form, or to have assumed everywhere a uniform and unalterable type. The society developed its arrangements as circumstances called for them. At first little more to its own consciousness than a Jewish sect, it only learned by degrees to gather in Gentile believers, and to organise itself on an independent footing. In its passage from the East to the West, from Hebrew to Greek, and from Greek to Roman, it necessarily underwent, as experience suggested them, changes in points of detail, which make its early history (so far as we are able to trace it) a history of variations superinduced on one elementary type. Even if we should fix on any single moment in the process, and desired to reproduce the Church, or a part of it, as it then stood—(say this first Church at Jerusalem, for example; or the Church at Antioch, as it existed at the synod of Jerusalem, about twenty years later; or the Church of Achaia, when St. Paul wrote his letters to Corinth; or that of Ephesus at the death of St. John)—it would be impossible for us to make out precisely all the arrangements then in existence, the office-bearers with their relative duties, the form of service and its parts, or the relation of separate congregations to one another. So much we know through merely incidental notices as to afford a few leading principles, and over even these modern Protestant Churches have fought long and obstinate battles. But no man who dispassionately studies the matter will affirm, I think, that the New Testament records enable us to construct with certainty a facsimile of any apostolic Church whatever, at any given year of its history. Tantalising, however, as this scantness of information must appear to those who like to have exact scripture precedent for every detail, it seems to me to harmonise better with the free spiritual character of the new institute. We see the Divine Creator of life given to the young Church, to create it, and inform it, and rule it. By degrees, and with struggles, the new society is found to shake itself loose from its Hebrew swaddling bands. We gather as we proceed, how, bit by bit, the new life it possessed worked out for itself, under the leading of the Spirit, fit utterance for its own feelings, a fit provision for its needs, and fit organs for its action. A gracious harmony of order with liberty prevails from the first. Few and simple observances nourish the young Church life. Disorders are corrected, fresh requirements are met, by the heaven-taught inventiveness of the Church itself. From first to last, the bond of union which hinders schism, and makes discipline possible, and gives to effort its purpose and its concentration, is not any outward restraining bond of statute, but the inward constraining bond of fraternal love. Only when we have receded a generation's length from the birthday of the Church, so that a mixture of foreign elements has crept in, do tones of authority begin to be heard, and the threat of apostolic penalty is needed to sustain persuasions to apostolic charity.

It is quite in keeping with this view that St. Luke should have given us, instead of a record of Church organisation, a vivid picture of Church life, as it existed in the earliest days. The features of this picture—its beautiful family unity, its prevailing kindliness, its idyllic simplicity, its unearthly impressiveness—let us try to set as vividly as we can before our hearts.

First, we must discriminate several stages in the historian's account. He describes the progress of the new converts (ii. 42); the feelings of the rest of the public (ver. 43); the internal state of the Church at large (ver. 44-47a); and the continuous growth of the Church by fresh conversions (ver. 47b).

(1) It might have been feared that the sudden accession of so large a number as three thousand to so small a number as an hundred and twenty or little more, would alter materially the character of the body. Through the grace of the Holy Ghost, such a result was avoided, as appears from the patient persevering attention with which the three thousand joined themselves to those who had previously been disciples. Since instruction[1] in the messiahship of Jesus and in His teaching was the point at which these new believers chiefly came short of those who had enjoyed their Lord's personal ministry, it fell to the Twelve to supplement this deficiency. This regular tuition of the new converts must have embraced two sections: first, the fulfilment in Jesus of Old Testament messianic Scriptures; and second, the truths which Jesus had Himself taught to the Twelve respecting the kingdom of God, both before His death and after His resurrection. Here we seem to recognise the germ of the Christian pulpit as an instrument, not of evangelistic preaching (for that we had at Pentecost), but of Christian edification.

---

[1] Here called "doctrine," by an old English use of that word, now grown obsolete.

To such teaching by the Twelve, were added the share which these new converts now took in the close social intercourse of the disciples,[1] and their assiduous attendance on two means of grace—namely, "breaking of bread" at home and public "prayers" in the temple.[2]

(2.) While those who had been won to the faith on its first great field-day were, in Peter's words,[3] desiring the sincere milk of the Word, like new-born babes, that they might grow by it, the Church's Lord was so displaying His glory in the midst of it, as to erect a wall of spiritual fire round about it. Considering the recent fate of Jesus and the feebleness of His followers, it was quite a possible danger that the hostility of the Jerusalem population, led by a powerful party in the council, might at once stamp out the infant Church. A little later, to be sure, persecution only made it grow; but just at present, persecution might have killed it, so new was it, so raw, so void of that confidence which comes by experience. Against this risk its watchful Head provided. A spiritual awe, akin to fear, partly produced by the deep solemnity of the sight when a whole crowd was smitten down in a day by the mere force of truth; partly kept up, too, by tokens of the divine presence and power which each fresh day reported; this spiritual awe lay on the souls of priest and Sadducee, and held them back from opposition as with a bit. Not for long, indeed, yet for long enough to give the Church time to consolidate her gains, to fortify her new converts, and to feel her strength. For of course each day that passed,

---

[1] Here called "fellowship," κοινωνία, ver. 42.

[2] I think καθ' οἶκον, in ver. 46, being opposed to ἐν τῷ ἱερῷ, must mean "at home," rather than "from house to house;" though Luke uses such a construction in Luke xviii. 1 and Acts xv. 21. But see Meyer *in loc.*   [3] 1 Pet. ii. 2.

with its miracles done and converts added and the fruits of spiritual life exhibited, brought fresh assurance to the disciples that Jesus was really aiding them from heaven. By this assurance it also knit them more closely into one body, with cohesion sufficient to withstand the storms which were to come.

(3) It was during this brief hour of childlike peace, while yet the fear of God cowed all the people, and left it safe room in which to unfold in fearless freedom its beautiful new life in the Holy Ghost, that the Church wore that gracious aspect sketched so long after by St. Luke. Thirty years later, from the midst of a Church often wet now with blood and tears, a Church which, all over the Mediterranean lands, had already begun its death-grapple with the pagan world; fresh from its perilous labours, perhaps at the very side of its chief missionary as he lay chained in a Roman prison, this man Luke cast back his eyes on the sweet prime and glad day-dawn to draw this picture, which has ever since entranced the weary, fighting Church of God, and shines in our far retrospect, as it shone in his, with the light of a golden age.

When we try to set before our minds the Christian life of those days in Jerusalem, I think one is most struck by its social, almost family, character. The number of the disciples was already a large one, but it was not yet felt to be too large for them to be all "together" in one place. Not that the historical "upper room," which held the hundred and twenty while they expected the Holy Ghost, and which had probably other memories to hallow it, could accommodate the thousands now baptised; but it may have remained still the head-quarters, and, as it were, family home, to which all had a right to come, and at some time or other came. The old close intercourse which, so long as the Lord lived on earth, His immediate followers had been used to, was too pleasant a thing to be lightly given up. With them He had been accustomed to lead a social life, which made them all, as it were, members of one large household. With the Twelve, at least, He had one purse and ate at one table. Others who at times kept Him company assisted of their means to meet common charges. All, in fact, who believed in Him, He reckoned as members of His family, as " brother and sister and mother." [1] About the time of His last sufferings and after it, this close fellowship of His disciples seems to have become closer. Many came up then to Jerusalem and remained in it after the tragical end. Common sorrow first, and afterwards common joy and hope, held them together; and the large " upper room " became more than ever a home to the disciples. This bond of oneness in their Lord, and of a peculiar brotherhood through Him, was so far from being slackened when the Holy Spirit came, that it was just His coming which intensified it and gave it permanence. Hence, when three thousand new believers were added to the old, the family circle was only widened enormously to take them in. They were admitted as a matter of course, and, as far as possible, to the old fellowship, the common table, and the daily household intercourse. This effort to realise on a wide scale the intensest and most perfect type of all society, the family, as a true expression for the new sacred bond of brotherhood which now knit them to the Father through the Elder Brother, appears

[1] See Matt. xii. 48-50.

to me to explain nearly everything which is peculiar in the arrangements of that primitive time.

Take their worship, for example. That was indeed curiously two-sided, because they had not ceased to be Jews in becoming Jesus' disciples. As yet they differed from their countrymen only in holding Jesus to be their national Christ, and they did not feel that this required them to withdraw from the national worship or become schismatics from their ancestral faith. What was new was only the legitimate outcome of all the old, the crown both of Mosaism and of prophetic Scripture; nor, in fact, did Christianity ever fully cut itself clear of its Judaic birthplace, till Judaism had of its own accord cast Christianity adrift. These first believers, at any rate, remained good Jews. Their "prayers" were, if not exclusively, yet primarily, the public prayers in the temple,[1] which they frequented as diligently, at the stated hours,[2] as if they had been Pharisees. The only distinction it was possible to establish in this conformity which they practised, was that they attended the temple in a body,[3] presenting to the worshippers the spectacle of a sect within Judaism, which believed all that other Jews believed and one thing more. It was no fault of theirs if Judaism, calling itself orthodox, by-and-by cast them out.

Another act of worship, however, was peculiar to themselves, and to it they gave the most social and family character possible: I mean the service called, in the earliest apostolic period,[4] the "breaking of bread." This

---

[1] The expression ταῖς προσευχαῖς, in ver. 42, can hardly refer to any other, I think.

[2] Cf. Acts iii. 1, of Peter and John.   [3] Cf. ὁμοθυμαδὸν, ver. 46.

[4] Not so used later than Acts xx. 7.

name appears by its very ambiguity to reflect the ambiguous character of the observance. It was not an ordinary meal (although the phrase "to break bread" is sometimes used of that [1]), nor the Eucharistic commemoration merely; but it included both. Every evening after sundown, at the customary hour for the principal meal of a Jewish household,[2] these brethren appear to have come together to a family table, very much as our Lord and the Twelve had done on the memorable night in which He was betrayed. It was the chief token and bond of their unity in their departed, but still spiritually present, Head and Householder. To make the bond tighter by more formally recalling its basis in His death Who sat no longer at the head of the board, they closed their meal by breaking bread as He had done, and had bade them do "in remembrance" of Him. So far as we are told, this was at first their only formal act of separate (or Christian) worship; and though it most probably would be accompanied, as the first supper had been, by words of comfort and the chanting of psalms, yet it was in its essence nothing else than a prolongation of that divine and unforgettable communion of daily family life which His followers had kept with the Son of God while He was on earth. That family fellowship of Jesus Christ with His own had been to them the seal of a deeper soul fellowship with One Whom they loved as their Saviour. At the table, it was so still. He had expressly consecrated table intercourse into a badge of unity, a memorial of His

---

[1] See Luke xxiv. 30, where, however, there may be an allusion to something peculiar in our Lord's way of doing it; and Acts xxvii. 35, where a religious reference seems excluded.

[2] So in Herzog, s.v. "Mahlzeiten;" and Smith, s.v. "Meal;" but Winer thinks noon, rather (see art. "Mahlzeit").

Passion and a seal of discipleship. By the "breaking of bread," therefore, there were naturally expressed, (1) the continuity of their intercourse with One in Whom, though now they saw Him not, yet believing, they still rejoiced; (2) their own fraternity, as the children of One Whom the Son had taught them to call "our Father;" and (3) their expectation of His speedy return Who had only gone away that He might make the Father's great house above ready for all the family. Let us try to forget, if we can, the abuses which, after a while and among the Greeks, darkened this primitive love-feast, and led to the separation of the Holy Supper from what had become an unholy repast. Let us still endeavour, as often as we renew the sacred rite, to catch its tender and homely interest. It is a reminiscence of days when men did eat and drink with the Eternal God in flesh. It is a pledge that all who still love Jesus Christ are members in Him of one "household of faith." Above all, it leads us to associate the religious sanctity of our inner life as a life in Christ with whatsoever we daily do, "whether we eat or drink."[1]

In the same endeavour to give to the brotherhood of believers a family character, I think we may find the best key to what has been (not very correctly) called their "community of goods." This social peculiarity of the Jerusalem Church during the early weeks of its existence is attended with a little difficulty, but that difficulty has been increased by the discussion which has raged over it. When we throw ourselves back into the circumstances of the time, what really happened becomes more than intelligible —it becomes natural. During the Master's ministry, He and His itinerant assistants, who formed, as I have said,

[1] 1 Cor. x. 31.

one household for the time being, had naturally one purse, out of which their common expenses were defrayed. This fund, when low, was recruited by the voluntary gifts of well-to-do and generous friends, especially females, who had received spiritual blessing from the Master. The unity of the brotherhood had thus been realised even in its financial arrangements. Now, matters were not felt to have materially changed. There was still a band of Twelve, who could not earn a subsistence because they had spiritual work to do, as well as a number of incapable, aged, and sickly brethren, widows, like the Mother herself, and young children. There was also a larger number than before of somewhat wealthy disciples, such as Nicodemus, Joseph, and Barnabas. All these, as brethren, ate daily at one common table, and counted themselves to be one large family of God, left by their divine Head, indeed, yet not orphans, since the Comforter had come.[1] But how can we speak of brotherhood in the family if the abundance of one brother is not to be a supply for another's want? Inequalities, indeed, are not inconsistent with the family idea; but destitution is. There is, to be sure, no suggestion of what moderns call "equality," as a result of this "fraternity;" only there is an intolerance of downright want. There must not be among them any who lack. The spirit of fraternity in Christ will at least forbid that; forbid it, not by any statute, but by the instinct of brotherhood working spontaneously, yet working irresistibly. The common expenses of the house and table, which belonged to all; the support of the apostles; the relief of destitute and widowed members: all these were from the first a very

[1] Compare Jesus' words in John xiv. 16–18, Greek.

pressing and patent care. For such purposes a fund was formed under the charge of the apostles. Into that fund all those who had landed property or real estate of any sort brought the proceeds of its sale. Besides, I think there is a hint that some capitalists distributed their wealth at their own discretion,[1] as well as through the hands of Church officers. Anyhow, the result was that, under the strong and general feeling of Christian charity which sprang out of Christian unity, men gave as freely as if what they had were not really their own, but only held by them in trust for others. Practically, what was any brother's came to be the brethren's; no man asserted his private proprietorship, or "said that aught of the things which he possessed was his own."

This free, fervent outburst of Christian brotherly-kindness offers to my mind features, not simply of clear distinction, but of sharp contrast with the communism of modern Socialists. No doubt both are rebellions against the same reigning principle of selfishness which has always moulded social relations, and on which it is thought to be a glory of the past century[3] to have erected a theory of political economy. That by each man doing the best for himself, and for himself alone, society will do best on the whole; since, through human selfishness, supply and demand will always regulate themselves, and the common wealth will increase the most: this is, I believe, the creed of economists since Adam Smith.

[1] In Acts ii. 44, 45, where "all the believers" are spoken of as "parting" their possessions to all as each might require. This inference, however, is not a sure one. *Qui facit per alium, facit per se.*

[2] Quoted from Acts iv. 32, where the subject is specially handled, and by which the reference in chap. ii. 44 is to be explained.

[3] The "Wealth of Nations" was published in 1776.

Against this, as an exhaustive or satisfactory account of society, and especially against its practical working with the cruel consequences which we daily see around us, early Christianity and modern Socialism both protest; only their remedies are unlike. Socialism is communistic; it annihilates property; it compels men to labour for a common, not for private, gain; it equalises incomes, and of course abolishes both wealth and poverty. It does this, or seeks to do it, by force of law; that is, by the strength of the majority. But this simply means to take by compulsion from him whose work is worth much, and give a part of his fair earnings to one whose work is worth less.

The Church at Jerusalem did no such thing. It did not abolish property; it produced no artificial equality; it imposed no constraint. It simply bred in men's hearts so intense a sense of their oneness as brothers in Christ, that the extreme destitution of any one became a sight intolerable to all the rest. Thus, by a free spiritual movement of charity resting upon sympathy, it solved, for a time and on a small scale, the problem of society. It is the only time at which that problem has been healthily and safely solved; the only way in which it can ever be. Religious communisms have generally rested, like the monastic orders, on an ascetic rather than a social basis. The fanaticism of the German Anabaptists, indeed, did not lack force, but it involved the ruin of society. Recent humanitarian attempts in France and America to realise a voluntary communism, wanting a religious motive, have broken down.[1] There is no real cure for diseased society except the regeneration of the

[1] See art. "Communismus," in Herzog.

individual, and the individual is regenerated when you have substituted brotherly-kindness for selfishness as the ruling motive or ground of character. This no system has even attempted to do save Christianity. Just in so far as any man takes in the peculiar teaching of the gospel, such as the saving mercy of the Father in heaven, our oneness in the incarnate Son, and the binding common life of the Holy Ghost—to that extent he will cease to be a difficulty in the way of social economics. He will help others as much, and grasp as little for himself, as possible. To penetrate society at large with such influences till society becomes Christian, has been the aim and hope of the Church from the first. Yet its success in this attempt has been, let it be sorrowfully confessed, very partial. The number of men over whom it has attained sufficient influence has never (unless in the case before us, or in a sphere as narrow and for a period as brief) been considerable enough to determine the condition of society. Vice is always breeding penury, as fast as, or faster than, such Christianity as we have can relieve it. We seem hardly, if at all, nearer to-day than ever to the return of that ideal state, touched once in Jerusalem, in which no rich man is illiberal and no poor man greedy.

(4) The original impact of new-born fervid faith upon the incredulous population of Jerusalem, which had with divine power carried thousands over at a rush, did not all at once cease to tell. There followed a steady daily gain of members, although at a slower rate. The persistent testimony of the original members, who had been eye-witnesses of the resurrection of Jesus, must have continued to convince numbers of their neighbours. The

sight of so warm and loving a society, radiant with a new gladness, may have attracted even more. There is a wonderfully fascinating power about genuine enthusiasm so long as it is new. Besides, among the people who had themselves seen and heard Jesus, there would be a great many within whose hearts His own life had left soft touches, over whom His own voice had months before put forth its charm; and though these very persons might have been dragged along when the popular judgment turned against Him, it is easy to imagine how the earlier and better instincts of their hearts would reawaken now that Jerusalem was once more ringing with the praises of a multitude who loved Him, and hailed Him as Israel's Lord and Israel's Christ. The Church had sprung to sudden life on a prepared soil. Its own warmth was contagious. New-born convictions always spread the fastest. The same Spirit of divine life, Who breathed and spoke in the Church, moved no less within the outside listening bystanders. So, one by one, "the Lord [Christ] added daily those who were being saved."[1]

It was very lovely while it lasted, that first flush of spiritual life. Before hypocrisy or discontent had grown up within, or wicked hands had smitten it without, the Church dwelt secure and innocent, like a happy family. I have called it the Church's "golden age." It was its infancy, and the beauty of it is the beauty of childhood. Simplicity marked it, called in our Bible "singleness of heart;" a gracious, childlike absorption in one happy thought, careless of the future; a simplicity, which is

[1] Τοὺς σωζομένους, ver. 47. This would be the first use of "The Church" in its New Testament sense, if the *textus receptus* could be trusted. But the weight of authority is against it.

to the sterner discipline of the Church's after history as infancy is to manhood, or as pastoral to civil life. Along with simplicity there was gladness too; such gladness as one notes to this day, when into a number of young hearts the blessed gospel first comes, and the Holy Spirit gives them assurance of the love of God in Christ. Then with joy they sing their artless hymns of praise, and the touching grace of their fresh pure life wins from the spectators favour. Shall we sigh over the disappearance of these primitive infantile beauties? There is reason that we should, if in their stead we have reached nothing manlier or more noble. Well indeed for those most happy souls who can keep their first childlikeness unfaded even through the toil and change and trial of spiritual manhood: yet it is better both for the Church and for the spiritual man to travel away from childhood, even at some risk of "forgetting things behind." There comes a day when all things that are now so old and withered shall be made new. Then we, too, shall renew our youth; and anointed with the oil of gladness—which is the Spirit of God—and sitting down as brothers with Christ at the feast-table of eternal life, we too shall "eat our meat with gladness and singleness of heart."

VII.

St. Peter's Second Apology.

"YE ARE MY WITNESSES, SAITH JEHOVAH,
AND MY SERVANT WHOM I HAVE CHOSEN."

"BEHOLD, I HAVE GIVEN HIM FOR A WITNESS TO THE PEOPLE,
A LEADER AND COMMANDER TO THE PEOPLE."

Acts iii. 1–iv. 4.

Revised Version.

Now Peter and John were going up to the Temple at the hour of prayer—the ninth. And a certain man who was lame from his mother's womb was being carried, whom they placed daily beside the door of the Temple called "Beautiful," to beg alms of those who were entering into the Temple: who seeing Peter and John about to enter into the Temple, asked to receive an alms. But Peter, gazing upon him with John, said: "Look on us." So he gave heed to them, expecting to receive something from them. Then said Peter:

"Silver and gold have I none. But what I have that give I thee. In the name of Jesus Christ the Nazarene, walk."

And seizing him by the right hand, he raised him: and instantly his soles and ankles were strengthened, and leaping up, he stood and walked and entered with them into the Temple, walking and leaping, praising God. And the whole people saw him walking and praising God, and recognised him that it was the same who sat for alms at the Beautiful Gate of the Temple, and were filled with wonder and ecstasy at what had happened to him. While he then was holding Peter and John, the whole people ran together to them at the Portico called Solomon's, amazed: which Peter seeing replied to the people:

"Men of Israel, why do ye marvel at this man, or why do ye gaze on us as if by our own power or piety we had made him walk? The God of Abraham and Isaac and Jacob, the God of our fathers, glorified His Servant Jesus Whom ye indeed betrayed and denied before Pilate's face when he decided to release Him. You it was who denied the Holy and Righteous One, and desired a man who was a murderer to be granted you, but the Leader of Life you killed, Whom God raised from the dead, of which we are witnesses. And by the faith of His name, this man whom ye behold and know, His name it was that strengthened him, and the faith that is through Him gave him this soundness in presence of you all. And now, brethren, I know that you acted ignorantly, just as your rulers also. But God did thus fulfil what He had foretold through the mouth of all the prophets, that His Messiah should suffer. Repent, therefore, and turn, for the wiping out of your sins, so that seasons of refreshing shall come from the Lord's face, and He shall send Christ Jesus, appointed beforehand for you, Whom heaven indeed must receive until the times of restoration of all things, of which [times] God spoke through the mouth of His holy prophets from the beginning. Moses indeed said: 'A prophet shall the Lord your God raise up to you of your brethren like me. Him shall ye hear in all things whatever He shall speak to you; and it shall be that every soul that will not hear that prophet shall be destroyed from among the people.' And all the prophets too, from Samuel and those that follow, as many as spoke, also announced these days. Ye are the sons of the prophets and of the covenant which

God established with your fathers, saying to Abraham, 'And in thy seed shall all the families of the earth be blessed.' To you first, God, having raised up His Servant, sent Him to bless you in the turning away of each one from your iniquities."

But while they were speaking to the people, came on them the priests and the Captain of the Temple and the Sadducees, displeased on account of their teaching the people and announcing in the [case of] Jesus the resurrection from the dead. And they laid hands on them and put them into custody till the morrow, for it was already eventide. But many of those who had heard the word believed, and the number of the men was made up to [about] five thousand.

VII.

THE beautiful hour of dawn was soon overcast: how soon we do not know; but glancing forward, we find only a succession of disasters, from without the Church and from within, till the Jerusalem Church is broken up, and the history of the kingdom of God shifts onward to Samaria and the ends of the earth. The beginning of persecution about the lame man was followed by the affair of Ananias and his wife; a second and more serious imprisonment of the apostles had at its heels the internal dissatisfaction which called for the new office of the deaconship; and that led finally to Stephen's martyrdom and the scattering of the disciples. This is, in brief, the history detailed by our historian in the next five chapters of his work; a history of evil overcome, discipline improved, suffering bravely borne, and progress achieved in the face of violence.

The first important incident in this nêw section of Luke's narrative[1] is the examination of the apostles before the Sanhedrim. It may be said to have been the Church's earliest confession of the name of Christ in the face of an adverse civil power. Very much for the sake of that examination is Peter's sermon in Solomon's porch re-

[1] Although the long passage, Acts iii. 1–iv. 31, can be broken into paragraphs, it is in fact one story, of which the main and central part lies in iv. 1–21.

corded; and very much for the sake of Peter's sermon does the miracle at the Gate Beautiful find its place. Among many acts of healing done in those days by apostolic hands,[1] this one alone is told at length; because it led to a discourse, which is itself worth reporting, because it in turn led to the arrest, imprisonment, and judicial trial of the Church's chiefs and spokesmen. In the present chapter it is only with the miracle and the discourse which followed it that I propose to deal.

At the usual hour for evening sacrifice and prayer, the two foremost apostles, setting before their converts an example of attendance on the services of their ancestral religion, were going up together[2] to the temple. Having passed through the outer court, open to Gentiles, they were about to enter the inner one by that central gate on its eastern side, which, because it led the worshipper right in front of the altar and the sanctuary, had been made by far the largest and richest of all the ten that afforded the faithful access to the second or more sacred enclosure. This noble gate is described by Josephus[3] as made of Corinthian brass, very richly overlaid with gold and silver plates, and so massive as to task the strength of twenty men to turn its leaves upon their hinges. Right by its portals, at the hours when the stream of worshippers was fullest, his friends were wont to lay an unfortunate man, now forty years of age, who had never been able to walk through congenital weakness

---

[1] Acts ii. 43.
[2] The reading which joins 'ἐπὶ τὸ αὐτὸ to chap. ii., and begins chap. iii. with πέτρος δὲ κ. τ. λ., seems indeed to be preferable (so A, B, C, and the Sinaitic); still the "together" of the A.V. is correct as to the fact. [3] See B. J. v. 5. 3; also vi. 5. 3.

ST. PETER'S SECOND APOLOGY.

of the ankle-joint. It is startling to find that after the Lord Jesus had gone in and out by this very gate so often for years past, and had healed so many, this man was still lying, as he had lain for long, an impotent beggar. It seems to me plain that during Jesus' own ministry he never can have had so much faith as to ask healing from Him Who had given sight eight months before[1] to a blind man sitting at another temple gate, and had even restored a sufferer at the neighbouring pool of Bethesda, at least more than a year before.[2] If he had ever asked, not alms, but healing, of that gracious Worshipper, would He have refused to give him what He had? I question very much whether it was our Lord's custom to confer miraculous aid on such as neither sought it for themselves, nor were brought to get it by their friends. That He sometimes did so, indeed, is proved even by the two cases just cited. Yet I think the prevailing tone of the Gospel narratives implies that such cases were exceptional, and due either to a certain inward fitness of the sufferer to receive what he lacked courage or perhaps opportunity to ask for, or else to some peculiar service to be rendered to the kingdom of God by the performance of a miracle.[3] Now, however, what this cripple had neither asked nor got from the Master, he received, to his own surprise, at the hand of

---

[1] At the Feast of Tabernacles, in October; John ix. 1; cf. Wieseler, *Chron. Synop.* p. 270.

[2] See John v. In March was a year before the Passion, if it was a Purim, and if Wieseler is right (see *Synop.* p. 205, ff.); but two years, if John v. refers to a Passover.

[3] Possibly the case of the blind man in John ix. comes under both these categories. Cf. his behaviour before the Sanhedrim, and the words of Jesus in John ix. 3. In the other case of the Bethesda cripple, there is only Jesus' question, " Wilt thou be made whole? " to guide us (John v. 6).

the servant. Had then Pentecost and the spiritual joy of the new converts warmed into life within his breast a faith which the presence of the Lord Himself had failed to quicken? Or did the earnest gaze of Peter[1] first move him to receive with faith a salvation which was now at last to single him out for blessing, because now God's time of gracious choice had come.[2] The time and mode of the genesis of the cripple's faith we cannot determine, but that his own faith was present at the instant of cure, as a concurrent factor, seems plain enough. What man in his case, who was utterly sceptical as to Peter's claims and Peter's Master, would have taken seriously a command to rise and walk, or grasped with instant compliance the outstretched hand which offered to help him up? His seizure of Peter's hand, and his own effort to raise himself at Peter's word, were both elements in the cure; and they both presuppose in him some idea that cure was possible, some hope that divine help might come. It is thus that a helpless soul, lacking the strength of grace within itself to arise and come away from sin to God, or to walk and run in His holy paths, is bound to meet Christ's offer of divine aid. Not in hopeless scepticism, but gazing into the honest searching eyes which gaze on it, to learn how serious and how capable this great Helper is, the soul is bound to welcome His help with hope and spiritual effort, rousing itself to grasp the Hand that is held out, and, in obedience to His call, letting itself be

---

[1] Cf. with Acts iii. 4 the exactly parallel cure by Paul at Lystra, Acts xiv. 8–10; esp. "steadfastly beholding him, and perceiving that he had faith to be healed."

[2] Can it be to call attention to God's sovereign choice of the subjects of miraculous help, that Raphael has put the second uncured cripple into his cartoon?

lifted up and strengthened, willingly. To attempt any spiritual rising or walking without straining that divine Hand with the weight of our acknowledged impotency, is a vain thing. At the same time no man can so grasp Christ as to burden Him with the soul's weight, unless he is putting forth an effort of his own will in the direction of obedience. It was therefore a speaking parable which Peter acted at the Beautiful Gate. In it the Church has always found an apt and helpful illustration of that mystery in religion, the concurrence of man's will with God's sovereign enabling grace, in the greater miracle of a sinner's conversion.

It is worthy of notice how entirely, in this first recorded miracle wrought by an apostle, the manner of Christ's own miracle-working is kept up. Careful students of our Lord's life know that the sort of miracles He did, and the way in which He did them, are as significant of His character as anything else about Him. Beneficent restorations of disturbed nature to order and health, symbolical all of them of deeper spiritual blessings, and therefore full of teaching; done, not at hap-hazard, but with choice and for a purpose; having, moreover, an appropriate moral bearing, both on the person healed and on others; accomplished, for the most part, through some close and very human contact betwixt Himself and the sufferer, so that personal compassion in Him awoke personal desire or receptivity in the patient: these were the most striking characteristics of His usual miracle-doing. Now, so closely is this of Peter's analogous to his Master's works, that I venture to say, that if one who was familiar with the four Gospels were to read this passage of the Acts for the first time, changed only in the name and leaving out the servant's reference to his Master as the source of power, he would accept it as entirely bearing the stamp of the miracles of Jesus. He would refer it to the Prophet of Nazareth. Shall we say, then, that Peter consciously copied the manner of his Lord, or that he had through long intercourse acquired it involuntarily? The first supposition would be fatal to the spontaneity and simplicity of the narrative, nor have studious copyists any such success as this. The second supposition is out of harmony with the history of Peter down to the day of Pentecost. For will any man who reflects on this apostle's behaviour and style of speech towards the close of his Master's life, say that he was steadily growing into such unconscious accordance with the spirit of Jesus' acts and words, that a close resemblance in manner betwixt the two might be expected? If it is possible, with some show of reason, to say this of John, no man would dream of applying it to Peter. Yet it is Peter, and not John, who here acts and speaks so entirely in the manner of Jesus. I submit that no explanation of this is possible save the one evidently implied both by Peter himself and by his historian. That is, that Peter acted here under the impulse of a divine Spirit, Who was the same Who informed and guided the public life of Jesus; in other word, that Jesus was, by a spiritual Agent sent down from Himself, prolonging His own life-work, through the hearts and lips and hands of these men, as His ministers and organs. This is the full New Testament significance of Pentecost. It is to be viewed as the resumption of work[1] on earth by the Lord Jesus, the Church's Head and Life. It was His virtual return in

---

[1] Cf. Acts i. 1: "Began both to do and teach."

spiritual power to do through His brethren such works as He had done in person, and greater works than these.[1] In this sense it must be presupposed if we are to explain so much as a single chapter in primitive Church history.

The temple received a new worshipper that afternoon, and a joyful one. Making the best use of his freshly-gotten strength, the man accompanied his healers (who had been one in the act, though only one of them could act in it) to evening prayer. There his excited conduct drew general observation. He kept the apostles' hands in his, and, as he walked, could not forbear, in the joy of a new power, to leap, as Isaiah foretold the lame should do, and lift up his voice as well, in ejaculations of thanksgiving to the God of Israel. As an old *habitue* of the gateway, his person was well known, and when the rumour of the wonder spread through the crowded court, he and the two apostles became the observed of many amazed and curious witnesses. After service, when they retired by the Beautiful Gate[2] to the outer court again, and crossed it to that double colonnade which ran along the exterior eastern wall of the temple area, in which the disciples (following in this their Lord's example[3]) were accustomed to meet, the multitude of worshippers hurried after them from every side, and thronged the portico, to catch a glimpse of them. In reply to eager looks and questioning words,[4] Peter delivered a discourse which

[1] Cf. John xiv. 12, 18, ff., with Rom. xv. 18, 19; Acts xv. 12, xix. 11.

[2] The associations connected with the spot would revive in the man his demonstrations of joyful gratitude to the two. See ver. 11.

[3] See John x. 23, and cf. Acts v. 12. In the former case for shelter from winter cold, but here, probably, to escape from the afternoon sun.

[4] The force of $ἀπεκρίνατο$ in ver. 12.

may well be called his second apology. One compares it naturally with the first, delivered on the day of Pentecost, and the parallel betwixt the two is remarkably close. Here he gives the true explanation of a miracle wrought by himself, as formerly of a miracle wrought upon himself. Here, as there, he starts with repelling the mistaken views of the crowd.[1] The lame man has not been cured by his or John's magical power, nor as a reward of their eminent virtue, any more than the gift of tongues was due to wine. Jesus is the Worker in both wonders. Here, as there, too,[2] his main drift throughout the earlier half of his address is to prove God's exaltation of Jesus as the true Messiah, in contrast with his hearers' treatment of Him; only, on this occasion, his reproaches of them for their share in the death of Jesus become even sharper and more keen than at Pentecost. He not only specifies their crime as betrayal, denial, and murder, but aggravates it by opposing the righteous Leader and Bringer of life, Whom they had put to death, to the insurgent murderer whom they had saved alive.[3] More incisive words he could not use. But again, as before,[4] he turns suddenly from their treatment of Jesus to God's—"Whom God raised from the dead;" and to the Man thus raised and glorified of God, he traces with the most absolute emphasis this day's, as he had before traced that day's, wonder. So far the former half of his present address closely answers to his earlier one. But it will be remembered that at Pentecost St. Peter followed up his first sermon, in which he mainly smote the hearers' consciences,

---

[1] Cf. Acts iii. 12 with ii. 15.   [2] Cf. Acts iii. 16 with ii. 33.
[3] Cf. Acts iii. 14, 15 with ii. 23. ἀρχηγός (also used by Peter in v. 31; only elsewhere in Heb. ii. 10; xii. 2) = Leader, Author, Cause even. See Bleek on Heb. ii. 10.   [4] See Acts iii. 16, cf. ii. 24.

by a second, in which, after some interval, he answered their alarmed inquiry, "What shall we do?" That later address must be very imperfectly reported, for it is condensed by St. Luke into a sentence.[1] Here, on the other hand, the second half follows at once on the word of conviction, and is apparently given with equal fulness, so that we get a substantial addition to our knowledge of Peter's public preaching.

Now, if this latter portion of the speech[2] be examined, it will be found that its central point, on which is thrown the chief weight of exhortation, is precisely the same as in Luke's abridged version of the former speech. "Repent and be converted, that your sins may be blotted out," he says here. "Repent, and be baptized for the remission of sins," he said then. A change and turning of the individual heart away from those sins which have pierced and grieved God, to seek and love and serve Him Whom we have grieved and pierced—this is the uniform plain demand of the gospel. To the sinner who does so turn and face round to God, God offers pardon, the "remission of sins;" or, as it is here, the blurring over and effacing of them as an indictment against the sinner.[3] Only this uniform demand and promise are to be variously recommended to men by considerations drawn from each man's special position. As though God were beseeching his countrymen through his lips, Peter here prayed them in Christ's stead to be reconciled to God;[4] and he used such motives as, in the mouth of a Jew speaking to Jews, were most fit and likely to persuade.

---

[1] See Acts ii. 38–40.   [2] Ibid. iii. 17–26.
[3] The words are, εἰς τὸ ἐξαλειφϑῆναι ὑμῶν τὰς ἁμαρτίας, ver. 19. Compare Col. ii. 14.   [4] Like Paul in 2 Cor. v. 20.

In the first place he suggested, as an extenuation of their guilt, that it had been contracted in "ignorance." It may not have been quite true of all, but it certainly was true of the vast mass of the people, who wheeled so readily from applauding Jesus to execrating Him, that neither when they did the one nor the other had they any real knowledge on solid grounds Who He was. While such ignorance was vastly more culpable in its spiritual guides than in the mob, yet it seems to have been true of the majority even of them, that they acted under this mistaken notion that, in putting a false pretender to death, they were doing God service. Even Paul says, that "had they known it, they would not have crucified the Lord of glory."[1] It ill becomes us to be harder on these Jews than, in their first excitement, the apostles were. It is perfectly true that the religious authorities were guiltily blinded by prejudice, preconception, and official jealousy. It is true, also, that the less biassed mind of the populace, till it was poisoned by its leaders, responded frankly enough to the words of Jesus. Still, this is to be said for the people, that few men at any time have the courage to follow their own instincts of truth against the force of tradition and the authority of experts who are supposed to know best; and for the rulers, this also, that where interest, class feeling, and educational bias are all on one side, few men have intellectual honesty enough to welcome, or moral honesty enough to confess, disagreeable discoveries. In the Hebrew nation at that day there were of course all degrees of sincerity on the one hand, and of criminal resistance against light on the other; but the broad fact remains that, for whatever reason, the

[1] 1 Cor. ii. 8.

bulk of those who voted, by next to universal suffrage, for Jesus' death, believed themselves to be voting what was either just or politic or necessary. Such ignorance as this does not excuse a crime, but it palliates it. It makes it more pardonable. Peter only followed here the example of his Master, and probably had in his mind those very words, so touching and so generous, which escaped His blessed lips when, extended on the bed of His shame, the anguish of the nails first wrung His flesh: "Father, forgive them, for they know not what they do."[1] Even if we apply that divine prayer, as I think we ought to do, primarily to the four Roman soldiers who at the moment were rudely piercing His tender limbs, and who, in obeying military orders, certainly little knew Whose body it was they handled; yet the principle applied of course to all others implicated in that crime just in so far as they too were doing it in ignorance. St. Paul, who certainly was as well taught a Pharisee as any, and not given to extenuate his own sins, tells us that the reason he "obtained mercy" after persecuting Christ was that he had done so "ignorantly in unbelief."[2] It was, therefore, no mere piece of oratorical craft, but a wise and generous concession to fact, when Peter blunted a little the edge of his own charges against his fellow-citizens, by conceding that in ignorance they had done it. Was he remembering that if they denied Jesus ignorantly, he himself had denied Him wittingly?

Further to open his hearers' hearts to penitence, he reminded them, as he had done at Pentecost,[3] how their very crime had been the fulfilment, all unknown to them-

---
[1] Luke xxiii. 34. [2] 1 Tim. i. 13. [3] See ver. 18, and cf. ii. 23.

selves, of those predicted sufferings which it had been God's will to inflict upon Messiah. Through their slaying of the Christ, God had ordained that the Christ should become their Saviour. The deep loving purpose of our Father takes up into His own hand our roughest-hewn deeds, and shapes them to consummate and noblest ends.

But the most singular motive by which Peter here pressed his countrymen to repent, is that, upon their doing so, had been made to hinge the return of Christ in glory, and that predicted era of blessedness which is to enter when His personal presence is restored to the earth.[1] Evidently, Peter has now clearer and truer ideas of the messianic kingdom than he had, when, before Jesus' ascension, he questioned Him, and got for answer that the times and the seasons are in the Father's power. He is far indeed from having abandoned the hereditary hope of his nation. The whole testimony of Old Testament prediction pointed him forward to a period when, under the mild sway of David's Anointed Son, Israel's long harassments, oppressions, and dispeace should have an end. After millenniums of turmoil, the land was at length to be refreshed with rest and enjoy its Sabbath;

---

[1] See Acts iii. 19-26. This difficult passage has been rendered, not difficult, but false, by a mistranslation. The Authorised Version reads: "Be converted, that your sins may be blotted out *when* the times of refreshing shall come;" as if the forgiveness of sins were a thing postponed till some future epoch. It ought to read: "Be converted, that your sins may be blotted out, *in order that* (ὅπως ἂν) times of refreshing may come from the presence of the Lord." These times or seasons (καιροί) of refreshing, and those " times (χρόνοι) of restitution (or restoration) of all things which God hath spoken " (in ver. 21), both seem to refer to the same great hope of the Church, and are connected with the second sending forth of Jesus Christ from heaven to earth.

wrong was to be reversed, tyrants displaced, suffering healed, and the torn and wasted tribes reduced to their old prosperity in a long glad final jubilee. Of prospects like these, Hebrew Scripture is full. To such a golden age pointed especially those six and twenty closing chapters of the book of Isaiah, where the Christ is spoken of as Jehovah's "Servant;" a prophecy clearly before the mind of Peter in this sermon, because he twice over applies that very title [1] to Jesus. Through his Master, therefore, Peter still expects the kingdom to be restored to Israel. In Isaiah's language, Judah's wilderness was to be planted with myrtle and cedar; the merchandise of Ethiopia and Egypt was to come over to her; Palestine was to be thronged with inhabitants, and Jerusalem clothed with beauty like a city of jewels, with its gates for ever open, and the Gentiles crowding to its light. Then should there be no more weeping in that holy city, nor anything to hurt; but long life, "abundance of glory," riches, peace, righteousness, and everlasting joy.[2] Gentile Christians have long since learned to read these splendid promises to the land and people of the Jews with hardly a thought of what they meant in a Jewish ear. We mentally carry them over to another "Jerusalem which is above," a new "holy city" of the saints, which, long after Peter spoke, his companion, who stood that day by his side in Solomon's porch, was to see in vision on a lone Ægean island,[3] after Titus's army had laid the earthly city and its temple in the dust. From Peter all this was still hidden. To

---

[1] Wrongly translated "Son" in ver. 13 and 26.
[2] Cf. Isa. xli. 19, xlv. 14, xlix. 19, liv. 11, lx. *passim*, lxv. 19-25, lxvi. 11.   [3] Cf. Rev. xxi. *passim;* and see Gal. iv. 26.

him the promises were national. "Ye," said he, "are the children of the prophets and of the covenant." If in Abraham's seed "all the kindreds of the earth were to be blessed," it was only through their "joining themselves to the Lord," "taking hold of His covenant," and being "made joyful" in that house which was to be "a house of prayer for all people." Not for a good while yet, and not without both vision and providence to teach him, did the apostle of the circumcision learn to "call no man common or unclean."[1] He was a still older man when he taught his brethren to hope for an inheritance reserved for them in heaven.[2] Though there was so much which Peter had not yet learned, this much he now saw, that such glorious times of refreshment and restoration—the "golden age" of the future—could not come till the words of the angel on Mount Olivet[3] should be fulfilled by the return of the ascended Jesus. The object of his Lord's retirement into the heavens he took to be the conversion of Israel to faith in Himself. So long as He was here, they had denied Him; now, in His absence, they were to return and call with tears upon Him Whom they had pierced. Had not a beginning of this happy conversion been already seen in the three thousand at Pentecost, and the daily additions since? Let the work go on. The faster Israel turned to Jesus, the sooner would Jesus return to Israel; for, as Peter wrote a great many years later, "the Lord is not slack concerning His promise" to return; He is only "long-suffering, not willing that any should perish."[4] With urgency, there-

---

[1] See Acts x. *passim*.   [2] 1 Pet. i. 4.   [3] Acts i. 11.
[4] It is interesting to compare with this address 2 Pet. iii. *passim*, and especially ver. 3, 9, 12.

fore, did the preacher that day press upon his "brethren," as "Israelites," to turn "every one from his iniquities," so that there might come the sooner those times of national reviving and restoration which had so often been predicted to their fathers.

While he was yet speaking,[1] came the leaders of his nation and put him in hold! It seemed a bitter mockery of this noble Jew's sanguine prospects and impassioned appeals. Israel was not then, by a long way, and it is not yet, at the end of its denial of its Christ. Is then the national hope which, through so long and brilliant a line of patriot seers, descended upon Peter, a defeated, or is it only a postponed, hope? Time will show; but I should incline to answer, even if defeated in the letter, yet, in its spirit, only postponed. "Through their fall salvation is come unto the Gentiles, for to provoke them to jealousy. Now if the fall of them be the riches of the world, and the diminishing of them the riches of the Gentiles, how much more their fulness? . . . If the casting away of them be the reconciling of the world, what shall the receiving of them be but life from the dead?"[2] So wrote that grandest Christian Jew who is also the *Doctor Gentium*. His discussion at a later date is the safest commentary on St. Peter's early sermon; and his words are worth our heeding when he adds this warning: "Because of unbelief they were broken off, and thou standest by faith. Be not high-minded, but fear." "Unto you," may we now read St. Peter's peroration as adapted to our modern and Gentile Church: "Unto you, not first, but second, God has sent His Son to bless you also in turning away every one of you from

---

[1] Λαλούντων δὲ αὐτῶν, chap. iv. 1.   [2] Rom. xi. 11–15.

his iniquities. Repent ye, therefore, and be converted, that your sins may be blotted out; so that those predicted times of refreshing may come the more speedily, which, so soon as the fulness of us Gentiles is come in, shall be to all Israel salvation, and to ourselves life from the dead."

VIII.
In Collision with the Sanhedrim.

"*I AM IN THE PLACE WHERE I AM DEMANDED OF CONSCIENCE TO SPEAK THE TRUTH, AND THEREFORE THE TRUTH I SPEAK, IMPUGN IT WHOSO LIST.*"

Acts iv. 5–31.

Revised Version.

Now, it came to pass on the morrow, that their rulers and the elders and the scribes assembled in Jerusalem, and Annas the high priest, and Caiaphas and John and Alexander, and as many as were of high-priestly lineage; and having set them in the midst they demanded:

"In what kind of power, or in what kind of name did ye do this?"

Then Peter, being filled with the Holy Ghost, said to them:

"Rulers of the people and elders [of Israel], if we are questioned this day concerning the good deed of the impotent man, whereby this man has been saved, be it known to you all and to the whole people of Israel, that in the name of Jesus Christ the Nazarene, Whom ye crucified, Whom God raised from the dead, in the same does this man stand before you whole. This is the 'Stone' which has been set at naught by you the 'builders,' which is become 'head of the corner.' And there is not in any other salvation; for neither is there another name under the heaven given among men in which we must be saved."

Beholding then the boldness of Peter and John, and having perceived that they were illiterate men and laymen, they marvelled and recognised them that they had been with Jesus; and seeing the man standing with them who had been healed, they had nothing to gainsay. But when they had commanded them to go aside out of the Sanhedrim, they conferred with one another, saying:

"What shall we do to these men? For that indeed an acknowledged sign has been done through them, is manifest to all the inhabitants of Jerusalem, and we are not able to deny it. But in order that it may not be still more spread to the people, let us threaten them [with threats] not to speak at all on that name to any man."

And having called them, they enjoined on no account to utter a word nor to teach on the name of Jesus. But Peter and John answering said to them:

"Whether it is just before God to hearken to you rather than to God, judge ye. For we [for our part] are not able not to speak what we saw and heard." But they, having further threatened, released them, finding no means by which they might punish them, on account of the people, for all were glorifying God for what had happened. For the man on whom this sign of the healing had happened was more than forty years old.

Now, when they were released, they went to their own [company] and reported whatever the high priests and the elders had said to them; who, when they had heard it, with one accord lifted up their voice to God and said:

"O Ruler, Thou Who didst make the heaven and the earth and the sea, and all things which are in them, Who by the mouth of our father David Thy servant, through the Holy Ghost, didst say,

"'Why did the Gentiles rage,
And peoples purpose vain things?
There stood up the kings of the earth,
And the rulers conspired together in one
Against the Lord, and against His Christ.'

"For there 'conspired' of a truth in this city against Thy holy Servant Jesus, Whom Thou didst 'anoint,' both Herod and Pontius Pilate, with the 'Gentiles' and 'peoples' of Israel, to do whatever Thy hand and Thy counsel forcordained to happen. And now, O Lord, have a regard to their threats, and grant to Thy bondservants with all boldness to speak Thy word in [Thy] stretching forth Thine hand for healing, and that signs and wonders be done through the name of Thy holy Servant Jesus."

And when they had prayed, the place was shaken in which they were assembled, and they were all filled with the Holy Ghost, and continued to speak the word of God with boldness.

VIII.

ST. PETER'S address in Solomon's portico on the cure of the cripple was even more important for its results than for its own sake. On the one hand, it won a large accession of members to the young Church: how many is not told, but the total list of believers, probably excluding women and children,[1] was brought up by it to the sum of five thousand. On the other hand, it brought the new sect for the first time into collision with the national authorities. That afternoon began the long and glorious story of Christian confessorship and martyrdom. The peaceful prosperity of the primitive Church met here with its earliest check.

The captain of the temple guard, as the officer on duty charged with maintaining good order throughout the extensive precincts of the holy house, had an obvious excuse for interference. For an excited crowd to rush about the cloisters, and be harangued by an unauthorised preacher, might fairly enough be described as a breach of the tranquillity which is usually supposed to reign in a sacred building. Those priests who had just been officiating at

[1] The use of τῶν ἀνδρῶν, in ver. 4, compared with the careful distinction of sex in chap. v. 14, leads to this inference. I take the figure stated to be the total number converted up to this date. Unfortunately we have no means of even guessing what time elapsed between Pentecost and the cure of the cripple.

evening service not unnaturally joined the temple police in the interests of order. So far the action of the authorities might not have meant much. It assumed a more serious complexion when these temple officials were seen to be backed up by members of the Sadducean party. This small but wealthy and powerful sect of rationalistic deists was, to be sure, no more popular at that time than it usually was; but it held the chief offices of state, it controlled the priesthood, it was noted for harsh severity where it had the power, and just then it had reasons of its own for resenting extremely the teaching of the new faith. All that the apostles preached turned upon one alleged fact, the return to life of Jesus Who had been put to death. Such a fact, if established, was fatal to the whole system of Sadducean unbelief. That God ruled men, indeed, in this world by temporal rewards and penalties, they held in common with their orthodox countrymen; but that the soul had no separate existence after death, and therefore could not reanimate the flesh in order to be judged or dealt with in another world, was then, whatever it may originally have been,[1] their prime tenet. To such a party of freethinkers, the report with which the apostles had for days been filling Jerusalem could not fail to be offensive. To the apostles the hostility of such a party could not fail to be full of danger.

The situation, therefore, was a grave one when, next morning, at its usual hour of session, the supreme court of judicature met for the trial of the two prisoners. This body was believed to be the lineal representative of those seventy elders who acted as assessors to Moses himself,[2]

[1] See the conjecture of Prideaux, that at first they only rejected tradition, in his *Connection*, part ii. book 5.

[2] Of the seventy elders, cf. Exod. xxiv. 1, 9, c. Numb. xi. 16, 24, ff.

and it still retained the largest authority over all spiritual causes, as well as over such secular matters as had not been seized by their Roman masters. In the eyes of a patriotic and religious Jew it was the most venerable and authoritative court on earth. Its president was God's high-priest, and the *élite* of the holy nation sat in it. Ex-high-priests, with the heads of the twenty-four classes into which the priesthood had been for convenience divided, formed a strong sacerdotal element; the learning of the age was represented by doctors of sacred law; and the old tribal division of the people was probably still recognised by the presence of heads of ancient houses.[1] In this body the great influence of Sadduceeism at that time probably centered in the descendants of Aaron. At the head of this ancient family of high-priests, by far the most powerful family in the nation, was the venerable Annas, who had long held the office, and who still, through his personal influence, shared the title with his own son-in-law, Caiaphas. Both these important members were present; both were Sadducees; and with them were other members of the same pontifical lineage, of whom two are named by the historian. Of John nothing further is known; Alexander may have been the head of the Jews settled at Alexandria, and a brother of the most eminent Alexandrian Jew of that generation, the great scholar and thinker, Philo.[2] It was before judges like these, august by descent, learning, and personal weight, as well as by official authority, that two men were that morning brought to the bar, of whom, when their Master stood before the

---

[1] See Alexander *in loc.* for some reasons for thinking that this is the class described as "the elders" (οἱ πρεσβύτεροι in ver. 5), but the conclusion is an uncertain one.

[2] Cf. Josephus, *Antiq.* xviii. 8. 1.

same tribunal a couple of months before, both had deserted, and one had expressly denied Him. It has never failed to strike the enemies as well as the friends of Christianity how extremely these men's conduct now contrasted with their conduct then. In fact, it struck their judges at the time. To every one who rejects the historical fact of the resurrection, with the special advent of a divine influence at Pentecost, this contrast must remain one of the stumbling-blocks of the narrative. Admit these two intervening facts, and everything is plain. Deny them, and the story becomes a puzzle.

The question put by the court to the apostles frankly assumed that the crippled beggar had been healed. It was idle to affect to question this. Nor was the question one which laid any charge against them. They were not yet in the position of accused persons, they were simply brought up for examination. The object was just to elicit their own explanation of the miracle. At the same time the interrogation was so framed as to entangle them, if possible, in an admission which should criminate themselves. For it ran thus:—"In what sort of power or in what sort of name did you do this?"[1] To understand this phraseology, it must be remembered that at that time, as for long before, there existed a numerous class (among Jews not less numerous than among Gentiles) who pretended by magical formulæ, and the invocation of names of more than mortal might, to expel demons, cure diseases, or in other ways change the course of nature. Jewish exorcists of this class were wont to trace their art to King Solomon. To this day, indeed, over all the East that monarch's name is held in popular reverence as the patron

---

[1] Ver. 7. The words are peculiar: 'ἐν ποίᾳ δυνάμει ἢ ἐν ποίῳ ὀνόματι.

and prince of magicians. Josephus, who seems even to have believed in the art, tells us that he saw with his own eyes a Jew cast out a demon, in presence of the Emperor Vespasian and a crowd of Roman officers, by using the name and the incantations of Solomon.[1] Such practices had been branded by the Mosaic law as profane, and made punishable by death,[2] but they never were extirpated from Jewish soil. We read of them in the reigns of Saul and of Ahab and of Manasseh. Isaiah speaks of them; so does Micah; so does Malachi.[3] In our Lord's ministry they were quoted to Him as rivals. Later they encountered Peter in Samaria, and Paul at Paphos and at Ephesus.[4] It is impossible to comprehend the history of the planting of our faith through a divine supernaturalism without realising how thoroughly the world, heathen and Hebrew, was then saturated with the conception of a demoniac and magical supernaturalism. It is in this light we must read the question of the Sanhedrim. A wonder is confessed. The doers of it are assumed to have done it in some ghostly "power" or by the charm of some compelling "name;" and they are adjured to say in what sort of "name" or "power," divine or magical, good or evil. Of course it was not obtruded on their attention that by virtue of the old Mosaic statute they might be stoned to death if they confessed to having used any other "name" than that of Jehovah; but, equally of course, this fact was present to their own recollection

---

[1] See *Antiq.* viii. 2. 5.

[2] Exod. xxii. 18; Lev. xix 21, xx. 27; Deut. xviii. 9–14.

[3] Cf. 1 Sam. xxviii.; 2 Kings ix. 22; 2 Chron. xxxiii. 6; Isa. ii. 6, lvii. 3; Mic. v. 12; Mal. iii. 5.

[4] See Matt. xii. 22–30 (c. ver. 43), and parallels; Acts viii. 9–19, xiii. 6–12, xix. 11–20.

not less than to the mind of the examiners. It was, if the court chose to make it such, a question of life and death.

Hence the courage of Peter's reply is to be estimated by the double danger which he ran. By avowing that, in the name of Jesus, not nominally in that of "Jehovah," the cure had been effected, he ran the risk of being condemned for sorcery. By preaching to their face the resurrection of Jesus, as the authentication of His divine power, he braved the strongest and most implacable party in the court. He shrank from neither danger; and the reason given by the sacred recorder is that there was then, for the first time, fulfilled a promise, spoken not long before by Jesus Himself, and preserved for us by the same pen: [1]—"They shall lay their hands on you and persecute you, delivering you up to the synagogues and into prisons, being brought before kings and rulers for My name's sake; and it shall turn to you for a testimony. Settle it therefore in your hearts not to meditate before what ye shall answer, for I will give you a mouth and wisdom, which all your adversaries shall not be able to gainsay nor resist." A special breath of God's Holy Ghost animated the first confessor of Christ in the hour of confession. The words which his Master gave him rang with a novel boldness in the ears of Israel's rulers. A senate, accustomed to overawe all men into such deference as only the conjunction of civil with spiritual power can inspire, was struck dumb with astonishment when two "unlettered laymen" dared to speak at its bar in tones of prophet-like authority. As St. Luke says, using the very word of

[1] See Luke xxi. 12–15, cf. xii. 11, 12, c. Mark xiii. 11. Cf. ver. 8. πλησθεὶς πνεύματος ἁγίου.

IN COLLISION WITH THE SANHEDRIM. 149

Jesus' promise,[1] they were not able to "gainsay" them. It seemed to high-priests and scribes like having Jesus among them again—risen from the dead in spirit, if not in the flesh. They looked at the two confessors till they recognised them for men who had been often seen in the company of the Crucified.[2] It is the very life of Christ Himself, breathed into His saints, which forms the characteristic of their Christian life. That Spirit of Christ looks through their serenely confident eyes, speaks in their free, undoubting sentences, even as it informs their gracious and mighty deeds; till they grow, in supreme moments, to be so like reproductions of that Christ Whom the world refused, as to vex the world's conscience with the recollection of its rejected Lord. It was a most notable instance of what has often occurred when the wicked world has striven to put out its moral lights. John is beheaded, but the fame of Jesus troubles King Herod. Jesus is crucified, but Peter charges the Sanhedrim with His death. Stephen is stoned, but Saul returns a mightier Stephen. There is a Light which the world cannot put out.

The unpremeditated, yet picked and close-packed words of Peter's defence need not detain us, since they are a briefer echo of his popular sermons. To the Sanhedrim, as to the crowd, he explains the miracle by the power of the risen Nazarene. On the Sanhedrim, more bluntly than on the crowd, he charges the death of Jesus as the rejection of God's Christ. They, not the people, were the official "builders" of God's temple on earth; yet they, more truly than the people, had refused that chosen and

[1] Ἀντειπεῖν, in ver. 14, is only elsewhere used in Luke xxi. 15, in the New Testament.

[2] See ver. 13; and cf. ἀγράμματοι κ. ἰδιῶται with what was said of Jesus, John vii. 15.

precious "Stone" on which alone the temple could rest. By his citation from Psalm cxviii.,[1] Peter probably recalled to some of his audience what he himself no doubt remembered, Jesus' own use of the same text a few days before His death. By it he paved the way for a strong unflinching assertion that only through Jesus could salvation come from God to any soul of man. To refuse Jesus, like the rulers, was to be lost; to receive Him, like the lame man, was to be saved. In speaking thus, Peter had travelled far past the cure which was the immediate matter of inquiry, but not without reason. To him, as to his Master, each minor salvation from any ill of body or earthly suffering was but a visible promise of the one catholic salvation from both moral and physical evil of every sort which Jesus came to work. It never escaped the view of Jesus or His apostles that there must be a *solidarité* about salvation simply because there is a *solidarité* in evil. This makes it vain to look for true help from the least evil, save from One Who can rescue from the greatest; but it also justifies this one true Deliverer's claim to deliver in six troubles, yea, even from the mystic seven.[2] He Who can save at all can save wholly; the conscience from guilt, the heart from lust, the will from infirmity, the reason from darkness, as well as the body from disorder and death. By one great Name has this cripple been "saved"[3] from lameness; by the same one

---

[1] Psa. cxviii. 22. See our Lord's use of it in Matt. xxi. 42; and cf. the same Psalm quoted previously on His entry, by the crowd, in Matt. xxi. 8. With this speech of St. Peter cf. his First Epistle ii. 4, and his own name of rock-foundation. In 1 Pet. ii. 4-8 he quotes both Isa. xxviii. 16 and Psa. cxviii.   [2] Job v. 19.

[3] Σέσωσται is the word used in ver. 9 of the cure, where the A. V. reads "is made whole."

Name alone, and by no other, can any one of us be saved from sin and everlasting death.

The Sanhedrists were Hebrew theologians, and must have known perfectly what Peter meant. He was charming with no name of demon or false god. It was not inconsistent with the strictest monotheism, nor any treason against Jehovah, to say that Jehovah had sent His foretold Deliverer, His Anointed, and that through Him salvation had come to Israel. Had Jesus Himself said no more about Himself than that, His condemnation would have wanted even the shadow of ground which it had. But the claims of Jesus to be Messiah, which Peter reasserts, rest now on new evidence, said to have transpired since His condemnation. It is on the resurrection that Peter, after his wont, bases his preaching of Christ, and the resurrection was to the council a new fact in evidence. Much as individual Sanhedrists must have heard about it since that morning when they bribed the Roman legionaries to keep silence,[1] this was the earliest occasion since then on which it came under the formal cognizance of the court. Mark how they treat this fresh light on the gravest question a Sanhedrim ever discussed, which has thus, by mere chance as one might say, struggled into their council chamber. Two Galileans are found haranguing a crowd inside the temple; and on examination it is brought under their official observation, (1) that the crucified Pretender to messiahship is affirmed to be alive again; and (2) that through His name and living power a miracle has been effected. Honest men under official

[1] Matt. xxviii. 11–15. The language of Matthew favours the impression that the report of the guard was communicated at a regular meeting of the council; but it may have been only an irregular gathering of the majority which had condemned Jesus.

responsibility to find religious truth for their countrymen, would have fastened on two such alleged facts as of primary importance, and would have either publicly admitted or publicly refuted them. What do these men do? They pass by the first and chief fact alleged—that of resurrection—in absolute silence. Was it because they already had on record the report of certain Roman soldiers who had spent a night on duty at the door of a certain tomb? To me, this absolute silence in the Sanhedrim respecting the statement of Peter that God had raised up Jesus, is one of the most noticeable things in the narrative. Granting that the Sadducean members were glad to let such a statement alone, were there not Pharisees in the sederunt who might eagerly have seized on it as a weapon against Sadducean scepticism? Or had the Pharisaic party, who had mainly pressed on the execution of Jesus, reasons of their own for avoiding that subject? To make a point in their polemic against the materialistic school, would be a dear-bought triumph if it could only be done by convicting themselves of having slain the Christ of God. There was, however, a second fact which could not be ignored. The healed beggar, who never stood before, was "standing" before their eyes, and the notoriety of his cure compelled them to notice it. Had even this fact been either inquired into or accepted in a candid temper, it must have led them to the truth. Yet when the court was cleared for private conference, the question which agitated these fathers was not what religious meaning such a fact might have, or what bearing on the Christ-hood of Jesus; but only this—How can the affair be best hushed up? A miserable result of official bigotry! When spiritual corporations know nothing better to do

IN COLLISION WITH THE SANHEDRIM.

with a new fact or fresh light than to keep it from spreading further, spiritual corporations are not far from their end. Christianity was once a new truth feared by the conservative and traditional religion which it came to supersede. Need Christianity itself fear to be in turn superseded by a truth which is newer still? Or it is the mere Rabbinism of Christendom, its narrow, interested, and traditional misgrowth, which, whether in Papal or in Protestant councils, fears the touch of light, and would smother up facts that they spread no further? All systems tend, when they get old, to grow timorous, as old men do, because they have a fashion of growing away from the vital truth which created them, till they come to stand at last like a husk without a kernel. If we did not believe that Christianity is not to be identified with any visible system, but carries in it an indestructible Spirit, Who can rejuvenate the old materials and recreate old establishments, we might fairly be excused if, at this hour of Christian history, we too gave way to alarm. Christian systems of dogma, of polity, of national religious life, of ancient worship, are cracking and toppling to their fall on every hand. They and the people whose lives are bound up in them may fear; but the simple Christian of a primitive and New Testament type, whose religion is in the spirit, not the letter, in the spirit, not the system, can afford to welcome (as the Sanhedrim ought to have done) every indication that, out of the *débris* of older forms, God the Spirit is about to build up afresh for us, in nobler beauty, the kingdom of Jesus Christ.

Weak as the decision of the court was, their subsequent behaviour was far weaker. It was a "lame and impotent conclusion" to forbid the apostles to preach. When the apostles refused obedience, to do no more than forbid them a second time, and then send them home, was much more "lame and impotent." Had this been lenity, or a tender sparing of misguided citizens, it would have been at least respectable. But it was no such thing. It was simply weakness. Hollow authority, authority filled up by no truth, had come into collision with the might of conscience informed by the truth. So often as this is seen, it is the earthen pitcher to the iron pot. And it has been often seen. Surely it is a mistake to represent this as the first occasion on which the human conscience asserted its inalienable right against spiritual tyranny. The first Christian instance of course it is, and Christian history has been much more full of similar instances than the history of any other faith. The genius of heathendom is unfriendly to supreme loyalty to truth. The circumstances of Judaism offered few opportunities for it. Still, the case of Daniel,[1] at least, will occur to most minds as a parallel before Christ to these words of Peter, nearly as notable as the case of Luther, after Christ. The Hebrew statesman at Babylon and the German reformer at Worms were both alike impelled by conscience to defy a full unbroken front of civil authority in its utmost strength, rather than, not deny, but conceal, divine truths given them to proclaim. This is precisely what Peter and John did. If there ever lay on a man's conscience an absolute moral necessity, a compelling duty, not to hide in his own heart the truth he knew, but

[1] The events of the Maccabean period are less generally known, owing to the excessive neglect into which all the apocryphal writings have indiscriminately fallen; yet the Maccabean period is the martyr age of Judaism, *par excellence*.

at whatever hazard to utter it in the ears of all men, it was lying on these two who said, "Whether it be right in the sight of God to hearken unto you more than unto God, judge ye: for we cannot but speak the things which we have seen and heard." To have been eye and ear-witnesses of facts in which was wrapt up God's salvation for the world, bound them to speak. To have been silent would have been disobedience to the supreme voice of God, and treason against the spiritual hopes of mankind. Woe unto them, as Paul wrote of himself, if they preached not the gospel![1] Silence those men, those few, poor, Galilean laymen, whom Christ chose for His witnesses, and you strangle in its cradle the kingdom of God. Not often has it happened that on the faithfulness of so few hung results so immense. Only at rare turning-times in the unfolding of divine truth to the world can so vast a responsibility be laid on a single soul or on a handful of men. Yet at all times, and on every man, there undoubtedly lies a measure of responsibility, small, but his own, to quench or conceal no light which God has kindled in him. Christian experience is also a sort of seeing and hearing; it implies a personal acquaintance with Jesus Christ in His spiritual power to save of such a kind as gives the man assurance of the truth. Therefore it turns every one who has it, as truly, though far less eminently than Peter, into a witness for Christ. Within a narrow circle, it may be, and to very few people, or through most quiet and hidden ways, yet really, each of us who has the faith of experience is bound to speak. Either by word or sign or act of life, we ought to tell forth, not whatever in our shallow conceit we may fancy we understand better

[1] 1 Cor. ix. 16.

than other men, but simply that which in the deep secrets of our personal religious life we have seen and heard of God's salvation. To do this on our little scale, with small issues hanging on it, is a duty not less binding on us, nor less testing to our loyalty, than was Peter's witness on that day when the history of the Church hung upon his lips. He who is not faithful in a little will not be faithful in much. To me it is a failure as grave and full of blame should I withhold my humble testimony, as to Peter it had been to stifle his through fear of death. It is his fidelity to duty, not the magnitude of his service, which approves the servant.

From the court-room they retired to the church. Christian confessors win their victories in the face of day; but the strength by which such victories are won is only to be got where Jesus got His, in secret. Remember Luther's broken cries as he lay on his chamber floor at early morning on the 18th of April, 1521.[1] In every crisis of strain and peril through which our lives must pass, at every moment of supreme difficulty, Sanhedrim threatenings, Worms Diet, or whatever less thing it be before which our faith and courage quail, there is for us no place of help like the secret footstool of Almighty God, nor any weapon like the cry of faith. Faith, grasping the word of God's promise as the first Church then grasped the Second Psalm,[2] and laying hold on the faithful help of Him " Who hath made heaven and earth and the sea," can procure that, not the chamber only shall be shaken,

[1] See D'Aubigné, *Hist. of the Reformation*, book vii. chap. 8.
[2] See the words of their prayer in ver. 25, 26, citing Psa. ii. 1, 2; as in ver. 24 they had already referred, without express citation, to Exod. xx. 11.

but kingdoms too, and principalities of evil, and ghostly powers of darkness ruling over human souls. The reporting at length of this noble prayer, and the answer which came with outward sign, almost like the signs of Pentecost itself, show us how critical the moment was felt to be for the infant Church. It is true that the council had been too weak and inconsequential to enforce its decision for the present. Still, it had decided; and its decision against the new faith was a sore blow and grievous discouragement. It meant, first of all, that any hope of a national recognition of Jesus' messiahship, by a formal reversal of the national judgment which condemned Him, was in the meanwhile at an end. The supreme national authority has again rejected the risen, as it before rejected the unslain, Messiah. Israelites may repent and believe, separating themselves one by one[1] from the guilty people; but Israel, through its chiefs and rulers, has deliberately repeated its crime, and refused the salvation of God. It meant more than that, however. The conversion even of individuals was now become immensely more difficult, since every man who joined the new sect must brave the Sanhedrim. Each word spoken for Christ must thenceforth be spoken at the risk of liberty. Even to listen to apostolic words was now a breach of law. Every fresh convert forfeited the rights of a good citizen, ran a chance of excommunication, and cast in his lot with a band of convicted heretics. Men who are clothed with a venerable name may grossly abuse their power, yet every new faith has to learn through stern experience how great is the power of venerable names. The Hebrew Sanhedrim was still a word to con-

[1] Comp. Peter's words to the people, Acts ii. 40.

jure with. Nay, it could bite as well as bark, as a few days more were to show.

What the Church needed under such changed circumstances, and what the Church prayed for, was, first, a spirit of courage in her spokesmen, "that with all boldness" the apostles "may speak Thy Word," undeterred by the threatenings of powerful and bitter foes; next, that a way might still be kept open for the Word into the hearts of the people. Here it is surely quite worth noting that the means chiefly relied on by the Church at Jerusalem for both these ends is miracle. To fortify the apostles' hearts, and carry forward the new kingdom, it begs for "signs and wonders to be done by the name of Thy holy Child Jesus."[1] This language is characteristic of the very earliest days of the Church. At no later period would such exclusive stress have been laid on this external aid of miracle. Long since have we outgrown it altogether, and learned to lean on the native, self-commending virtue of the gospel message, enforced to the heart by the inward virtue of the Holy Ghost. But just then, living in an atmosphere charged with the miraculous, and in a city accustomed to be fed on wonders,[2] fresh too from a sudden cure which had added multitudes to their "company," the young Church asked, what under the circumstances was probably the best thing it could ask, a continuance of those special manifestations of divine might by which it had been founded and its witness at first authenticated. The prayer was heard. Once more the name of Jesus was proved to have power with

---

[1] Or rather "Servant," as in ver. 27 (also Acts iii. 26), where the same word παῖς occurs.

[2] Cf. John iv. 48 c. 1 Cor. i. 22 also Matt. xii. 38 and parallels.

God. However strictly the exhibition of that power may have been limited, since the apostolic age, to the spiritual sphere alone, it is the same power still, and not less efficacious now than it was then for the pardon of guilt and for the renewal of spiritual life in men. It is not less true now than then, nor a whit less solemn for us to hear than for the Jews, that "there is none other Name under heaven given among men whereby we must be saved."

IX.
Ananias and Sapphira.

UT POENA DUORUM HOMINUM SIT DOCTRINA MULTORUM.

Acts iv. 32—v. 11.

Revised Version.

Now, the crowd of those who had believed was of one heart and soul, and not one said that anything of what belonged to him was his own, but all things were common to them. And with great power did the apostles continue to give their testimony to the resurrection of the Lord Jesus, and great grace was upon them all. For neither was there among them any one in want; for as many as were owners of lands or houses, having sold them, kept bringing the prices of what was being sold and laying them at the feet of the apostles: and it was distributed to each as he had need.

And Joseph, who was surnamed Barnabas by the apostles, which is being interpreted "son of consolation," a Levite, a Cypriote by birth, being owner of a field, sold it, and brought the money and laid it at the feet of the apostles. But a certain man, Ananias by name, with Sapphira his wife, sold a property, and put aside from the price for himself, the wife also being privy, and having brought a certain part, laid it at the feet of the apostles. But Peter said:

"Ananias, why did Satan fill thine heart, that thou didst lie to the Holy Ghost, and put aside for thyself from the price of the land? While it remained, did it not remain thine own, and after it was sold, was it not

in thine own power? Why was it thou didst put this deed in thine heart? Thou hast not lied to men, but to God."

Then Ananias hearing these words, fell and expired. And great fear came on all who heard. And the younger men rose and wrapt him up, and having carried him out, buried him. And it happened about a space of three hours after that his wife, not knowing whath ad happened, went in. To her answered Peter: "Tell me if for so much ye sold the land?" And she said: "Yes, for so much." Then Peter to her:

"Why is it that ye agreed between you to tempt the Lord's Spirit? Behold, the feet of them that have buried thy husband are at the door, and shall carry thee out."

Then she fell instantly at his feet and expired. And the young men when they came in found her dead, and having carried her out, buried her beside her husband. And great fear came on the whole Church and on all who heard these things.

IX.

OPPOSITION from without, when it drives the Church to prayer, becomes a source of strength and a crown of honour. The real foe of the spiritual kingdom is corruption within. Two apostles may lie in ward all night, and be tried for their lives in the morning; but the Church, like every community and every man, is disgraced only when she disgraces herself.

It is also to be noticed, that as the ripest fruits are nearest rotting, so the first sign of internal decay which alarmed the Church of Jerusalem showed itself in that which had been her noblest boast. The love which, in Calvin's words, " made that common to the needy which was proper to every man;"[1] the strong sense of brotherhood, which, acting as a bond of unity, levelled the inequalities of fortune, and for a time realised a virtual community of wealth: this was, of all features in the primitive Jewish Church, the rarest and loveliest. Yet precisely here corruption entered.

I have already had occasion in an earlier chapter to speak of the unity of the Church and the nature of that charity which at first signalised it. In these respects we

---

[1] " Tunc quod proprium erat singulis, commune egenis faciebat caritas."—Calvin *in loc.* I quote in the text from the translation by Fetherstone, 1585, reprinted by Calvin Trans. Soc. 1844.

are informed that the general condition of the Church was little affected by the recent threats of the Sanhedrim. Large as the number of the disciples had now become, and critical as was their relation to the public authorities, their internal harmony remained unshaken. The storm drove the flock closer—it could not scatter it. Nor was the witness which the Church's spokesmen bore to the resurrection of Jesus (which was their special proper work,[1] and the burden of their preaching) one whit less bold or telling because the highest court of law had forbidden it. Filled anew with holy courage, Christ's confessors set at nought the prohibition of the rulers, and obeyed God rather than men. In this they were supported by the whole body of believers. To take up such a position of open defiance to the lawful heads of their nation was a serious step. It was likely to entail the most painful consequences. Excommunication, social ostracism, scourging and imprisonment of the leaders, scattering of the followers; all these things were coming,[2] and any man might foresee that they were sure to come. Nevertheless, the brethren showed themselves prepared to face such hazards by the cordiality with which they clung to one another. Left alone, they sought mutual support, and made up for the pain of their isolation by the warmth of their brotherly-kindness.

The chief way in which at that time a member of the Church could express his unshaken devotion to the common cause, or his willingness to sacrifice to the last penny for the common weal, was by placing his realised capital at the disposal of the brotherhood. The en-

---

[1] This is the force of the article in τὸ μαρτύριον (ver. 33).
[2] See chap. v. 18, 40, and vii. 57–viii. 4.

dangered position of the little community thus tended to inflame the fervour of its charity, and gave a new impetus to that common relief fund which had been started at Pentecost. It probably became more than ever the fashion for well-to-do believers to sell all that could be sold of their property; and in the heat of the moment (for the time was one of growing spiritual excitement) some doubtless did from a mixture of imperfect motives what the best did purely for love. I can hardly suppose Ananias to have been the solitary case, though he was an extreme one, of a disciple who followed others in doing what the public opinion of the body prescribed as the right thing to do, when, if left to himself, he would rather have let it alone. The specific sin of Ananias did not lie in this, but in something worse than this; and such deference to public opinion from mixed motives is far too common for us to believe that he stood alone in it. The wealthy part of the Church[1] was no doubt made up of two classes; men who were full of the new Spirit, and so hearty in the cause of Jesus, that they were forward of their own accord to put all they had into the Church treasury, in order that no lover of Jesus might lack; and men honest enough in their belief, only less enthusiastic or generous, who gave, partly indeed from good-will, but partly also through the force of example or the fear of censure. To whatever extent this latter class existed, it formed a dangerous element. When high-pitched virtue becomes a fashion, men learn to pay to it the homage of hypocrisy.

Of each of these classes, Luke has preserved an extreme

[1] For this narrative only concerns the propertied members. The poor of the Church had another and a different temptation in store for them, as appears from Acts vi.

example. In what respect, indeed, Joseph,[1] the Cyprian Levite, whom the apostles called Barnabas, surpassed other warm-hearted benefactors, is not told. I should suppose mainly in the purity and strength of his motives, since all we know of him leads us to judge that he was a singularly unselfish and generous Christian. Emphatically he was "a good man."[2] To his ready friendliness St. Paul himself was much beholden. He was the fittest to be sent to encourage the infant Gentile Church in Antioch. His gift of prophetic speech was chiefly a gift (as Luke's translation of his by-name shows)[3] of consolation and heartening. It was like him, therefore, to be forward with his sale of land, so that, reverting to the primitive Levitical life,[4] he might with unembarrassed hands give himself to better than Levitical work. Possibly the promptitude of his benefaction, or something in his manner of making it, caused him to be singled out for mention as an example of the better class of givers.

For an example of the worst class, there could be no doubt whom to choose. There might be several Josephs: there was, let us hope, only one Ananias. Even if we are justified in the conjecture that others, as well as he, followed the example of men like Barnabas with some reluctance or from a wish to stand equally high in the Church's esteem, still no one probably except himself and his wife allowed vanity and greed together to lead him

[1] The true reading of his name in Acts iv. 36, is Ἰωσήφ, on the authority of A, B, D, E, not Ἰωσῆς, as in the *Textus Receptus*.

[2] As he is called in Acts xi. 24; cf. besides, chap. xi. 22-26, ix. 27, and xiii. 1.

[3] Barnabas (from נְבוּאָה), rendered υἱὸς παρακλήσεως in chap. iv. 36.

[4] Levites by law could not own land (Num. xviii. 20; Deut. x. 9), except round about the Levitical cities (cf. Jer. xxxii. 7); but this may have fallen into disuse in later Judaism.

into downright falsehood. So long as imperfect motives, wrong motives even, secretly mix themselves with the spiritual life of a religious community, as they always do, Church discipline can take no notice of them. In the case of this wretched pair, all the baser ingredients which marred the splendid charity of those days came conspicuously to the surface in very gross sin, and the sinners became at once the mark for an ecclesiastical judgment of the most awful description. The crime for which Ananias died was certainly not the first appearance of evil in his heart. Men never do such things, never do them at least so deliberately, without a previous period of moral deterioration. The crime is the fruit of a plant of unrighteousness which has been tolerated or fostered for a while. Nor were Ananias and his wife the only disciples who were tempted to give less than all they had to spare to the Church plate. Others there might be who, grudging to give so much, gave less, and frankly called it less. Others still may have given their all with some little grudge, yet gave it. And there were probably some who battled with the temptation to lie, as Ananias lied, but overcame the tempter. The peculiar sin of this pair lay here, that, being tempted by two evil things—the love of money and the love of applause—they suffered both these unchristian passions to enter and occupy their souls, to fill them up bit by bit, driving out the love of men and the fear of God, till, grown blind and hard and reckless through sin, they plotted in cold blood to cheat the Church and lie to the face of God. Had they been covetous only, they would have kept their property; vain only, they would have given it all. In either case the motive had been a bad one, but in neither case would the offence have grown into a scandal. It was the effort to reconcile two conflicting passions, to be close and seem generous, to keep their gold yet win the credit of giving it, which betrayed these Christians into the first open and shameful breach of Christian morality. Out of the confluence of covetousness with vanity came forth a lie.

In tracing thus the genesis of their great sin, we must not leave out of account that extra-human tempter to whom St. Peter pointed. Ananias and Sapphira were the Adam and Eve of that early Christian paradise, and their fall is referred to the inspiration of the same agent. Or, if you like, the covetous hypocrisy of him who fell from his seat in the apostolate was reappearing even within the new Church of the Holy Ghost; and Peter recognised the presence of the same spiritual adversary who had filled Judas' heart.[1] Men may and ought to resist his suggested evil. It is their own fault if they suffer him "to fill their heart." Yet his presence is not to be forgotten, nor may his influence ever be more surely detected than in a lie; above all, such a lie as sin tells when it would pass for virtue. The "father of lies" is in character when he comes among the sons of God as "an angel of light."[2] With that strong desire to get rid of the inexplicable which almost dominates recent literature, men are more ready just now than ever before to explain away the personality of the devil. There can be no doubt, however, among impartial students of Scripture, that all Scripture authority, including that of our Lord Himself, represents man as set betwixt a twofold world of invisible moral influences. From the Above and from the Beneath alike, real per-

---

[1] Cf. what is said of Judas in John xiii. 27.
[2] See John viii. 44; 2 Cor. xi. 14; and Job i. 6.

sons operate upon this doubtful border-land of mingled good and evil where we spend our period of probation; and in the background of man's spiritual being they are represented as rival actors, inspiring, though they cannot determine, the activity of his will. To any one but a materialist, this conception of antagonist spiritual influences, a Spirit of God Who leads upwards to good, and a spirit against God who heads the realm of evil and tempts downward, need offer no serious difficulty. To a careful thinker, it may even appear to answer some of the darkest questions of history, and explain many of the deepest experiences of spiritual life. To me it seems to complete the scheme of the personal world by linking all its members into one whole, and binding our own moral history with those vast realms of spiritual existence which lie on either hand of us. Neither the Holy Spirit nor the unholy needs to trench upon the sacred awful region of human responsibility. Men resist the Holy Ghost; men, too, "resist the devil."[1] Welcome either, yield to either; lean this way or that; and the power of withdrawal from your chosen spiritual ally may be indefinitely diminished. You may become, by a law of personal life, more and more the "slave"[2] of him whom you elect to obey. Yet after such an appalling supremacy of evil over good has become most pronounced, so that a man has come to fulfil with little scruple the worst suggestions of the devil, it can still be said to him, as was said to Ananias, "Why did Satan fill thy heart?" There is no answer to that "*Why?*" save the first guilty consent of the free will which opened up the heart to the foul one's breath and laid the springs of action in his hand.

[1] See Eph. iv. 30, and Jas. iv. 7.   [2] Cf. John viii. 34 (Greek).

It was in a full Church meeting, possibly at one of the hours of daily prayer, that Ananias came to offer his gift to the Lord. The apostles, as the office-bearers of the society, were the official custodians and dispensers of this charity. Devoted to the service of the Lord's poor, the money was evidently looked upon as consecrated to the Lord Jesus Himself, and the oblation of it formed therefore an act of public worship. It was laid solemnly "at the apostles' feet" while they sat in their seats as presiding teachers and heads of the holy family. One wonders much more at the audacity of the man who ventured to lay down before God, as the whole price of his estate, so much only as he and his wife could find it in their hearts to part with, than one does at the spiritual insight of the apostle. It sometimes happens that pure-hearted women[1] and little children shrink with involuntary dislike from false bad men whose real character is still by the world undetected. So, where the Holy Spirit dwells eminently in the heart, as He then dwelt in Peter's, He may bestow what will look like supernatural insight into character by simply heightening to greater acuteness than in other men the sensitiveness of the true soul to the approach of the false. In the One Man in Whom the Spirit

---

[1] Cf. what Marguerite says of Mephistopheles, in "Faust:"—

"Der Mensch den du da bei dir hast
Ist mir in tiefer inn'rer Seele verhasst;
Es hat mir in meinem Leben
So nichts einen Stich ins Herz gegeben
Als des Menschen widrig Gesicht."

* * * * *

"Seine Gegenwart bewegt mir das Blut."

* * * * *

"Auch wenn er da ist, könn't ich nimmer beten."

u. s. w.

dwelt without measure, this insight into the hearts of men reached its maximum,[1] and He it was Who gave a measure of the like insight to His chosen servants.

Precisely this eminent presence of God the Holy Spirit in the assembly of believers, and in their chiefs above all, was the fact which aggravated the offence of Ananias. In secretly purloining[2] part of the money which he had already devoted to God's treasury, he did what, if not exactly a sacrilegious robbing of God, like the sin of Achan, is extremely like it. In presenting the remainder under the pretence that it was the whole, he, at any rate, committed a lie in act; and since God the Spirit (Whose personality and divinity are here unmistakably assumed) was the informing Breath of the new Church, the Guardian of its purity and the Inspirer of its worship, the man's lie passed beyond his human brethren to that dread august Personality Who inhabited them. What Peter says, is not that Ananias bore false witness *of* the Holy Ghost, in representing his own offering as dictated by the spirit of love, when it was only wrung out of the grip of greed by a desire for praise. That is true: but what Peter says is that Ananias bore false witness *to* the Holy Ghost, lied to Him, as though he would, if he could, deceive God.[3] Or, to state it as Peter stated it, three

[1] See examples of this in our Lord, in John ii. 23–25, and (regarding Judas) in John vi. 70, and xiii. 27. Cf. the case of Paul, in Acts xiv. 9.

[2] Ver. 2, ἐνοσφίσατο (only elsewhere in Tit. ii. 10, of theft) = "put aside for himself" (in Mid.). Of Achan, see same word in LXX., Josh. vii. 1 (though used generally of Israel). Cf., on robbing God, Mal. iii. 8–10; and on this use of our text, see Hooker's *Eccl. Pol.* vii. 24, 17.

[3] The expression is ψεύσασθαι σε τὸ πνεῦμα = "to deceive by a lie." (With acc. of the person is classic usage, though only here in N. T. See Meyer *in loc.*)

hours after to the woman, this couple put God the all-knowing Spirit to the proof, tried Him whether He would let Himself and His holy Church be taken in with a lie.[1] The exceptional guilt of this falsehood did not consist in its attempting to deceive men. A false statement made out of doors to any curious questioner would have borne that complexion and no darker one. Here was the exceptional feature that, in trying to impose on the Church of God, they tried to impose on God Himself—"lied not unto men," as Peter strongly put it,[2] "but unto God" the Holy Ghost.

It seems to me that we have much need to lay to heart the lessons of this incident. Christ's Church has long since come to include so many false or unspiritual members, and to be so blent with the world, that we fail to realise its ideal sanctity as the body of Christ, animated in a peculiar manner by the divine presence. We fail to feel that to offend against the saints is to offend Christ;[3] that to fetch our worldly sins of conceit, ambition, envy, or covetousness, into sacred services, is to affront God to His face; that to defile the Church is to defile God's temple, and "if any man defile the temple of God, him shall God destroy." Nay, more than this. We are apt to lose out of our hearts that faith in the Third Person of the adorable and undivided Trinity, which realises Him as One Who can be wronged, grieved, insulted, or lied to; One Who, though He keeps Himself out of view, is

---

[1] Cf. ver. 9, πειράσαι τὸ πνεῦμα κυρίου.

[2] Ver. 4, οὐκ ἀνθρώποις ἀλλὰ τῷ Θεῷ. Cf., on the rhetorical absoluteness of this negation, Winer, *Gr.* p. 440.

[3] Compare our Lord's words in Matt. xviii. 5, 6, with Paul's in 1 Cor. viii. 12; and for an Old Testament parallel, see Zech. ii. 8.

yet sensitive to the treatment which, in the persons of righteous men, He daily receives from the profane. We are apt to treat the collective Church and the individual Christian as if God were not in any special way resident in them; forgetting that when we commit a sin against them as a Christian man or as the Christian community, our sin goes past the human object of it, to strike against One Who informs the Christian's life and guides the service of His Church. Priestly assumption, by monopolising for her official members alone the whole of that reverence which is due to the Church at large; and superstition, by extending a like reverence over places, times, emblems, robes, and other ecclesiastical adjuncts, have between them disgusted sober and manly thinkers. On the other hand, the rude irreverence into which some sections of evangelical society are in danger of falling, as if the Church of God, as the body of His people, had no greater sanctity than any other society of respectable persons, is clearly against Holy Scripture and spiritual facts. Official ordination does not make a man holier than other men, any more than consecration makes a building holier than other buildings. But the organised society of God's saints, in whose hands are the keys of the kingdom of heaven, is a more sacred thing than other societies are. To malign Christ's little ones; to deceive the Church; to turn God's worship into a performance; to use Church influence for private profit; to break the vows of our holy religion or profane its sacraments; to be called a Christian yet outrage the proprieties of Christian conduct; to despise the services, the ministers, or the discipline of the Church — these things are not, and cannot be, just the same as similar offences against a secular and self-made society. The peculiarity which makes this Society the kingdom of God, if it is the kingdom of God at all, must aggravate offences done against it; and the special presence of the Holy Ghost, if He is specially in it, must stamp all contempt or outrage with a sacrilegious die.

It is to mark the sanctity of that enclosure which is now for the first time called " the Church,"[1] that this narrative of judgment is set thus in the forefront of its history. On the earliest appearance of open sin within the Church follows the earliest infliction of Church discipline. Because it is the earliest, it is taken out of the hands of servants, to be administered with appalling severity by the hand of the Master. For it ought to be well observed that it was not Peter who slew Ananias and Sapphira. Not even as the executioner of a divine sentence can he be said to have slain them. In the first case, that of the husband, Peter only exposed and denounced the crime; he neither threatened nor foretold—probably did not even expect—the punishment. I can well believe that it took the apostle by surprise, as well as any bystander, when right at the back of his words, as if these words had been blows, the wretched man fell prostrate and dying to the floor. In the wife's case, Peter, after he had first given her space for confession, foretold, indeed, what he now foresaw to be her parallel fate; he foretold, but did not threaten, still less inflict. In both cases the stroke was struck by an unseen Hand. In the days of His flesh, Jesus, Who came " not to destroy men's lives, but to save

[1] In Acts v. 11. The reading in chap. ii. 47 is very doubtful—not found in A, B, C, or the Sinaitic. Here it is undoubted. The word occurs before this in only two passages in St. Matthew (xvi. 18, xviii. 17), as used by Jesus. After this, twenty-two times in Acts, and in the Epistles *passim*. See Bruder.

them," used His power over human bodies in beneficence, never in judgment. He refused to call down fire upon His enemies.[1] But Jesus raised to the right hand of God is clothed with the responsibilities as well as the prerogatives of divine rule, and one of these is judgment. What did not become the subject Son lies as a duty upon the exalted Lord. He has a kingdom to govern: to defend its purity, to vindicate its sanctity, to avenge its dishonour, are plain functions of His royal office. From the Lord Jesus Christ, then, the Head of His insulted Church, came, as I take it, the blows which stretched these two confederates upon the ground. It was awfully severe: it was meant to be awful in its severity. As an exercise of earthly discipline it was entirely exceptional, a warning not to be repeated. Church discipline, administered in its normal form through ministerial human hands, is a discipline by words, not blows. It employs spiritual deprivation, not corporeal chastisement. But since it pleased the offended Lord to step down for once into the earthly congregation of His saints and execute before men's eyes the supreme sentence of law on the earliest profaners of His House, no one can say that instant loss of life was a judgment too heavy for the greatness of their sin. The lives of all men are in His hand. Daily He is cutting them off in a moment—even hot with lust or red-handed from crime. His doom now and then antedates the slower processes of human law. The time and fashion of all our deaths is with Him. The life which we are daily forfeiting for transgression is daily spared through mercy. If one day His mercy turned to judgment, and He took from the earth two forfeited lives for the warning and the

[1] See Luke ix. 52–56.

bettering of many, who shall say either that the lesson was dearly bought or that the penalty was undeserved. It is well that men should be taught once for all, by sudden death treading swiftly on the heels of detected sin, that the gospel, which discovers God's boundless mercy, has not wiped out the sterner attributes of the Judge. "He that despised Moses' law died without mercy under two or three witnesses. Of how much sorer punishment, suppose ye, shall he be thought worthy who . . . . hath done despite unto the Spirit of grace?"[1]

I am far from saying that this awful manner of death implied of necessity the perdition of Ananias and Sapphira. They were members of the first Church, baptized as believers in the Lord Jesus; and though they had suffered Satan in this thing to fill their hearts, it is not for us to say that even sin so gross was quite inconsistent with grace, or that even a death so sudden quite shut out repentance. With the final fate of these two culprits, in short, we have nothing whatever to do. Only the time, the place, and the manner of their death were meant for the teaching of the Church—as a protest that the Holy Ghost is in her, as a warning against hypocrisy. To be false in their hearts, and to thrust this falsehood into their religious worship and pretended service of God in His Church, was the offence for which they died. There never has been a time from that day to this in which the Church has not needed the lesson. Let each Christian lay his hand upon his heart and say if he does not need it. Do none of us try to gain the world and save our soul at the same time? Who never renders to God a divided worship? Is it so rare

[1] Heb. x. 28, 29.

to seem better than we are? to cultivate a cheap repute for piety? to give that we may be seen of men, while we grudge what we give and love dearly what we keep? Are our prayers at no time false, as though we sought to deceive God? Or do modern Christians never show themselves devout before fellow-worshippers with a pretence of devotion? Is there no Holy Ghost now to be lied to? Or is He grown indifferent to insults through long endurance of them? Because judgment against our evil works and evil worship is not executed so speedily as on Ananias, shall we dream that God the Spirit has ceased to care, or God the Son ceased to rule? Two tombs only outside Jerusalem, rifled perchance long since, and clean forgotten now: but over how many Ananiases and Sapphiras hangs the unexecuted sentence? God grant us repentance to the acknowledging of our sins, and fill our hearts with the spirit of reverence, truthfulness, and godly fear, lest another spirit fill us with lies, with greed, with vain-glory, and with presumptuous impiety.

X.
A Second Collision with the Sanhedrim.

IF ANY MAN SUFFER AS A CHRISTIAN, LET HIM NOT BE ASHAMED.

Acts v. 12-42.

Revised Version.

Now by the hands of the apostles were many signs and wonders wrought among the people. And they were all with one accord in the Portico of Solomon; but of the rest, no one dared to attach himself to them; on the contrary, the people magnified them. But all the more were believers added to the Lord, crowds both of men and women. So that along the streets they brought out the infirm, and laid them on couches and mattresses, in order that at least the shadow of Peter passing might overshadow some one of them. There was also coming together the crowd from the towns around Jerusalem, bearing infirm persons, and those vexed by unclean spirits, all of whom were being healed.

But the High Priest rising up, and all who were with him, being the sect of the Sadducees, were filled with zeal, and laid their hands on the apostles, and put them in custody in gaol. But an angel of the Lord, by night, having opened the doors of the prison and led them out, said: "Go, stand and speak in the Temple to the people all the words of this life." And when they heard that, they entered at day-break into the Temple and were teaching. But the High Priest coming, and they who were with him, called together the Sanhedrim and the whole eldership of the children of Israel, and sent to the prison-house to have them brought. But the officers when they came did not find them in the prison. So on their return, they reported, saying: "*The prison-house we found shut in all security, and the guards standing at the doors, but when we had opened we found no one within.*" *And when the Captain of the Temple and the High Priests heard these words, they were at a loss concerning them, what this should come to. But one came and reported to them:* "*Behold, the men whom ye put in the prison are standing in the Temple, and teaching the people.*" *Then went away the Captain with the officers and brought them, not with force, for they were afraid of the people, lest they should have been stoned. And having brought them, they set them in the Sanhedrim. And the High Priest asked them, saying:*

"*We straitly enjoined upon you not to teach on this Name, and behold ye have filled Jerusalem with your teaching, and mean to bring down upon us the blood of this Man!*"

Then Peter and the apostles answering said:

"*One must obey God rather than men. The God of our fathers raised up Jesus, Whom ye murdered by hanging upon a stake. This Man God exalted with His right hand a Leader and Saviour, to give repentance to Israel and remission of sins. And we are His witnesses of these matters—* [we] *and also the Holy Spirit Whom God gave to those who are obedient to Him.*"

Now when they heard, they were cut through, and were consulting to take them off. But there stood up a certain Pharisee in the Sanhedrim, Gamaliel by name, a teacher of the law honoured by the whole people, who ordered to put the men outside for a little, and said to them:

"Men of Israel, take heed to yourselves in regard to these men, what action ye are about to take. For before these days rose up Theudas, saying he himself was somebody, to whom adhered a number of men, about four hundred; who was slain, and all as many as obeyed him were scattered, and came to nothing. After him rose up Judas the Galilean, in the days of the census, and drew people after him. He also perished, and all as many as obeyed him were dispersed. And now I say to you: Refrain from these men, and let them alone. Because if this plan or this work be of men, it will be destroyed; but if it is of God, ye will not be able to destroy it, lest ye should be found fighters against God also."

So they were persuaded by him; and having summoned the apostles and scourged them, they charged them not to speak on the name of Jesus, and released them. They therefore went rejoicing from the presence of the Sanhedrim, because they had been deemed worthy to be disgraced on account of the Name, and every day in the Temple and at home they ceased not to teach and preach Jesus as the Christ.

X.

ST. LUKE has given no data for fixing with certainty the chronology of his narrative, during the first ten chapters of it at least. If we could tell exactly the date of Saul's conversion, we should know pretty nearly when the Jerusalem Church was broken up by the martyrdom of Stephen, or rather by the outburst of persecution which followed it. This there are no materials for doing. Still we can approximate more or less to chronological correctness; and we shall be tolerably safe in saying that from Pentecost to Stephen's death must have been a period of from five to eight years. A less number indeed has been assigned by some; but the balance of authority and the results of the latest and most reliable chronologists lean to the longer rather than to the shorter period. It is, therefore, a great mistake to suppose, as I fancy many people do, that the events related in the first six chapters of the Acts were all crowded into as many months. The growth of the earliest Church was a much more gradual thing. Her times of trial recorded in detail by her historian were separated by considerable intervals of peaceful progress, over which he passes more lightly. She was allowed for year after year to consolidate her position and loosen herself from the Jewish state, before her membership was scattered about Syria by the violent blast of a general persecution.

When we glance over the incidents preserved to us out of this period, such as the first arrest of Peter and John, the death of Ananias, the second imprisonment of the apostles, or the election of deacons, we find ourselves unable to say in what part of these years any one incident occurred, or how long an interval elapsed between any two of them. Those general descriptions of the Church's state by which Luke separates the particular incidents [1] are obviously meant to cover considerable intervals of time; but how long the interval may have been in any case, we have no means of determining. At the same time, I think there is an internal probability that the interval of popular favour and wide increase which succeeded the death of Ananias and Sapphira must have been one of considerable duration. The immediate results of that first dreadful act of discipline had time to work themselves out. One natural effect of it was to cut a sharper line of demarcation betwixt the new converts and the body of their countrymen. To the Church itself it taught the lesson of its own peculiar sanctity as a divine society, inhabited by the Holy Ghost, and ruled from heaven by its departed Founder. Now, for the first time, it began to wear its characteristic name of "Church," *ecclesia*, or select community; [2] and now more than ever it had its meetings in a recognised quarter of the Temple buildings. That portico on their eastern side, in which Jesus had been wont to teach,[3]

---

[1] As at Acts ii. 42, *seq.*, iv. 32, *seq.*, v. 12, *seq.*, v. 42, vi. 7.
[2] See ver. 11.   [3] John x. 23.

where Peter, too, had addressed the crowd on the healing of the cripple,[1] became at this time an accepted rendezvous[2] for the twelve chiefs of the young spiritual commonwealth which was so fast developing itself. On the mind of the public outside, the fate of two unworthy members had impressed a wholesome respect for the new sect. It checked any disposition to make light of the apostles or of their doctrine, and it cleared a free space within which the Church could develop her peculiar life, shielded by popular admiration from Sadducean hostility.

One of the most noticeable things about this period is the contrasted attitude of the common people on the one hand, and of the influential classes on the other. It is the experience of Jesus Himself repeated in the experience of His cause. So long as the mass of plain country people in Galilee and Judæa were favourable to the Prophet of Nazareth, all the weapons of His enemies among the learned and official classes fell harmless. They feared to touch Him because of the people.[3] It was not till the passions of the mob were for a moment enlisted on the side of bigotry that His condemnation (resolved on long before) could at last be carried out.

---

[1] Acts iii. 11.   [2] Ibid. v. 12.

[3] See specially such passages as Matt. xxi. 45, 46, xxvi. 4, 5; Mark xi. 18, 32; Luke xiii. 17, xix. 47, 48, xx. 19, xxii. 2. Such passages are very strong. St. John rather represents the other side of the situation—the popular fear for the displeasure of the ruling party. See vii. 13, ix. 22, xi. 42. Yet the fourth Gospel also contains incidental confirmations of the popular enthusiasm for Jesus (*e. g.*, vii. 47–49, xi. 48, 55–57, xii. 11, &c.), which make it probable that the repeated failures of His enemies to arrest Him really arose from His being in such favour with the mob. Cf. John v. 16, vii. 30, 44, viii. 20, 59, x. 39, xi. 53–57.

So it fell out with the Church. The Sanhedrim had prohibited preaching in the name of the Crucified; yet so overwhelmingly was public feeling in Jerusalem against the Sanhedrim, that not only did the apostles every day defy that prohibition within earshot of the council chamber, but even when the authorities ventured to arrest them, it had to be done " without violence, for they feared the people lest they should have been stoned."

Various causes, no doubt, contributed to this popularity. There is a charm to the common mind in the audacity with which the apostles of any new creed must brave the resistance of established authorities; and the creed which was now proclaimed was one that always awoke an answer in Hebrew breasts, for it was the advent of the Messiah. Besides, the holy separation of the disciples, with their mutual charity and unearthly enthusiasm, probably told on the imagination of their countrymen. There can be no doubt, however, what the chief source of attraction was. It was the same as had for years been drawing multitudes about the feet of Jesus Himself—miracles of healing. The number of these miracles wrought by the apostles increased after the affair of Ananias, and St. Luke gives us a lively picture of the eagerness with which the citizens crowded for aid to these new wonder-workers, just as they had lately crowded to that greater Wonder-worker Whom they preached. For as, in the days of His flesh, men and women pressed on one another to touch Jesus, reaching eager fingers past their neighbours to clutch so much as His robe's fringe;[1] so now, when His apostles made their way on foot through the narrow streets of Jerusalem to and from the Temple, householders hasted to carry to the

[1] Compare Mark v. 27, vi. 56.

door the bedridden invalids of their homes, in the hope that, as he passed along the sunny street, Peter's tall form might at least cast its shadow across their open doorway; and if it fell for a moment on the wasted frame over which love had bent and watched and prayed in vain, their simple hearts leaped in them for joy. It may have been a silly superstitious faith, at which we who know so much can afford to smile; but I do not find that God mocks the hope of any simple soul that really trusts in Him, because its faith clings too foolishly to external aids. A little knowledge may puff us up to despise our ancestors who knew no better than to seek their Saviour through charms and relics, or to sneer at the contemporary devotion of untaught and mistaught Christians; but, thank God! He Who is the wisest is above despising any. This enthusiasm created by miracles extended beyond the city walls. It infected the villages which lay within easy access of the capital. It drew a concourse of sufferers from the country; and these all, as they returned cured to their rural homes, must have helped to spread far and near the better tidings which every day to all comers the apostles preached. In that first medical mission, as in every one which we plant to-day in order to utilise in the service of the gospel those unmiraculous "gifts of healing" which our Master has given to this generation, the thing which is of all things most touching to be noted is how sadly in earnest men are, and how painstaking, to have the ills of this brief and not too joyful life relieved; while, as to the true ill of an impenitent and unholy heart, which has not the love of God in it, they have no mind to try that rare remedy which the Son of God hath brought us in His holy gospel. Not that it was so with all. For the Jerusalem Church went on growing—grew faster than before: at that prosperous time when God had put a bit in the mouth of her enemies, even timid women found courage openly to join her communion.[1] Yet not all who laid their sick in Peter's way received Peter's Master; else would the populace not have turned by-and-by so suddenly upon Stephen, as they had before turned on Jesus, to clamour for his blood. Christianity counts it no conquest to draw a crowd, to win its *vivas*, to be sued for temporal blessings or praised for granting them. That only is true success which takes captive by the cross the hearts of men, and binds them for ever in unselfish loyalty to the kingdom of God.

To this friendly attitude of the common people there stood contrasted, exactly as during Jesus' ministry, the displeasure of the official and educated classes. Priests, rabbis, Sanhedrists, all who had been active in procuring the death of the Man Whom Peter affirmed to be alive, had now the strongest motive for shutting Peter's mouth. To be sure, those who were Pharisees had not that additional ground of quarrel which the Sadducees found in their denial of any possible resurrection. Somewhat later a number of the rank and file even of the priesthood went over to the new faith.[2] At this period, however, all the sacred and ruling orders appear to have been kept aloof from the Church by a public opinion of their own, so strong that no individual member of these orders had as yet the courage to oppose it. "Of the rest durst no man join himself to" the apostles.[3] Members of the priesthood and of the rabbinical

---

[1] See ver. 14.   [2] Acts vi. 7.
[3] Cf. ver. 13. Doubtful whether "the rest" refers to the general public, or to that section of it only which stood contrasted with "the people."

schools, who were also high in civil authority, must have watched with special uneasiness the progress of the Church. Not only was their official mandate set daily at defiance by the apostolic preachers, but every day, too, Jerusalem rang with words about the resurrection and the messiahship of Jesus, which were a direct accusation against those who had sentenced Him to an impostor's death. It is clear that for a while nothing held the magistrates back from fresh arrests except the apprehension of a popular rising. It is also clear that a point was sure to come, sooner or later, at which this fear of irritating the mob would be balanced by the rising displeasure with which the rulers heard themselves denounced as the murderers of God's Christ. Caution must some day yield to rage. Nay, there came to be a new danger even in delay. The very populace whom they had hounded on to cry out for Jesus' blood, might now be provoked, under the excitement of Peter's oratory, to turn and rend those who slew their Prophet. It would have availed little in such a case to remind the infuriated people that everything which had been done on that Friday had been done with their own loud acclamations of consent. Policy therefore concurred with irritation in impelling the rulers to strike. So a day came at length when the apostles—the whole of them apparently—were suddenly arrested and lodged in gaol. This arrest, like the former one,[1] was made at the instance of leading Sadducees, who supported that political party of which the high priest was the head. Like the former one, too, it took place late in the day, with a view to an early examination next morning. But when the Sanhedrim

[1] Acts iv. 3.

assembled for that purpose, and with it apparently some special convocation of other experienced and aged citizens,[1] it was discovered that the prisoners had been mysteriously set free. The design of this miraculous rescue is not at first sight apparent. That Jesus[2] sent a messenger from heaven to liberate His witnesses was certainly not due to any intention to extricate them out of a difficulty, for it did not postpone their trial even for a day. Its main purpose could only be to encourage their confidence in the gracious concern He felt for them, and in His power to protect them if He chose. It matters comparatively little through what straits or pain it pleases God to lead His saints for the high ends of His cause or for their own discipline; but it does matter a great deal that their hearts shall not fail or sink within them under pain and straits, that they lose their hold neither on the love nor on the power of God. So on the eve of a very trying day, their first day of actual physical suffering for Jesus' sake, the apostolic company was comforted by the words and emboldened by the temporary aid of an angel, even as Jesus Himself had been on the eve of His own great passion. At the same time I cannot help thinking that this strange rescue of prisoners was designed to carry its lesson also to the Sanhedrim. I recall that very strange incident at the arrest of our Lord in the garden, when, before the silent meek majesty of the Man, Who a few moments earlier had been prostrate in sorrow, the band of Temple police and Roman soldiery "went backward

---

[1] This seems the most probable sense to be given to the very unusual word γερουσία, in verse 21.

[2] That the divine messenger came from the Lord Jesus, is implied in the words ἄγγελος δὲ κυρίου.

and fell to the ground."[1] That was no vulgar attempt to escape from apprehension. Their victim waited till they recovered, and held out His wrists to be bound. Neither was it, obtrusively, a miracle; no prayer from His lips called angels out of heaven to beat His assailants back. It was a secret, silent hint only of a power above their own, into the origin of which no man cared too curiously to look. Very similar was the incident before us. That it was an angel who had opened the prison the Sanhedrim could not know unless they chose (and they did not choose) to inquire. Yet there was enough of wonder about the occurrence to suggest Whose hand had possibly undone the bolts. This, too, was no vulgar rescue; for the men stood quietly in the Temple to be recaptured. Miraculous aid was the first explanation which would occur to any Jew of that day, whose mind was habituated to miracle, and who knew that these men's Master had spent His ministry in doing miracles, and that they themselves were filling Jerusalem still with miracles done in their Master's name. It follows that, had the authorities even now been only tolerably open to spiritual warnings, this very midnight deliverance, wrought for His servants by the Man Whom they had slain, might have warned them back from the fresh persecution which they were already plotting against Jesus and His cause.

The defence offered by the apostles through Peter's lips is in substance the same as he had made at the former examination. There is the same assertion of a divine necessity laid on them to preach, which overrode the authority even of God's magistrates; the same bold

[1] John xviii. 6.

charge against the court of having compassed the Messiah's death; the same testimony to the fact of the resurrection; and the same preaching of the good news through the exalted Christ under cover of an apology for preaching. But an examination of the two speeches will show that, while covering the same ground, a quite different tone characterised this second one. It is less respectful and less elaborate. The question put this time by the court had been edged with personal fear and spite : " Ye intend to bring this Man's blood upon us ? " Caution, therefore, and courteous reserve, would plainly be thrown away on such judges. The strife has passed into a bitterer stage. Peter spoke, not with less dignity or skill, yet with a more unsheathed directness, such words as the Holy Ghost gave him to say.

The main historical interest of the scene, however, lies in the speech of Gamaliel. This remarkable man is the only member of the court who possesses importance in the contemporary history of his country. The son of one distinguished Hebrew doctor, and the grandson of a greater, Gamaliel has personal claims on our attention which outweigh those which are hereditary. In his own day he stood at the head of that most eminent school of rabbinical interpretation which his grandfather Hillel had founded. Posterity reckoned him as the first of seven doctors who were dignified by the title of " great."[1] As the mediæval scholastics were dignified with sobriquets by their admirers, so was he surnamed in the Hebrew schools " the Glory of the Law ; " and after Christ won from him his scholar Saul of Tarsus, he left no worthy successor in the rabbinical colleges. The speech by which

[1] Rabban or Rabboni = " Our Master," in the sense of excellence.

on this occasion he sought to moderate the blind fury of his colleagues is his only appearance in sacred history, and we shall fail to do him justice unless we consider how the question had now shaped itself. Previously, when Peter and John came up for examination on the cure of the cripple, the point to be determined had been a theological one. It was this: "Was the miracle due to divine or to demoniac power?" Had the senators decided that it was divine, they ought to have received the apostolic teaching; had they decided that it was demoniac, they ought to have put the apostles to death. But they decided nothing. They shirked their proper duty as guardians of the national religion, and contented themselves with an idle order, which was no better than a police regulation, that the apostles should not preach. Now, the charge on this second examination did not bring up the original question—the moot point about the miracles. It turned simply on disobedience to the prohibition of public teaching—a mere technical charge, affecting the authority of the court, but nowise touching the real merits of the case. It will be noticed, however, that at the moment when Gamaliel interposed his advice, the majority of the court were on the point of taking a step which would have thoroughly foreclosed the larger question. Stung by Peter's words into momentary forgetfulness of their own dignity, and of their position as a judicial body, they were consulting how to have the apostles put to death. Rage blinded them to the fact that they could have no pretext for putting the accused to death, unless they found them guilty of miracle-working through demoniac aid, whereas the apostles had not been arraigned on this capital charge, but merely on a charge of disobedience. It was of course open to Gamaliel to point out, if he chose, that his brethren were assuming a matter to be settled which was not even before the court; but what hope could he have of saving life by thus recalling them to the graver question? Nothing had been easier than to put the men once more on their trial then and there on the old issue— " By what power or by what name have ye done this?" and such a trial, in the heated temper of the assembly, could have no end save one. To recall his colleagues to this undecided point, by what spiritual help Peter wrought his wonders, might have given a colour of legality to the sentence of death, but would hardly have saved innocent life. Gamaliel therefore kept the matter away from the dangerous region of theology altogether, and argued it on the only ground on which it came technically before him, the ground of public policy. For his immediate purpose, his argument was extremely judicious. Had the old Rabbi been, what later Christian tradition called him, a secret ally of the apostles, he could not have pled their cause more skilfully. First he sent the prisoners from the chamber, because the sight of them was inflaming his passionate colleagues. Next he went calmly back upon historical examples, as if to gain time and let their excitement cool. He appeased them, too, by contemptuously likening these new popular leaders to certain political fanatics, whose brief career had come to a speedy and miserable end. It was only at the close of his speech that he found them sufficiently calm to be open to a superstitious fear lest they might after all be fighting against God. All this is very clever, and deserved to succeed. Still, there is no doubt that a blunder lay at the bottom of his reasoning. He took for granted that the divine or human origin of the new sect (for he says nothing of demons) could not be decided as yet; that no data were accessible by which the Sanhedrim could come to a judgment on this head; and that the source of the movement was to be tested only by one test of slow application—success or failure. If it broke down, as other risings under false Messiahs were ever and anon breaking down in that troubled and fanatical period, then it too would be proved to be a mere upheaval of popular discontent. If, which he seemed to think not unlikely, it succeeded in dislodging the Romans and establishing a messianic kingdom, then it would have established its claim by the best of evidence—by succeeding. Clearly this is the logic of a shrewd politician, not of a religious teacher. It might be quite right to turn for the instant the torrent of fanatical zeal in his heady colleagues by such cool and wary counsel as practical statesmen would comprehend; but it was quite wrong for Gamaliel, as a great Rabbi and chief guide of God's people, to judge the pretensions of the new gospel by no higher touchstone than the vulgar device of letting it alone. Nothing in the text shows how far he acted throughout on the principles of his speech. Only the fact that he lived to see his best scholar demonstrate the new faith, even by his own and the world's argument —success—and yet died in the faith of Judaism, dictating with failing lips a prayer against the Nazarene, suggests the apprehension that he grew narrower as he grew older, and never honestly did his duty by an impartial inquiry into the claims of Christianity. I question if many of us are entitled to fling a stone at the devout old Jew. Experience is always showing how hard it is for men who have grown grey in traditional ideas to welcome new light; and Gamaliel, the master, may well have lived and died in the faith of Moses, even though Saul, the scholar, became an apostle of the faith of Jesus.

Be this as it may, Gamaliel's speech saved the lives of the apostles from Sadducean violence. That their lives could be so easily saved, and that a leading Pharisee could be found to do it, shows how very little any one anticipated the fierce conflict which was so soon to be waged betwixt the Church and Pharisaism. It remains to be seen how, under the influence of a new leader, those elements of spiritual freedom and catholicity were developed, which as yet only slumbered in the bosom of the society represented by Peter; and how, so soon as they were developed, they called forth from the very school of Gamaliel a bitterness of hostility which nothing but blood could quench. As yet neither Stephen nor Saul had entered into history.

There was no inconsistency in scourging men whom it was resolved not to kill. Contumacious resistance to the authority of the court had laid the apostles open to a punishment which was commonly inflicted for minor offences. These nine and thirty stripes, however, mark a fresh point of departure in the history of Christianity. For the first time, pain and public penalties are borne, as Jesus foretold they should be, for Jesus' sake. The first martyrdom has not come yet, but the first persecution has, and the Church's baptism of blood begins. That the chiefs of the new faith—those divine witnesses who were divinely witnessed to by such glorious signs of favour from God—should be openly stripped and flogged by the common executioner, was a serious blow. Then appeared beneath the lash the novel strength of that power which had begun to work among men. Christianity has no monopoly of martyrs. Besides Judaism, the faiths of Mahommed and of Buddha have had their witnesses unto death. But to rejoice in suffering for one's faith, as in a crown of honour, was a new thing on the earth. Its explanation lay here, that these men bled not for an abstract truth, but for the love of a Man Whom they knew to be the very God in flesh. For the beloved Friend Who for them had been, a few weeks before, stripped and scourged before He died, showing how low the love of God could lead God to stoop for men—for His sake to give the back to the smiter and so be brought nearer in likeness to Himself, and offer Him back blood for blood and blow for blow, this was not only, as Horace sang of patriot deaths, " a sweet thing and a seemly "[1]—it was (as Peter wrote long after) a thing " thankworthy," a blessing for which Christian men might glorify God with great rejoicing.[2] To be borne up and inspired to meet shame and pain in such a spirit as this, was a more wonderful thing than to have one's prison bolts withdrawn by the hand of an angel. This spiritual glorying in tribulations, of which apostles set the example, has never died out of Christ's Church. An army of martyrs has gone to death since then, not only with the natural gallantry of brave men, but with the strange unearthly joy of one who goes to greet a heavenly spouse. If we would not be unworthy followers of those who carry palms in heaven, we must seek to be so possessed with the love of our most blessed

---

[1] " Dulce et decorum est pro patriâ mori."
[2] See 1 Pet. ii. 19-21, iii. 14-18, iv. 12-16.

God and Saviour, and with the spirit of His passion, that when shame comes on us for His sake, or loss, or evil names, we too shall rejoice that we are counted worthy to fill up that which remains of the sufferings of Christ for His body's sake.

XI.
Hellenist and Hebrew.

THESE JEWS ARE ALREADY GOTTEN INTO ALL THE CITIES, AND IT IS HARD TO FIND A PLACE IN THE HABITABLE EARTH THAT HATH NOT ADMITTED THIS TRIBE OF MEN AND IS NOT POSSESSED BY THEM.—*Strabo, quoted by Josephus.*

MOSES OF OLD TIME HATH IN EVERY CITY THEM THAT PREACH HIM, BEING READ IN THE SYNAGOGUES EVERY SABBATH-DAY.

Acts vi. 1-6

Revised Version.

But in those days, when the disciples became numerous, there arose a murmuring of the Hellenists against the Hebrews, because their widows were being overlooked in the daily ministration. So the Twelve, having summoned the multitude of the disciples, said:

"It does not please us that we should abandon the Word of God to minister at tables. Look out therefore, brethren, seven men of you, well spoken of, full of the Spirit and of wisdom, whom we shall appoint over this business. We on the other hand will apply ourselves constantly to prayer, and to the ministry of the Word."

And the word pleased the whole multitude, and they elected Stephen, a man full of faith and of the Holy Spirit, and Philip, and Prochoros, and Nicanor, and Timon, and Parmenas, and Nicolaos a proselyte of Antioch, whom they set before the apostles; and having prayed, they put on them their hands.

XI.

FROM the first the Church of Jerusalem had held within its bosom two opposed tendencies. So long as its numbers were not too large, and its original enthusiasm had not yet spent itself, this underlying division created no difficulty. A moment, however, was at length reached, fruitful in results for the after history of Christianity, when the jealousy of Hellenist and Hebrew began to give promise of that deep schism which was by-and-by to cause prolonged and anxious strife, and to end only through the withering up of one of the divisions of Christendom altogether. Here also that saying came true—"The elder shall serve the younger." Hebraic Christianity has long since disappeared; Hellenic Christianity has overshadowed the earth.

It is quite needful for the understanding, I do not say of this first incident only, but of the whole subsequent history, that we should pause at this point to ascertain what this distinction betwixt Hellenist and pure Hebrew meant, and how it came about. Its origin goes back to the time of the Captivity. Down till the day when Nebuchadnezzar's general burnt Jerusalem and swept off the flower of Judah into slavery, the Jews had dwelt as far as possible alone, a people of husbandmen, clinging every man to his ancestral plot of sacred soil, fearing and shunning Gentile contact. The Captivity changed all that. A small colony of Jews was deported into Egypt, a larger one to Babylonia: thence they spread through Persia, through Media, in fact, through all the huge empire, stretching from India to the Ægean, which owned the sceptre of Xerxes. The numbers who returned to the Holy Land under Zerubbabel, and again under Ezra, fell very far short of the total number then to be found scattered over the East; and although a connection as close as possible was kept up betwixt the Jews in Judæa and the Jews of the Dispersion,[1] yet it was impossible but that contact for centuries with pagan nations should greatly modify the old Hebrew customs and modes of thought. Especially was this the case after the conquests of Alexander the Great, and during the wars of his successors, when Palestine itself became a battle-field to the kings of the north and south,[2] of Syria and of Egypt. It was the settled policy of Alexander, as well as the natural effect of his rapid victories, to break down the barriers of race, and, by facilitating peaceful interchange between nations, and making the Greek tongue the universal medium of intercourse, to fuse East and West into one world. It resulted that the characteristic feature of several centuries before Christ was a general flux and confluence of peoples which before had been sternly kept asunder. No race of the East felt this outgoing, colonising movement, more than the Jews. Already their ancient tie to their own land had been seriously weakened. A new spirit of commercial and industrial enterprise now

[1] Or, of the *Diaspora*, by which accepted designation they are named in the inscription of St. Peter's first Epistle. See 1 Pet. i. 1: ἐκλεκτοῖς παρεπιδήμοις διασπορᾶς.

[2] So called in Daniel's prophecy, chap. xi.

awoke within them as a new world opened to their wandering feet. Large colonies of them settled not only in Alexandria itself, that typical city, which the great conqueror created to embody the new ideas which he had impressed upon history; but in Antioch, and all along the coasts of Asia Minor, in the Greek cities, in the Mediterranean Islands, and in North Africa. They went wherever openings for trade were to be found. The ancestral faculty for acquiring wealth which their Palestine life had crushed, developed itself. The restless activity proper to a homeless and landless nationality fitted them for a period when men were more cosmopolitan than they have ever been before or since.

Some of the effects of all this close and active intercourse with the great Græco-Gentile world upon a race so exclusive and peculiar as the Hebrew were very remarkable. Home Jews who continued to live in Palestine recoiled from defiling contact with foreigners, sharpened all the lines of national demarcation, grew prouder, bitterer, and more narrow, as well as more rigid, in their religion: hardened, in short, into Pharisaism by way of needful reaction, or under an instinct of self-preservation. Those Jews, on the contrary, who lived abroad, took on a strong tinge of Greek culture. Very early they abandoned the use of their Semitic mother tongue, and spoke Greek. The Alexandrian translation of the Old Testament became their Bible. They began to give their children Greek names. Many of them studied Greek literature. In Alexandria especially, a school arose which strove to bring their own sacred books into affinity with Greek speculation. Above all, the spirit of secular gain broke down among them that feeling of separatism, or, rather, that sense of divine consecration to a holier work than God had given to profane Gentiles, which had been the very kernel of ancient Judaism. So powerful were all these influences together that nothing save their deep religious antagonism to polytheistic idolatry, an antagonism now fairly burned into their nature by the long captivity and the Maccabæan wars, could have saved them from being submerged in the stream. That they held fast by. Strict monotheists in face of whole pantheons of gods, spiritual worshippers where all other worship was material, sensuous, and idolatrous, the dispersed Jews gained far more proselytes than they lost. It is very noticeable indeed how the exigencies of their dispersion, in so far as these modified their religion at all, modified it for the better. Cut off from the Temple ritual on Mount Zion, they carried with them neither priest nor sacrifice; they carried only the Septuagint and the synagogue. The local, temporary, external parts of Mosaism, its cumbrous dress of liturgy and washings and victims, had to be left behind. What they retained was just what was portable; and that which was most portable was that which was most spiritual. Wherever they went, they built them a synagogue. They met to pray, they read the law, they sang the psalms; and by this simple unsacerdotal worship they really were both prepared themselves and helped to prepare the Greek world for the preaching of a more spiritual faith.

When at last Christianity arose and ventured forth into heathendom, it found everywhere in the synagogues its first base of operations. We see it groping its earliest way through Asia Minor and Europe simply by laying hold on synagogue after synagogue. From the scanty records which remain, it is impossible for us fully to estimate how far Hellenised Judaism served to prepare susceptible minds even among the native Greeks to receive a faith still more spiritual than itself. But this much is certain, that it was among Hellenised Jews that Christianity found its first and its best missionaries to the Greek and Roman world. They formed the true link betwixt the ancient Hebrew cradle into which Christianity was born, and this western European world where its manhood was to grow to strength. Men who were Jews by birth, and Greek by training; thorough Hebrews in their monotheism and their hope of the Christ, but with less Hebrew bigotry or traditionalism than their Palestine countrymen; men who added to the intensity of religious fervour and moral gravity which the law had given them, a width of human sympathy due to intercourse with the Hellenic race: such men as Stephen was, and Paul ultimately became; men like Barnabas, Apollos, Timothy;— these were the men to whom we chiefly owe it, under God, that the Church of Jesus grew out of all risk of continuing a Judæan sect, and became the religion of civilised mankind.

From the very day of Pentecost, the Jerusalem congregation had embraced a number of these Hellenists or foreign-trained Jews,[1] though we have no means of knowing what proportion they bore to those born in Palestine, called by Luke "Hebrews." It is certain that their influence must have been out of proportion to their numbers. They were men of higher average intelligence and energy than the

[1] Cf. the list given in recording the gift of tongues, Acts ii. 9–11. "Hellenists" is rendered "Grecians" in vi. 1 (A. V.).

villagers of Judæa or the small traders of the capital, and were not likely to acquiesce silently in any neglect which, from being in a minority, they might suffer at the hands of the home-born. Whether they had just ground to complain that the poor widows belonging to their section of the Church received less than their share in the daily distribution of money and rations, or only fancied that they had, is of no moment. In either case, the complaint was a mere symptom on the surface of far deeper elements of incongruity and severance. There was always a tendency on the part of Palestine Jews to pride themselves on retaining the purest type of orthodoxy, and to suspect, as well as dislike, their countrymen who had taken on Gentile manners. On the other hand, it came very naturally to the foreign Jew to look down on stay-at-home and old-fashioned Hebrews as narrow or bigoted as well as ignorant. A grave danger threatened the young Church if her members imported into her communion such mutual jealousies as these; and that slight " murmuring " about the widows' rations meant nothing less. The apostles took alarm. So far as one can see, the murmurs of the Hellenists reflected on the apostles, and on no one else. As yet the society appears to have possessed no other officers. Christ's Church was not launched fully equipped, with all her machinery complete, as Moses, at God's bidding, launched the Hebrew polity. The Church is a body in spiritual communion with an invisible Head. It is that in the first instance, and, at first, it was no more than that. Just as contact with the world and the forces of secular society compelled it into more material relationships, did its wants grow more complex. It was called upon ere long to provide for the affairs of an external and visible corporation. But for each emergency as it arises it has it in its power to provide. Its Lord left no cut and dry system of officialism, of ceremonial, or of government. He did not profess to legislate beforehand for the details of a kingdom which was meant to be as wide as mankind and as enduring as history. For this the deepest reason is that He has not truly left His kingdom. He is still in it, at the head of it. He rules it at each new turn in its affairs through a Spirit of wisdom Whom He inspires into it. The shifting forms, therefore, of self-manifestation and self-rule, through which the Church passes in successive ages, are none of them meant to bind it for the future, or to lie on it with the weight of a tradition; but are good only so long as the need for them shall last. As often as new needs call for new arrangements to meet them, so often is Christ prepared to lead His servants into fresh ways of expressing the old gospel, or of living out His own undecaying life, or of accomplishing their unchanging task of saving men's souls. The Church Catholic is above her own traditions, since the Lord Jesus is not to be bound even by His own past. The Church has an inherent autonomy, a right and power of self-government, which nothing can take from her; no, not one generation even of her own members from the one which succeeds it. But when I say this, I do not mean the Church as divorced from her Head, but the Church as one with her Head: a Church over which the Head, Christ, retains His true, practical, and unhindered sway, by the gift of the Holy Ghost within the hearts of believers.

It may indeed be hard to hold fast such an ideal of Church life as this when one recalls the past course of ecclesiastical history, yet it seems to me to lie clearly in the sacred text. Hitherto the Twelve whom Jesus named His witnesses had been the only officers of the young society. They personally, or such substitutes as they employed, had hitherto served out the daily supplies which the charity of the rich provided abundantly for the poor. Now the work had grown beyond their power of personal supervision, and when one side of the Church grumbled that the distribution was unfair, some new arrangement was clearly called for. Even the apostles were no autocrats in Christ's house. They assumed no power to institute offices at their pleasure. If the Church was governed by an oligarchy of Twelve, it was an oligarchy which rested on a democratic basis. The "crowd of the disciples,"[1] or body of faithful men constituting the Church, is that in which supreme legislative power was felt to reside. What the apostles did was at first to suggest, initiating measures; and at last, to confirm appointments, consecrating officers. But the adoption of the measure, the establishment of the office, and the election of the office-bearers, were all the work of "the whole multitude." It pleased them to have deacons, and they chose seven, and they set them before the apostles for ordination. I do not for a moment suppose that, in creating a new office to meet a difficulty, the Church at Jerusalem thought it was acting out vital principles of Church polity, or setting an example which should be authoritative for all time. I do not suppose it thought about principles of polity at all. It simply obeyed the instinct of social Christian life. It followed what it felt, and truly felt, to be the Spirit of its Master; and in doing

---

[1] Τὸ πλῆθος τῶν μαθητῶν in ver. 2. Cf. 'ενώπιον παντὸς τοῦ πλήθους in ver. 5.

this it became an unconscious exponent of primitive Church principles. It showed, all the better that it did not mean to show anything, how unfettered the new kingdom of Christ is by external regulations, how full of self-regulating power, how unhierarchical, how free; how unlike great modern Church establishments; how like a large family of brothers administering their own affairs, by subdividing among themselves the work to be done. The mode in which this election of the seven was gone about did virtually embody, as essential to perfect Church life, such principles as these:—The right of the Church to transact under Christ its own business; the ministerial, not lordly character of even its highest offices; the subordination of all material interests to its spiritual work; and the ultimate seat of Church authority in the whole body of believers. In carrying out these principles, it is true, no Church can long retain arrangements so simple as those of the first Church. This very narrative tells how the first Church itself began to devise a more complex machinery. Still, any Church system whose arrangements flatly contravene these principles, must be held to have departed by so much from primitive order.

Another thing which the act of that day did, and was recognised even at the time as doing, was to begin the severance betwixt the spiritual and temporal work of the Church. It had become impossible any longer to combine the serving of tables with the ministry of the Word. That the work might be well done, a division of labour was called for, and the apostles could not hesitate which side of their double office they should abandon. To bear witness to the saving work of Jesus Christ is not a secondary or accidental function of the visible association we call the Church. It is its very end, its *raison d'être*, its one task, to which all else is a mere accessory. For that it exists, and to that all other things must minister, if they can; or, if they cannot minister, they must be sacrificed to it. While the supreme dignity and weightiness of its spiritual functions were thus fully recognised, the early Church declined, on the other hand, to treat even its secular work as wholly unspiritual. It deserves to be remarked how carefully the new office and its duties were lifted up out of the atmosphere of mere business into that of worship. The particular duty in question is the least secular of all secular transactions— the disbursement of alms in the name of Jesus. The men eligible to office are to be full of the Holy Ghost as well as of wisdom. They are set apart to their work with equally solemn religious services and symbolical acts of consecration as if their work had nothing to do with serving tables. The only two among the seven of whom we know anything are known for the zeal, success, and saintly enthusiasm with which they preached Christ, added to His Church, refuted gainsayers, and witnessed unto death. Stephen and Philip were each of them a good deal more than a treasurer or an almoner. I think it probable, indeed, that so long as this office stood alone, it sustained a more evangelistic and pastoral character than afterwards came to belong to the order of Deacons[1] which grew out of it. We do not know when or on what occasion the more spiritual order of presbyter - bishop arose, which we find existing from the eleventh chapter of

---

[1] The word διάκονος is not used in Acts as an official name. It only occurs in Phil. and 1 Tim. (and of Phoebe in Rom. xvi. 1).

St. Luke's history onwards,[1] and which takes precedence of the diaconate in St. Paul's first letter to Timothy. It is at least possible that the institution of such a purely spiritual class restricted somewhat and defined the functions of the diaconate. Yet the earliest instinct of the Church was a perfectly just one, that no office in the kingdom of God can be discharged as it ought to be, no matter how exclusively external or secular it may appear, unless it be discharged by a spiritual man and in a spiritual way. All the servants of the Church must be first servants of her Master, "men of honest report, full of the Holy Ghost."

With the ordination of these seven men a new page of early Church history opened. It marked a stage in the Church's progress towards separate existence. This is clearly no mere fresh sect of Hebrews which the apostles are founding, since it rounds itself off as a self-governed body, and begins to swing clear of both Temple and Synagogue. It was also the first step towards permanence. The apostles cannot live for ever; but if the new society has the power, under Christ, of founding new orders of office-bearers fit to share in the ordinary labours of the apostolate, then it carries within itself the conditions of self-preservation, self-adaptation to changed times, and perpetual progress. More important than all, this election brought a new element to the front. Every one of the seven bears a Greek name; and though this is not a conclusive proof that they were all Hellenised or foreign Jews, since even within Palestine it had become an affectation with some to adopt Greek alternative names, yet the presumption is that most of them belonged to that

[1] It is first named in Acts xi. 30.

section of the Church whose complaints had led to the election. At all events, one of them was not even a Jew by birth at all, but a Gentile who had adopted the Hebrew faith; while the man whose name stands first, and whose martyrdom was to crown the young diaconate with its earliest honours, appears, from his connection with synagogues of Hellenists, to have been certainly a Hellenist. The result, therefore, was this, that through the murmurs of a few widow women, those members of the Jerusalem Church were lifted into office who represented its most free, most spiritual, most un-Hebrew and catholic elements. One man especially was, by this incident, thrust forward into public life who was destined to rouse the narrow and ultra-national party of the Pharisees to persecution, as Peter had already roused the Sadducees, and whose death was to be a signal for the scattering of the whole Church over Syria. It was even to lead more remotely to the conversion of another man who should one day fetch into the apostolic college itself and vindicate as an inheritance for Christendom that larger and more spiritual view of Christianity of which Stephen was the first exponent.

The ministry and trial of Stephen will presently unfold more fully this change in the state of the Church — a change which nearly amounted to a revolution. Already, however, we can see how it was through the natural development of events, under Christ's providence, that all this was brought about. The Lord, Who, from His seat of oversight in heaven charges Himself with the conduct of His cause on earth, saw that the Jerusalem Church was ripe for change. It had been shielded from violence till it was now strong enough to bear it. Represented as it was by native-born men like Peter, strongly attached to the Temple and the Law, nothing had yet been done to alienate from it Pharisees like Gamaliel, or to offend popular prejudice; while any irresolute blows which the sceptical Sadducees dared aim at the new sect only increased its popularity. So long as the Church wanted shelter and time for quiet growth, these were the best conditions for it. Now, however, it had grown large and vigorous. Increase of numbers even threatened its purity. Subtle elements of discontent and worldliness were creeping in. A little more favour with the mob might corrupt it. A little closer approximation to the narrower side of Hebrew orthodoxy might shrivel it up into a local and national sect. The time had therefore come for it to enter on a new career, to understand itself better, to develop its essential antagonism to ultra-Judaism, to make proof unto blood of its own spiritual force, to be scattered as a bearer of the free gospel of divine grace to Samaria, to Cæsarea, to Damascus, to Antioch. No miracle from heaven accomplished this needful change in the Church's attitude and destiny. No supernatural revelation alone led the apostles into the new path. In the spiritual kingdom, events are determined in accordance with natural law, and men are led mainly by the thread of circumstance.[1] The voices of poor women comparing their own dole with that of their neighbours is the first link in a chain of events of which one later link is the martyrdom of Stephen, another the call of Saul, and a third the conversion of the Gentiles. St. Peter and his

---

[1] Later it needed both circumstance and supernatural visions to persuade St. Peter to accept frankly the new catholic basis of the kingdom. See the history of Cornelius.

fellows saw a very little way ahead when they advised the appointment of official almoners, but One above St. Peter saw a long way indeed. From this collision of Hellenist with Hebrew He meant to strike a spark which should set the civilised world on fire.

The story, surely, speaks a rebuke to our shortsighted alarms, to whom the small dissensions and apparent disasters of the hour appear so serious. We see the divided congregation; we hear its murmuring voices; we try our little remedy, not knowing if Stephen and his fellows will allay the mischief; we even bury our martyrs with tears of despair, and lose all heart when the Church is rent and blown to the winds. One thing we forget to see: even Him Who sits now above the clouds which darken men's horizon, searches the far future with a serene eye which sees the end, and lays His mighty hand on human hearts, and secular powers, and spiritual helps, on politics, and science, and speculation, and all the complex factors of history, that He may bend the fortunes of His Church towards some "far-off divine event." Shut up within our little world, creatures of our own age, to us affairs look like confusion. They are tangled fragments of thread in a web God is weaving. Let us have faith and be quiet. Let us trust Him and be hopeful. Let us do, by His help, our little part, seeking to put straight whatever crooked thing lies before our face, not too timid to trust the Spirit of wisdom Whom Christ gives us. We, too, are Christ's members. We, too, touch our Head at first hand. The long centuries which lie between us and Stephen do not lie between us and Jesus. If we lack wisdom, let us ask; and whatever He puts into our heart and head to do for the better ruling of

His house or the greater honour of His gospel, that let us do with a frank courage which looks to spiritual results and is not shackled by the past. Above all, let us beware of dreaming that we and our age are the Church of Christ. The Church has a long life. The generations are its years. It is no hot-bed plant; but has to take many a buffet from the winds of heaven, to outlive scorching summers, to bear fruit for far-severed centuries. Its roots go deeper than we fancy. Its boughs shall yet spread wider than we know. Only let us, who are as tiniest twigs on its latest outshoot, and know next to nothing of the mighty tree we hang on, make sure that we are livingly attached to Him Who is our stem and root. By leaf, or flower, or fruit, each of us may display a little of His sacred beauty, and help to make this world a trifle pleasanter or wholesomer to the few who know us.

XII.
The Proto-Martyr.

NOMEN HABES CORONATI;
TE TORMENTA DECET PATI
PRO CORONA GLORIÆ.

Acts vi. 7–viii. 1.

Revised Version.

And the word of God increased; and the number of the disciples in Jerusalem went on multiplying greatly, and a great crowd of the priests became obedient to the faith. Stephen, too, full of grace and power, was doing great wonders and signs among the people. But there stood up some of those of the synagogue called that of Freedmen, and of Cyrenians, and of Alexandrians, and of those from Cilicia and Asia, disputing with Stephen, and were not able to withstand the wisdom and the Spirit with which he spoke. Then they suborned men to say: "We have heard him speaking blasphemous matters against Moses and God," and stirred up the people, and the elders, and the scribes, and having come upon him, seized him, and led [him] to the Sanhedrim, and set up false witnesses to say:

"This man does not cease speaking matters against the holy place and the law. For we have heard him say: 'This Jesus the Nazarene will destroy this place and will change the customs which Moses delivered to us.'"

And, gazing upon him, all who were sitting in the Sanhedrim saw his face as the face of an angel. But the high priest said: "Are [then] these things so?" And he said:

"Men, brethren, and fathers, hearken. The God of the Glory appeared to our father Abraham when he was in Mesopotamia, before he dwelt in Haran, and said to him: 'Go out from thy land and [from] thy kindred, and come to the land which I will show thee!' Then, going out from the land of the Chaldeans, he dwelt in Haran; and thence after the death of his father He removed him to this land in which you now dwell, and did not give him an inheritance in it, not a foot's breadth, and promised to give it to him for a possession, and to his seed with him, when he had no child. But God spake thus: That his seed should be a stranger in a foreign land, and they should enslave it and ill-treat it four hundred years. 'And the nation to which they shall be enslaved will I judge,' said God, 'and after that they shall come out and serve Me in this place.' And He gave him a covenant of circumcision; and thus he begat Isaac, and circumcised him on the eighth day, and Isaac Jacob, and Jacob the twelve patriarchs. And the patriarchs, envious at Joseph, sold him into Egypt; and God was with him and delivered him out of all his troubles, and gave him grace and wisdom before Pharaoh, king of Egypt, and he appointed him governor over Egypt and his whole house. But there came a dearth upon the whole of Egypt and Canaan, and a great trouble, and our fathers were not finding fodder. But Jacob, having heard there was grain in Egypt, sent out our fathers first; and at the second time Joseph was made [again] known to his brothers, and Joseph's race became manifest to Pharaoh. But Joseph sent and called for his father Jacob and the whole kindred, in all seventy-five souls. And Jacob went down [to Egypt] and died, he and our fathers, and were carried over to Sychem, and laid in the sepulchre which Abraham bought for a sum of money from the sons of Hamor of Sychem.

"But as the time of the promise which God swore to Abraham drew near, the people increased and was multiplied in Egypt, until there arose a different king who did not know Joseph. The same being crafty against our race, ill-treated the fathers, so that they exposed their infants that they might not be preserved alive. In which time was born Moses, and was fair to God, who was nourished up three months in the house of his father. But when he was exposed, Pharaoh's daughter took him up and nourished him up as a son for *herself. And Moses was educated in every branch of wisdom of the Egyptians, and was powerful in his words and deeds. But when he had completed a period of forty years, it arose in his heart to inspect his brethren the children of Israel. And seeing a certain one wronged, he defended and took vengeance for him who was being oppressed, smiting the Egyptian. But he supposed his brethren to understand that God by his hand would give them salvation; but they did not understand. The following day also he appeared to them as they fought, and was reconciling them to peace, saying: 'Men, ye are brethren; why is it that ye wrong one another?' But he who wronged his neighbour thrust him away, saying: 'Who set thee up a ruler and judge over us? Dost thou wish to kill me in the way thou didst kill the Egyptian yesterday?' But Moses fled at this word, and became a stranger in the land of Midian, where he begat two sons.*

"And when forty years were completed there appeared to him, in the wilderness of the Mount Sinai, an angel in the fiery flame of a bush; and Moses, when he saw, wondered at the sight. But, on his drawing near to examine, came the Lord's voice: 'I am the God of thy fathers, the God of Abraham, and Isaac, and Jacob.' But Moses, beginning to tremble, durst not examine. And the Lord said to him: 'Loose the sandal from thy feet, for the place on which thou standest is holy ground. I have surely seen the ill-treatment of My people which is in Egypt, and their groaning I heard, and am come down to deliver them. And now, come, let Me send thee to Egypt.' This Moses whom they refused, saying: 'Who set thee up a ruler and judge?' the same has God sent [to be] both ruler and redeemer, with the hand of the angel who appeared to him in the bush. This man led them out, doing wonders and signs in the land of Egypt, and in the Red Sea, and in the wilderness forty years. This is the Moses who said to the children of Israel: 'A prophet will God raise up to you of your brethren, like me.' This is he who was in the church in the wilderness, with the angel who spoke to him in the Mount Sinai, and [with] our fathers, who received living sayings to give to us, to whom our fathers were not willing to become obedient, but thrust [him] away and returned in their hearts to Egypt, saying to Aaron: 'Make for us gods who shall march before us; for this Moses who led us out

from the land of Egypt, we do not know what is become of him.' And they made a steer in those days, and brought a sacrifice to the idol, and delighted themselves in the works of their hands. But God turned and gave them up to serve the host of heaven, as it is written in the Book of the Prophets: 'Did ye offer to Me victims and sacrifices forty years in the wilderness, O house of Israel? Yea, ye carried about the tabernacle of Moloch, and the star of your god Rephan, the figures which ye made to worship them; and I will carry you off beyond Babylon.' Our fathers had the Tabernacle of the Testimony in the wilderness, according as He Who spoke to Moses directed to make it after the figure which he had seen; which also our fathers, having taken it over, carried in with Joshua in their possession of the nations whom God drove out from the face of our fathers, until the days of David, who found grace before God, and requested to find a tent for the God of Jacob. But Solomon built for Him an house. Only not in what is made with hands does the Highest dwell, as the prophet says: 'The heaven is a throne for Me, and the earth a footstool for My feet. What sort of house will ye build for Me, saith the Lord, or what is the place of My rest? Did not My hand make all these?'

"O stiff-necked and uncircumcised in the heart and the ears, ye do continually rush against the Holy Spirit: as your fathers, so you! Which of the prophets did your fathers not persecute? And they slew those who announced beforehand the coming of the Righteous One, of Whom now you are become betrayers and murderers; you who received the Law at [the] arrangements of angels, and did not keep it."

But when they heard these things, they were cut through in their hearts, and gnashed their teeth at him. But, being full of the Holy Ghost, he gazed into heaven, and saw God's glory and Jesus standing on the right hand of God, and said: "Lo, I behold the heavens opened, and the Son of Man standing on the right hand of God." But they, crying with a loud voice, stopped their ears and rushed with one accord upon him, and having cast him out of the city, proceeded to stone him. And the witnesses laid down their robes at the feet of a young man called Saul. And they were stoning Stephen, invoking and saying: "Lord Jesus, receive my spirit." Then falling on his knees, he cried with a loud voice: "Lord, lay not this sin upon them;" and saying this he fell asleep.

But Saul was a consenting party to his execution.

XII.

AMONG the four hundred and eighty synagogues which, according to the Rabbis, existed in Jerusalem before its fall, there were some frequented exclusively by foreign Jews of the Dispersion. Families which had removed from the same distant region of heathendom, to settle for purposes of devotion in the holy city, clustered together for daily prayer in the same congregation; exactly as, to this day in Jerusalem, Polish and German Jews only are found in some synagogues, Jews of Spanish origin in others.[1] The language of St. Luke leaves it doubtful whether all the Hellenistic settlers named by him belonged to one synagogue or to several. They fall naturally, however, into three divisions. First, the Libertines (*Libertini*) or Freed-men from Rome. Some ninety years had now passed since the Syrian campaigns of Pompey carried off a multitude of Jewish captives to Rome;[2] and their descendants, most of them manumitted by their masters, had either settled in the Trastevere [3] or been banished from Italy.

[1] Spanish Jews (called Sephardim) have dwelt in Jerusalem since 1497, and have now four synagogues. German and Polish Jews are called Askenazim. See Porter, *Handbook*, i. 83.

[2] Jerusalem was taken by Pompey, B.C. 63. Cf. Prideaux, *Connection*, vol. iv. p. 514 (ed. 1807).

[3] The southern portion of that part of Rome which lies on the right bank of the Tiber is so called, and was a poor and populous suburb in the days of the early Empire. It is still inhabited chiefly by the working classes.

It is possible that many of the four thousand whom Tiberius is known to have deported to Sardinia in the year A.D. 19,[1] had by this time found their way back to their own land. Next come Jews from the north of Africa, from Alexandria, that is, and from the city Cyrene, which stood where Tripoli now stands. Cyrene was then the capital of a province (Libya) which had under one of the Ptolemies been added to Egypt, and since then had swarmed with Jewish immigrants. Lastly, Asiatic Jews are mentioned; two provinces of Asia Minor being named, the one known in Roman official language as "Asia," and always so called in the New Testament; the other Cilicia, from whose capital came the young Pharisee whose name was Saul.

With these various representatives of Hellenised Judaism, the Church now came for the first time into conflict. The elevation of Stephen, along with others, to official rank, had this for one of its results, that the spiritual and intellectual gifts with which God had gifted this man found at once a wider and more public sphere. His duties as almoner brought him into daily contact with poor believers of his own section of the Church, and through them with their neighbours who did not believe. These opportunities he used for the preaching of the gospel. Stephen was a great deal more than an almoner. He was a deep student of the Old Testament, a theologian of unusual insight, a powerful reasoner, and an advanced Christian. In him first we find those gifts of healing, which Jesus had given to the apostles,[2] exercised by a man who was no apostle. In him, too, we find that

[1] See Tacitus, *Ann.* ii. 85, and Josephus, *Antiq.* xviii. 3. 5.

[2] And to the Seventy, Luke x. 9, 17. See, in this connection, Matt. x. 1, 8; Mark iii. 15, vi. 7; Luke ix. 1.

promise fulfilled which had hitherto been fulfilled to Peter,[1] the promise of such wisdom in speech as no adversary could gainsay. His manner of speech, however, was unlike that of Peter. Peter was a witness, and preached by witness-bearing. Stephen was a student, and preached by exposition and controversy. These synagogues of foreign Jews, to which no doubt he himself belonged, were homes of learning and of bigotry. In them men of keen wits, sharpened by Greek culture, applied the methods of traditional interpretation to the sacred books. Pedantic as much of that Hebrew scholasticism was, and given up already to allegorical conceits or ingenious trifling, it bred fiery passions. Schools in which youths like Saul were "profiting in the Jews' religion," being "exceedingly jealous of the traditions of their fathers,"[2] could scarcely fail to become nurseries of a passionate fanaticism. Intense enough, and terribly sincere, were the disputants whom Stephen thus encountered, but proud, narrow, self-righteous, and bitter; just the men to argue themselves into bad temper, and, when beaten in logic, to fall to abuse.

One is ready to wish that we knew more of these controversies in the Hellenistic synagogues. We are left to gather their subject from their result. From the angry charge brought against Stephen, from the evidence of the suborned witnesses, and from his own defence, we must infer as best we can the character of his doctrine. The great question under discussion was plainly this—What is the bearing of the new faith of Jesus on the old system of Moses? In his very earliest sermons, Peter had hinted that the advent of Jesus, His passion,

---

[1] Cf. Luke xxi. 15; c. Acts iv. 14.   [2] Gal. i. 14.

and His resurrection, formed the consummation towards which Mosaism had from the beginning pointed—were, in fact, the accomplishment of that great hope which all the prophets had foretold, and for which Israel waited. The whole of the apostolic preaching up to this time had gained a favourable hearing, just because the new faith did not profess to be more or less than the completion of the old. It came, in its Founder's words, "not to destroy, but to fulfil." Orthodox Jewish citizens did not cease to be either Jews or orthodox when they received baptism into the name of Jesus Christ. Up to this time the question seems never to have been raised—What if the Jewish hierarchy and commonwealth reject God's new revelation through His Son the Christ? Is then the new faith so tied to the old framework of holy places and holy rites that it cannot live without them? By this time, however, it was getting to be not at all unlikely that the Sanhedrim might excommunicate the Church, might banish it as a heresy from its quarters within the temple courts, and forbid its presence at the sacrifices. Suppose it did, was that to be conclusive against the Church? Must that be of necessity a false revelation which the majority of the Jewish people called false? Was Mosaism to last for ever? Was no glory of the divine Presence possible, nor any worship acceptable, save within the temple and before the altar? Must every new economy of grace be fettered by the limitations of the old? Or was God perchance leading His people towards a wider and more spiritual dispensation? Nay, did not the very coming of Him to Whom the whole symbolic ritual pointed, require the abolition of symbolic ritual, and initiate of necessity a new worship?

How far Stephen went in this direction, what questions in this line his polemic led him to put, or what to answer, it is impossible now to tell. But it is clear that it was in this direction his face was set. He was the first man who dared to think that the gospel of Jesus was a divine step forward, a new economy of God, which the existing Hebraic institutions might indeed refuse to accept, but which in that case would not only dispense with, but in the end overturn, the Hebraic institutions. In the hot discussions which in those days went on within the Hellenistic synagogues, he probably went a good way in apparent depreciation of the Mosaic system. He certainly appears to have regarded it as a system which, if not yet superseded, was at least liable to change. To be sure, those were "false witnesses" who represented him as blaspheming Moses and the law; and his words which they professed to report, about Jesus destroying the temple and altering the ritual, were probably twisted to a sense quite as inaccurate as the similar words quoted against Jesus Himself when He was on His trial.[1] Still, something like this Stephen must have said, nor is it hard to guess in what sense he said it. The whole of Mosaic worship on its external national side was anchored to that sacred rock on which the temple stood. There was nowhere else any altar, any priesthood, any expiation, any shrine, any holy of holies, any symbolic ritual. Moreover, the current faith of the people, which found in Pharisaic rabbinism its scientific form, believed in all this external system of temple worship, and believed in little else. That was its palladium, its idol. So long as that stood, God was propitious and Israel blest; no matter how full the temple

[1] Cf. Matt. xxvi. 61; c. John ii. 19.

might be of cheating, or Jerusalem of uncleanness. To the painful observance of ritual, the average Jew ascribed a magical virtue which made righteousness or the fear of God practically superfluous. When told to "amend their ways," they still, as in Jeremiah's time, trusted in lying words, saying, with idle insistency, "The temple of Jehovah, the temple of Jehovah, the temple of Jehovah are these."[1] This was the system which threatened to reject the gospel of the Son of God. As it had already slain Christ, it seemed about to cut off from its fellowship Christ's Church. Its hierarchical council of rulers, its sacerdotal order, its colleges of learned men, its red-hot zealots, its popular masses; all seemed, so far as Stephen could read the indications, to be fast making up their mind against the new Saviour Whom God had in these last days sent to His chosen people. What did that prognosticate? The downfall of Christ's cause, or the downfall of the temple system? Stephen had read the history of his nation with other eyes than those of the rabbis. Underneath all the changes of Hebrew story, he had learned to trace a divine progress, a slow but blessed unfolding of the gracious thoughts of God towards some still unaccomplished spiritual end. He had not found in this latest phase of national religious life, that of the temple and its services, such a finality as his countrymen dreamed of. The most material, local, symbolical, and unspiritual of all forms which Hebrew worship had ever worn, did not seem to him the form most likely to be everlasting. But one thing he had found to mark the whole of his long ancestral history. As often as it had

---

[1] See Isa. vii. 2-15, and cf. the charge against him in xxvi. 11, 12, referred to by Baumgarten, *in loc.*

pleased God, through chosen messengers of His will, to lead Israel forward through a new moment of change into a fresh spiritual epoch of blessing, so often had God's thoughts been misunderstood, His purpose hindered, and His messenger rejected, by the bulk of Israel. This had been their national failing—to cling to the present and the material, whenever God was calling them to higher spiritual good. This they had done so often, that their doing it now, by rejecting a spiritual Christ and idolising a material temple, was only of a piece with their entire history.

Here, then, we seem to have the key to Stephen's long speech in self-defence before the council. Arraigned at last on a charge of blasphemy by the discomfited controversialists, and set before hostile judges in presence of a crowd of foes, Stephen discovered his profound insight into Scripture, and the rare adroitness of his intellect, by constructing an "apology" under the veil of an historical *resumé*. Not till he had patiently traversed the whole period from Abraham to Solomon, selecting such facts as made for his own case and setting them in skilful array, did he suffer one word to escape him at which even his most adverse hearer could take open exception. Then, when he had insinuated out of their own boasted annals the true answer to all their charges against himself, then only did he permit himself to draw from the same story a scathing invective against them, and used the last moment allowed for speech in charging home upon their consciences their own guilt.

Into a detailed exposition of this very remarkable oration, it does not belong to our present plan to enter. It is notable for the freedom with which the facts and words of the Old Testament are handled;[1] for its coincidence with contemporary Jewish literature on points where Holy Writ fails us;[2] for its parallels in thought and expression to the writings of St. Paul, and especially, or still more, to the Epistle to the Hebrews;[3] but most notable of all, as the first attempt in the New Testament to read the outstanding lessons of the Old. I pass over the many minute and casual touches by which the speaker made it obvious that he was no blasphemer, but a venerator of the fathers of his nation, of the law of Moses, and of the temple of God.[4] These will suggest themselves on a careful perusal. I can only indicate the main ideas which seem to be kept in view all along, and by which his treatment of the Old Testament narrative appears to be determined. These are two.

First, that a mode of worship limited to a single spot and fixed ritual was by no means essential to God's service, but had been late in its origin and temporary in its purpose—being only one most recent stage in a very long and gradual process of divine manifestation; second, that at every critical turning time in Israel's history, Israel had mistaken the leadings of God, and resisted those whom He sent to save it.

---

[1] See Dean Stanley's art. "Stephen" in Smith's *Dictionary*, for twelve deviations in speech from the Old Testament. In at least three instances the facts themselves cannot, with fairness, be squared with the scriptural statements. I cannot see, however, how the inspiration of the canonical books is at all implicated in the question whether or not Stephen erred in details through ignorance or inadvertence. [2] *E.g.*, cf. v. 22 with Josephus and Philo.

[3] For these parallels, cf. Wordsworth *in loc.*, and Conybeare and Howson, i. p. 87.

[4] Cf. especially, verses 2, 17, 38, 44, 46, &c., and his frequent use of the expression, "our fathers."

In the historical development of these ideas, Stephen fastens on three chief epochs, which he connects with the names of Abraham, Joseph, and Moses. Under the first he is able to conciliate the nation's pride in its Abrahamic origin, by noting the call, the promise, and the covenant by which "the God of glory" so signally distinguished His Mesopotamian "friend," and elected him to be the father of all believers. At the same time, Stephen quietly hints how far Abraham's privileges were from being tied to any spot of sacred soil. His call found him first in Mesopotamia. Again it found him in Haran. He got no inheritance in the Land of Promise. Nay, his seed were to be slaves to the foreigner for four centuries before they could set up so much as an altar on holy ground. This leads on to the life of Joseph, who, though chosen by God to be the saviour both of his own people and of a foreign land, was despised, refused, and sold into bondage by his very brethren. Joseph is Stephen's first instance of Israelitish misconception of God's meaning, and rejection of God's chosen one. His next is Moses. But as the name of that great legislator was associated with the law of ceremony and ritual which Stephen was charged with blaspheming, it was worth while to handle his history more in detail. Here, therefore, lay the main weight of his defence. Some five and twenty verses are devoted to showing how the Israel of Moses' own day misunderstood and refused him, first as champion, then as liberator, and finally as prophet; just as their posterity were now refusing and misreading that One, like unto, but greater than, Moses, Whom he foretold.

From the outset, God designed Moses to avenge, deliver,

and judge His people. Yet when he first stood forth as their protector, in virtue of his position in the royal house of Egypt, "they understood not" that "God by his hand would deliver them," but "thrust him away." Forty years after, indeed, he returned to them with a message from God, and succeeded in setting them free. Then, however, God meant him to be something more than a deliverer. He was God's prophet. To him God gave "lively oracles" for the people. He was in "the church in the wilderness with the Angel" Whose presence made the desert bush and the mount Sinai "holy ground." Yet even then the people once more thrust him away, refused his law, and went back in their hearts to the idolatries of Egypt. So rebellious were they to this boasted law, on its first promulgation, that God, in anger, gave them up to a continual series of apostacies, which were only avenged at last by the crowning disaster of their captivity in Babylon.

Here he might have ended; but the second item in the charge against him [1] leads Stephen to add a sentence on the exaggerated value which his opponents set on the local seat of worship. Was it blasphemy to speak of divine service anywhere but in the temple? There was no temple in Moses' day, only a movable tent of witness. There was none in David's day, much as he desired it. When Solomon, at last, did build a temple, it was only as an "house" to harbour the ancient ark, and in the very moment of its consecration the spirituality of its great Indweller and of His worship were solemnly re-

---

[1] He had spoken "blasphemous words against Moses . . . and the law." He "ceased not to speak" also "against this Holy Place" (chap. vi. 11, 13).

affirmed. For Solomon himself, like later prophets after him, exclaimed, "The heaven of heavens cannot contain Thee! How much less this house which I have built."[1]

Thus, by a very skilful use of facts selected out of the national history, this man, on whom rested so much of that Unction Which teacheth all things, this early "wrestler" for a spiritual gospel, as Adam de S. Victor calls him,[2] replied, without seeming to reply, to the charges of his enemies. He evinced true reverence for Moses' law, by acknowledging its divine origin and binding force. He paid honour to Solomon's temple-house, without treating it with such superstitious worship as idolatrous Israel paid to "the tabernacle of Moloch, or the star of their god Rephan." He vindicated the free spiritual elements which had always existed in Hebrew religion against the hard and dry Pharisaism which boasted in the law, but did not keep it, and trusted in the stones of the temple more than in the Most High Whose hand made heaven and earth. He set forth the progressive and gradual character of divine revelation, and made it fully probable that, as the outward framework of Judaism had been slowly built up to serve special ends, so, on the advent of a nobler and wider faith, of a Prophet greater than Moses, it might be taken down again.

But Stephen did far more than stand on the defensive. His speech is a polemic quite as much as an apology. More than either, it is an indictment. Not he is the blasphemer of God's revelation, or of God's messengers,

[1] 2 Chron. vi. 18.
[2] "Agonista, nulli cede,
Certa certus de mercede
Persevera, Stephane." (See Bäszler, p. 220.)

but they are. He charges it on his nation that, from the first, they have been blind to God's signs and deaf to His words; that each step in spiritual progress has been taken in spite of them; that as the patriarchs treated Joseph, and the Hebrews treated Moses, so it was their way to refuse fresh light and kill new prophets. As he develops this accusation in the later history of Moses in particular, his words grow keener and take a sharper edge, and his allusion to the recent fate of Jesus of Nazareth shines clearly through the veil of narrative. After he has closed his historical sketch, or been interrupted in it,[1] he abruptly breaks out upon his unwilling audience with some home-thrusting words, which stick like arrows and scorch like flame. The prisoner, who began in self-defence, ends by hurling at his judges the most audacious charges. They were stiff of neck. They were uncircumcised heathens at heart. They resisted God's Holy Spirit, like their fathers. They had betrayed God's Righteous One; they had murdered Him. They possessed the law, but this was how they had kept it. So far they heard. At this point a howl of execration from mouths which clashed with rage drowned the voice of the accuser. Stephen paused; his face changed again; the tumult died. Men recalled the look which he had worn before his speech began. When they first set him in presence of the council, they gazed upon a face so radiant with spiritual confidence, courage, and gladness, that, like the face of Moses of old, it seemed to shine with an unworldly light. Very unlike such angelic serenity and sweetness are these words which have just been flying like shafts of fire from his impetuous

---

[1] It may be either, but I rather incline to think he has finished all that he designed to say on the history of his people.

tongue.[1] Only when the heat of passionate indignation and the severity of deserved rebuke are the heat and severity of a noble unselfish soul kindled with zeal for God, or inflamed beyond itself through the breath of the Holy Ghost, are they like that wrathful fiery face which looked out from the midnight cloud to throw Pharaoh's host into confusion, but left the sweet light of heaven shining from within the cloud upon the trustful eyes of Israel. Stephen's heart abode still in the light of God. From the instant he heard that cry which told him the end was come, he ceased from rebukes which wrought no penitence, but only rage. He fell back from men whom he could not save upon the Master for Whom he still could speak. He raised his eyes from those bitter faces pressed back upon stiff necks, and shooting anger through their eyes; he raised them to the invisible, which opened itself to his soul's sight. To the strong gaze of faith, that which was in heaven became as real as earthly things to sense. The glory of God bathed him with its light, and a familiar Form, which in its mortality he had known below, was recognised amid the unapproachable splendour of the celestial throne. The old radiance stole back again upon his countenance, when,

"— looking upward, full of grace,
He prayed, and from a happy place
God's glory smote him on the face."[2]

Angry voices ceased, and angry eyes grew awed to see the silent rapture of worship with which he stood and bent his upturned shining countenance on what they could not see. At last he spoke—spoke amid the hush words

[1] Cf. Psa. lxiv. 3; Jer. ix. 3.
[2] "The Two Voices," see Tennyson, *Poems*, p. 299. (The lines refer in the original to a moment a little later.)

which broke the spell: "Behold, I see the heavens opened, and the Son of man standing on the right hand of God." That hated name let loose the tide of rage which awe had for a moment frozen, and with illegal tumult, councillors and bystanders, turned through sheer passion into a mob, swept him from the chamber with a rush and hurried him for execution beyond the northern city gate.

This first martyrdom of a Christian, like the death of Christ Himself, was a mixture of legal forms with popular violence. The people now, and not the Sanhedrim alone, were bitter against the new faith. They had come to understand its spiritual nature, and their fanaticism saved the Sanhedrim from a difficulty. It might have been too serious a stretch of jurisdiction to sentence and execute a blasphemer without reference to the Roman Procurator. It was easy to plead their inability to hinder a mob from taking the law into its own hands. At the same time, the execution was as legal as such an execution could be. The place, the mode of death, the first stone thrown by the witnesses, were all in exact accordance with ancient precedent and express Mosaic statute.[1] By such formalities they sought to represent their bloody work as a solemn vengeance of national law upon a blasphemer of Jehovah. One at least in the crowd (and I doubt not far more than one) thought he was doing God service[2] by consenting to the martyr's death. I take it for a kindness to the Church and her future apostle, that the young man from Tarsus had no direct hand in stoning

---

[1] See Lev. xxiv. 13–16; Deut. xiii. 6–11, xvii. 2–7.
[2] Cf. John xvi. 2; c. Acts xxvi. 9.

his great predecessor. It was enough to bear his full share in the day's guilt, "standing by," and "keeping the raiment of them that slew him;" a sin that to be remembered and deplored to his old age,[1] without his hand being actually upon him to shed his blood. Touching, however, as was Saul's presence there that day, and full of meaning for his future life, all other interests pale before the Christ-likeness of the martyred saint himself. To see for the first time what has so many times been seen since then, how one who trusts and loves Jesus can walk along His own royal road of pain, and carry with a like meekness His cross behind him; to mark the divine spirit of charity in which Jesus died descend on a frail and evil man who calls Him Lord; to hear the divinest words of the dying King echoed by the lips of His follower; to realise that transfiguration of death in its most horrid shapes into a gate of life,[2] which it is the praise of Christ to have wrought for His saints; to watch how the peace of God which Jesus gives can lay a man to the easy and serene repose of his last sleep, though his bed of death be hard as stones, his body bruised, and his ears filled with the din of curse and jibe:—this makes to all Christian ages the preciousness of the martyr's death. Many a soul, weaker than this hero of Christ, has proved a brave soldier in the long and "noble army of martyrs" which has followed Stephen's steps and won Stephen's crown. But of all the Church's blessed palm-bearers,

---

[1] 1 Tim. i. 12-16.
[2] "Tibi fiet mors natalis;
Tibi pœna terminalis
Dat vitæ primordia."
Adam de S. Victor, *ut supra*. [St. Stephen's Day is next after Christmas, 26th Dec.]

not one has quitted himself with a diviner meekness, or rendered back to Jesus' hands his ransomed spirit with a sweeter forgiveness of enemies, or a more assured expectation of glory, than he whose honour it was to lead the host, and set to Christ's confessors an example of dying. It was Jesus Who, from the cross as from a pulpit (as Augustine writes [1]), taught to Stephen the law of devout living; and it was Jesus, too, Who, when His scholar had well learned that rule and fully practised it, rose from His throne to crown him. Before us we too have the same Unchanged One to gaze at, nor can the long procession of succeeding saints hide Him from our eyes. He Who for the joy set before Him endured the cross, hath set open unto us also the gates of everlasting life. From beside the throne of God He beckons unto us as He beckoned Stephen. Stephen, by His grace, followed and entered in, but entering did not break the bridge (to quote Augustine again [2]), nor shut the gate behind him. Martyrs we may not be unto blood; but witnesses, and sufferers, too, for Christ we all must be. In our lives, if not in our deaths, we surely need great Stephen's steadfast courage, and his clear-eyed faith, and his heaven-piercing hope, and his godlike charity. After such life, death shall be sweet as a falling on sleep, and beyond it is the crown laid up, and the conqueror's palm, and the welcoming Lord.

[1] "Sedebat in cathedrâ crucis Christus et docebat Stephanum regulam pietatis." (Augustine, quoted by Wordsworth, *in loc.*)
[2] On this passage, cf. the rest of Augustine's sermon, *ut supra*.

XIII.

Simon Magus.

Simon Magus, welcher überhaupt durch die Anschauung der ersten Jahrhunderte zum Repräsentanten und Vorgänger aller häretischen Richtungen der späteren Zeit gestempelt zu werden pflegte. *Neander.*

Acts viii. 1–24.

Revised Version.

Now there took place on that day a great persecution against the Church which was in Jerusalem, and all were dispersed about the districts of Judæa and Samaria, except the apostles. Yet devout men carried Stephen [to burial], and made a great lamentation over him. But Saul was ravaging the Church, going in from house to house, [and] dragging both men and women, he committed them to prison.

Those then who were dispersed went about preaching the Word. And Philip, coming down to a city of Samaria, was proclaiming to them the Christ, and the crowds gave heed to the things which were said by Philip, with one accord, when they heard and saw the signs which he was doing. For [as to] many of those who had unclean spirits, shouting with a loud voice, they went out, and many paralytics and cripples were healed. And there was much joy in that city. But a certain man, Simon by name, was already in the city, using magic arts, and amazing the people of Samaria, saying that he himself was some great one; to whom they all gave heed from the least to the greatest, saying: "This man is the power of God which is called great." But they gave heed to him on account of their having been amazed for a considerable time with the magical arts.

But when they believed Philip preaching about the kingdom of God and the name of Jesus Christ, they were baptized, both men and women. And Simon himself also believed, and having been baptized was continuing with Philip, and beholding the signs and great deeds of power which took place, was amazed.

Now, the apostles in Jerusalem, when they heard that Samaria had accepted the word of God, sent to them Peter and John, who having come down, prayed for them, so that they might receive the Holy Spirit. For not yet was He fallen upon any one of them, but only they were persons who had been baptized into the name of the Lord Jesus. Then they laid their hands on them, and they received the Holy Spirit. But when Simon saw that through the laying on of the hands of the apostles the Spirit was being given, he offered them money, saying:

"Give to me also this power, in order that on whomsoever I lay hands he may receive the Holy Spirit."

But Peter said to him: "Thy silver with thyself go to destruction, because thou didst mean to buy for money the free-gift of God. To thee there is no part nor lot in this matter, for thy heart is not right in the presence of God. Repent therefore from this evil of thine, and pray the Lord if possibly the purpose of thy heart may be pardoned thee. For into a gall of bitterness and a bond of iniquity I see thou art [fallen]."

But Simon answering said: "Pray ye on my behalf to the Lord, so that nothing may come upon me of the things ye have said."

XIII.

STEPHEN'S martyrdom was the signal for a general persecution. From St. Luke's words[1] one might almost gather that the crowd which stoned him outside the gate, rushed back with its blood up, or, as Calvin says, like a wild beast which has once tasted blood, and threw itself there and then upon the company of brethren who perchance had met to pray secretly in their upper room for the brother who before men was playing so well his honourable and perilous part. At all events passions were awake which a single victim could not satisfy. Circumstances, too, had brought about a coalition of dangers for the Church. Now at last Sadducee and Pharisee agreed in their hostility. The Sanhedrim had at last committed itself by the execution of one disciple. The people's favour for men who healed their sick had turned into popular fanaticism against men who blasphemed Moses. Even the Roman authorities seem to have been accessory or supine. In brief, a favourable juncture had come when the bigots, who hated this growing heresy, and really cared to crush it, might hope to do so. With the hour

---

[1] Which literally are ἐν ἐκείνῃ τῇ ἡμέρᾳ, "on that day;" an expression which seems never to occur in any other than its literal sense, except in reference to some vague future "day," such as the time of the Judgment, of the Second Advent, or of the New Dispensation. See Bruder.

had come the man. One young Pharisee, at least, born to do with his might whatever he did, and be, for good or ill, a leader of men, took to persecution as a pious task, and pushed himself into notice as the arch-inquisitor. Saul was "exceedingly mad against" the saints.[1] Not content with breaking up the Christian assemblies, driving their prominent members into exile, and silencing the public preachers, he hunted up and down among the synagogues for concealed adherents. He even stooped to domiciliary visits. He forced the timorous to recant and blaspheme their Christ; when the more resolute refused, he dragged them by violence to the authorities. Women he spared no more than men. He had his victims imprisoned, he had them flogged. Nay, we have it on his own authority that he voted in the Sanhedrim for their death,[2] so that others besides Stephen must have won at his hands the crown of martyrdom. Thus, says St. Augustine, there raged against the flock that wolf, who was soon to be made, through grace, a lamb first, and then a shepherd of the sheep.[3]

Two features have been preserved to us which relieve the darkness of that first persecution. While its opening fury lasted, men were found, not Christian men probably, but godly adherents of the law of Moses,[4] who dared to reverence the poor broken flesh of God's martyred confessor, and, gathering it up from among the stones, to bear

---

[1] Acts xxvi. 11. [2] The exact force of κατήνεγκα ψῆφον in xxvi. 10.
[3] "Exue te lupo; esto de lupe, ovis; de ove, pastor." See Wordsworth, *in loc.* Also used by Calvin, *in loc.* See Kuinoel, *in loc.*, for uses of ἐλυμαίνετο, v. 3.
[4] εὐλαβεῖς seems to me to be chosen for its vagueness, to include disciples and Hellenists and Palestinian Jews indifferently. Probably some of each were engaged in it. The one point of contact was, they were all pious men.

it, as Nicodemus and Joseph had borne his Lord, to an honourable and lamented burial. Christ, Who cares for His servants' dust, found stranger hands to pay those last decent offices which His gospel has hallowed into a service of piety. The character of a man like Stephen, his charity, his wisdom and his courage, are often found to win affectionate admiration from true-hearted onlookers, even among such as do not share his faith. The other fact is the behaviour of the Twelve. Since this outbreak was primarily directed against Hellenistic believers, it is possible that the apostles were at first in less personal danger than they had been at an earlier period. Still, for the chiefs to remain after all other well-known members of the flock had fled the city, was obviously to provoke or to invite an attack. Yet nothing but their remaining could, at that moment, have secured the permanence of the Church. Out of Jerusalem it had as yet no seat. Within Jerusalem it had, except themselves, no leaders. Had they given way, either by following that tempting permission[1] of their Master to flee to another city, or by scattering themselves about the rural neighbourhood for the purpose of concealment, the Church would have ceased to have any organisation, any head-quarters, or any visible corporate existence. The strength of its footing in the holy city would have been for the time, perhaps for ever, lost. What they did was the wisest thing they could do. As many of the male members as could leave, especially all prominent or active members like the rest of the Seven, were sent hither and thither for safety. The Twelve themselves remained in the city, to comfort the women and those who could not leave, to watch over the interests

[1] Given to the Twelve during Jesus' lifetime at least: s. Matt. x. 23.

of the arrested, and to form a strong base of support and means of intercommunication for the scattered brethren. By this means the very disaster which threatened to extinguish the Church served to disseminate it. Every exiled believer became a travelling missionary. From the central apostolic college, lines of evangelism began for the first time to radiate throughout Judæa and into Samaria. By degrees they even came to stretch beyond as far as Damascus, Antioch, Cyprus, and Sidon; so that the indefatigable persecutor, when he had done what he could to break up the sect in Jerusalem, had to follow its adherents "even unto strange cities."[1] To use the image of a great Father, already quoted, the foolish Jews, who thought to stamp out the fire, only scattered embers all through the wood.[2]

Into the footsteps of only one out of those many banished evangelists does the historian lead us; but the spark which fell upon Samaria was a very bright one, and the wood into which it fell was very dry and ready. Philip was that deacon, second on the list, who stepped to the front when Stephen fell. After the two incidents recorded in the eighth chapter of the Acts, he disappears for many years from the history. He seems to have returned to the capital no more, but to have settled with his family in Cæsarea, where, if he could not any longer act as "one of the seven," he had at least ample exercise for his functions as an "evangelist."[3] Like Stephen,

[1] See Acts ix. 13, xxvi. 11.
[2] "Stulti Judæi . . . carbones ignis in silvam mittebant."—Augustine, *ut supra*.
[3] Perhaps this connection with Cæsarea explains why in the Sinaitic MS. (and it alone) we find καισαριας in v. 5, instead of Σαμαρειας. See xxi. 8, 9.

SIMON MAGUS.

he belonged to the freer section of the Church. It was quite in the line of Stephen's teaching when Philip broke clean away from Judæa and the Jews altogether, and carried the gospel into Samaria. It is true Samaria was an exceptional fragment of the Gentile world, peopled by an ambiguous race, which could be looked on, and did look on themselves, as either pure Gentile or almost Jewish, at pleasure. The Samaritans were descended from Assyrian colonists settled in the land of Israel after its own inhabitants had been carried off to captivity.[1] It is uncertain whether these colonists from the far East found any Jewish remnant left in the land to mix with.[2] At any rate, the infusion of Hebrew blood could have been but small, if any. The chances are that they remained, what they look to this day,[3] almost pure Gentiles by race. Not, however, by religion. They early combined a sort of Judaic worship with their ancestral idolatries. They practised circumcision; they built a temple to Jehovah; they revered the Pentateuch and kept the Passover. In process of time they grew to believe or to claim that they were more orthodox Jews than the Jews themselves. Josephus, however, complains with some bitterness that they called themselves Jews only when it suited their interest to do so; whereas, when doing so entailed trouble, they had no scruple to declare themselves (what they were) heathens, Sidonians or Cuthites or Assyrians, as seemed best.[4] This ambiguous position of the Samaritans was, no doubt, the reason why our Lord on one occasion preached the gospel to them, although on every other

[1] See 2 Kings xvii. 24–41.
[2] See this discussed in Smith's *Dict.* Art. "Samaria."
[3] See Robinson, *Bibl. Res.* ii. 282 (3rd Ed.). But cf. Stanley, *S. and P.* p. 240. [4] See *Antiq.* xi. 8. 6, xii. 5. 5.

occasion He steadily avoided doing so outside the territory of the chosen people; and why, in sketching the progress of His Church, He named them as a link between "all Judæa" and the "uttermost part of the earth." [1] So far, therefore, the gospel was already come—thanks to its persecutors—as far as to Samaria.

It is uncertain what Samaritan city Philip selected for his mission.[2] The city of Samaria, the old capital of King Ahab's dynasty and of Jehu's, after many a disaster had been lately rebuilt by Herod the Great, and colonised by his discharged foreign troops. To it, Philip was less likely to go than to the true centre of Samaritan life and worship, the city of Sychar or Shechem, some six miles off, where, too, he would be exactly on the footmarks of his Master. In that town Jesus had found fields white to harvest, and into His labour Philip was now to enter.[3] The welcome which the Shechemites had given to the words of Jesus, and the great joy which Philip's preaching now brought to the city, show how open the Samaritans then lay to a new revelation of religious truth. They were, quite as eagerly as the Jews, looking for the advent of a Messiah, and their expectations from Messiah when He came were rather less political, rather more spiritual, than those of the Jews. But events had been happening among them between the date of Jesus' visit and that of Philip's, which indicate that their religious susceptibility was less an intelligent desire for moral help than a vague and restless craving after anything which promised to bring the supernatural near. In this, indeed, they only

---

[1] See Acts i. 8.

[2] Instead of "the city of Samaria," in verse 5, we should probably read, "a city of Samaria," although both A and B have the article. So has ℵ, only with "Cæsarea" for Samaria,

[3] John iv. 5–42; cf. esp. verses 35, 38.

shared a characteristic of their time. All over the known world, the nations were at that critical hour in history agitated by a vague unrest and a feverish anticipation of some impending change. Everywhere men turned dissatisfied from their ancestral divinities and worn-out beliefs. Everywhere they turned in their uncertainty to foreign superstitions, and welcomed any religion which professed to reveal the unknown. The frightful calamities wrought by war and pestilence and slavery, which had accompanied the break-up of national life and the submergence of the whole world under the military power of Rome, had worn out men's hearts, and taught them to sigh for help. The earth groaned for a deliverer, who should reveal to the individual, at least, a better hope beyond this life, if no better national life could be looked for on this side of death. Along with this came a strange longing to penetrate the secrets of the world, to communicate with the invisible, to break the cruel dumbness of nature and get at the soul of things—the God Who hides Himself there, behind this universe of appearance and of matter. To persons in this expectant and restless condition, there could be no lack of prophets. Asia bred them, Egypt ripened 'them, the West swarmed with them. He who reads the book of Acts to its close, will come on many traces of them. Even Samaria, the half-Jewish land which owned the Pentateuch and looked for a Messiah, had found some for itself. Contemporary with our Lord, we read of one Dositheus, whose scholar Simon is said to have been, who gave himself out to be the prophet whom Moses foretold—a severe, ascetic man, who rigorously kept the Mosaic law, and fasted himself to death in a cave. After him had come one of a different stamp: a crafty, ambitious, able man, who deceived others more than he deceived himself, and knew how to cover both greed and lust under a cloak of spiritual pretension. Simon was a Samaritan, born in a village not far from Sychar;[1] but he had been educated, we are told (though on rather doubtful authority[2]), at Alexandria. He certainly had picked up ideas which were not Samaritan: the occult learning of his time, its black arts, and those endless speculations on the hidden powers of nature, the spiritual emanations from the Godhead, and the like abstruse and profitless subjects, which, under the name of Gnosticism, were, for two centuries after, to be the plague of the Christian Church. Thus equipped, he had returned to astonish his countrymen, and Philip found him already in established possession of the ground. We shall probably understand Simon Magus best, if, to skill in the art of magic, we add a tacit claim to be an incarnation of the divine. He was first a magician, then a pseudo-Messiah. It was to the wonderful performances which he effected through magic that he owed his earliest influence over the Samaritan mind. Ignorant and superstitious people, who find the whole world about them to be full of unknown powers, and whose chief longing is to break the bonds of material, commonplace nature, so as to reach the occult, the superhuman, or the divine, lend greedy and credulous ears to any one who seems to have a spiritual power which others have not, to be able to lay his finger on those secret springs which influence events, or, by

---

[1] Gitton, now Kuryet Jit. s. Robinson, ii. 308, *note*. So we learn from Justin Martyr, also a Samaritan, born only some sixty or seventy years after this date. The Simon of Josephus (*Antiq.* xx. 7. 2) I incline to think must have been a different person.

[2] That of the Clementines.

some mysterious force, to effect the desired and achieve the marvellous. The men who at that period traversed Asia and Europe in shoals, winning fame and wealth by their art, worming themselves into the secrets of the great and ruling the fears of the superstitious, were not all of them mere vulgar cheats or juggling charlatans. Magic, on its best side, springs from a certain mystical religiousness; and in that age it rested largely on philosophical and theological theories as to the relation of God to the universe. In its professors, there was no doubt to be found some self-deception, combined with some real knowledge of nature, and some conscious pretence, and all three elements in varying proportions. But it is of the essence of magic, at its best, to depend for its wonders upon secret powers, superhuman or divine, which obey other than moral laws. It never aims at moral results, never works through moral processes. A pure heart or penitent will is no condition of its power. It lends itself as fast to the foulest as to the holiest ends. It serves spiritual pride, or passion, or revenge, or covetousness, equally with the noblest thirst for goodness. It is, therefore, essentially irreligious, because unethical. Besides, it professes to discover laws, or charms, or hidden fates, which compel the divine will and make the power of God an involuntary minister to the desires of man. Instead of serving God, it thinks to make God serve human caprice. Thus it is again irreligious. It is so in its newest form of spiritualism, which also has its apparent wonders and gifts of healing; for spiritualism, which is only a recoil from the scientific materialism of our century, is an attempt to obtain power over unknown and spiritual agencies, without regard to those moral and religious conditions of purity and piety under which alone God will discover Himself to man.

Simon was a bad man but a good magician. On the ground of his apparent miracles, he spoke vaguely of himself as something more than mortal—" some great one." It seems, however, to have been the deluded people who called him " the great power of God,"[1] rather than he himself who claimed that title. Whatever distinct idea they attached to these words, it is pretty certain that they took the man for an incarnation of the Very Highest —a manifestation than which no greater could be had of the Divine Almightiness. They took him for the Christ— the Divine Man, Who was to come. He suffered them to take him for that, although he knew he was not that. His *rôle* evidently was to use his superior knowledge and skill for the acquisition of spiritual power over men's minds, and then, by encouraging their extravagant devotion to him, to trade upon and make gain of them. Spiritual ambition, working through imposture and ministering to covetousness, will perhaps fairly enough describe the base of this man's character. The main interest of what follows lies in the effect on such a person of the gospel of Jesus. Here, no doubt for the first time, Christianity encountered a rival wonder-working Christ, and set its claim to be " the power of God unto salvation " in front of a sham " power of God." The issue therefore is interesting as a test of Christianity, but it is more interesting as a critical moment for Simon. To him, as to every man, the coming of the

---

[1] " The power of God which is called Great," is the true reading. That is, than which is no greater.

message of God through His Son proved a turning time in his personal history, on which hinged all his after life.

Let us briefly recite what happened.

To a people so thirsty for wonders and so preoccupied by the marvellous arts of their prophets, as these Samaritans, Christianity first addressed itself through miracle. As Moses in Egypt withstood Jannes and Jambres,[1] so Philip met the delusive sorceries of Simon by counter wonders. Only the miracles of the evangelist, like those of his Master, bore their best commendation in the fact that they were miracles of healing, fit to usher in and symbolise a spiritual salvation. What Simon had done had put the people beside themselves with amazement.[2] What Philip did filled the city with great joy. When foul spirits left the possessed, and the lame man walked, and the palsied limb grew supple, these gracious exercises of a strength which was proved to be divine by its being beneficent, only led the wonder-worker on to discourse of a kingdom of God in which, through penitence and faith, the soul is cleansed from foul affections, liberated from spiritual impotence, and restored to moral soundness and purity. He led them through miracle to Jesus; told them of His mission of love from heaven, reminded them of His teaching in their own towns, related the story of His cross, and preached to them His resurrection. In the name, not of himself, but of the crucified, glorified Son of God, he proclaimed to them reconciliation to God, forgiveness, and the renovation of the whole inner life. Philip's victory was complete. His message filled the hearts of the people, for it satisfied cravings which Simon had not

[1] 2 Tim. iii. 8.   [2] Cf. ἐξιστάνων in ver. 9; and see ver. 7.

satisfied. This was real help from God, not feigned
help; gratuitous, as all heaven's gifts are, not to be
trafficked for; spiritual help, too, and not magical; a
very gospel of glad tidings; and "there was great joy in
that city." All, save one, were glad. Simon saw his
influence sapped, his occupation and his gains gone.
The defection of his adherents, as they flocked to receive
baptism at the hands of the new teacher, compelled
Simon's attention to the works and doctrine of his rival ;
and after a while he too believed and was baptised.
There is no need to weaken the force of Luke's words,[1]
or to question the sincerity of that profession of faith
which Simon made at his baptism. It is quite true that he
had unhappily a motive for conversion. It was his interest
to believe. Still, I am not disposed to say that the man
feigned a belief which he did not entertain, just in order
to find out wherein Philip's superior power lay. What
Simon professed was a conviction that Jesus, not he himself, was the true Christ, the incarnation of the power of
God, and that by His name true miracles were done, greater
than he had himself attempted. There is no reason
to doubt that this was an honest profession, and it implied a great deal. He was for the time beaten out of
his own blasphemous pretensions. Recognising in the
works of Philip a power above his own, he turned to it,
reverenced it, and believed in it. But Simon's fault was
this—and it was a fatal one—he was still bent, not on
holiness, but on power. He saw in the gospel a new and
superior sort of wonder-working, but he saw nothing more.
He cared now no more than he had ever done for moral
nearness to God, for truth or purity or nobleness of life.

[1] "Simon himself believed also," ver. 13.

His faith had not a moral, it had only an intellectual basis. He expressed no compunction for having deceived the people and blasphemed God. The whole ethical side of Christianity, its power of bringing man into peace with God, and of making man like God, was shut against him. For that he had no ear. Against that his heart was closed. He believed therefore without being converted; accepted Christ as divine, and bowed to His name, without realising any personal need of Him as a Saviour and Sanctifier: a faith this which is so far from being unusual amongst ourselves, that its occurrence in the case of Simon need bring us no surprise.

From the primitive habit of administering baptism without probation, on a mere verbal profession of faith in Jesus, the shallowness of the change produced on the false prophet could not be at once detected. What brought it to light was the visit of Peter and John. It was very natural that the extraordinary success of the gospel in Samaria should attract the attention of the apostles, who had remained in Jerusalem just on purpose to overlook from that centre all the scattered disciples at work in the various provinces of Palestine. It was natural, too, that a deputation of leading men should be sent down to inspect, to advise, and to sanction so important a step as the foundation of a Samaritan Church. This step implied neither jealousy of Philip nor any incompetency on his part. The apostles were the responsible chiefs of the whole body. They were bound to see to its welfare, and in every way to aid its progress. It was of the utmost moment that a branch Church, formed among an alien and hostile people, should not fall out of the unity of brotherhood with the mother Church at Jerusalem.[1] Besides, it is plain that the formal recognition of the converted Samaritans as members of the kingdom of Christ was expressly reserved for the apostolic deputies. Baptism had put them into the position of the hundred and twenty before Pentecost; but the full bestowal of spiritual influence, evidenced by visible or audible tokens like the gift of tongues,[2] took place only when, after solemn prayer for the assembled brethren, Peter and John laid their hands successively on the head of each. It was during the progress of this most sacred and awful transaction, when, as in the upper room at Pentecost, a quite manifest *afflatus* of divine enthusiasm possessed one after another of the converts, and set them on loud and rapturous utterance of His praise Who had called them to His kingdom and fellowship, that Simon, in his excitement, betrayed how utterly out of sympathy he felt with the whole spirit of the Church. Such a scene stirred in him also that which was deepest in his heart. The deepest thing in him was neither the burden of an evil and unspiritual life, nor the yearning after God, nor the gladness of a pardoned sinner. It was just what it had always been — ambition, the lust after spiritual power. As he gazed, amazed, on the sublimest exhibition of spiritual power which he or any other man had ever seen—the descent of the Holy Ghost on the souls of men, so as to master their bodily organs as well, and to lift the whole man into an ecstasy of devotion,—the one desire which leapt up in him and sprang to his lips was, that he too might possess power like an

---

[1] So Calvin *in loc*. See Alford on the reasons of this visit.
[2] Cf. the case of Cornelius before baptism, Acts x. 44–48.

apostle, to give power like this to men! But there was in unhappy Simon, as there had been in Balaam of old, a baser passion than even ambition. To him spiritual power was valuable because he could turn it to profit; take captive the silly by it, and wheedle them out of their money. What will win gold, is worth gold. What can be sold may also be bought. To one who had affected to traffic in what is superhuman till he had ceased to believe in what is really divine, the two apostles were only deeper magicians than himself. They possessed some more potent formulas. They could work upon some mightier spirit than he knew. If they were like himself, they might be bribed to share their secrets with him and enter into profitable partnership. Thus, in presence of the holiest, the unholiest in Simon came to light. Tested and discovered by his own words, he was gibbeted by the indignant imprecation of a very different Simon. "Thy money perish with thee!" So he became the godfather of all those who, from that day to this, have either sought or used the spiritual powers of God's house for ends of secular gain.

The horror and severity of Peter's first words yielded to Christian pity. He seems to have feared lest the wretched prophet might have committed the unpardonable sin, by blaspheming the Holy Ghost; yet with such plain speaking as shook the sinner's soul with terror, he blended an earnest exhortation to pray, "if perhaps the thought of thine heart may be forgiven thee." Poor Simon Magus knew not how to pray. Into his soul no hint of shame, or penitence, or grace found entrance. The awfulness of that threat, from one in whom he recognised a power above his own, crushed him only in abject and cowardly terror.

He shows no relenting — not even remorse. He dreads the perdition which one mightier than himself has hung over his head: his sin he does not feel. The very sense of guilt has been lost in the man because he has lost faith in God. It is very horrible; to be so near the kingdom of God; baptised into it, too; and yet so dead in soul — dead in pride and earthliness and lies and greed!

Simon Magus disappears here from inspired history, but not from Christian literature. His name for centuries became the centre of legends which grew as legends grow.[1] From the witness of his countryman, Justin, who was born little over half a century after this event, we may conclude that the man who had come so near to Christ and been self-repelled from Him, grew afterwards into a more daring and more wicked impostor than ever. He founded a sect which lingered long in Samaria. He travelled as far as Rome in the pursuit of his profession. Everywhere he opposed the gospel. He appears as the bitter foe of Peter in particular. He added lust to covetousness, calling the paramour whom he had taken from the stews of Tyre a divine emanation like himself. If he does not deserve to be termed, as the Church fathers term him, the parent and type of all heresy, he seems at least from that memorable day to have gone ever further off from the pure faith which once he had professed, and from that blessed hope which in His mercy God once brought near him.

[1] Lechler (in Lange *in loc.*) and others seem too summarily to set the legends aside. Why should not the main features of his after history be trusted?

XIV.
The Ethiopian Courtier.

ETHIOPIA SHALL SOON STRETCH OUT HER HANDS UNTO GOD!

Acts viii. 25-40.

Revised Version.

So then, after witnessing and speaking the Word of the Lord, they were returning to Jerusalem, and were evangelizing many villages of the Samaritans. But an angel of the Lord spoke to Philip, saying:

"Arise and go toward the south, to the road that goes down from Jerusalem to Gaza: it is a desert [way]."

And he arose and went. And behold, a man, an Ethiopian, an eunuch, a statesman under Candace, queen of the Ethiopians, who was over all her treasure, [who] had come worshipping to Jerusalem, and was returning, [and] sitting on his chariot, and read the prophet Isaiah. And the Spirit said to Philip:

"Go near and join thyself to this chariot."

And running forward, Philip heard him reading Isaiah the prophet, and said:

"Well, but dost thou understand what thou art reading?"

And he said:

"How then should I be able, unless some one should guide me?"

And he besought Philip to come up and sit with him. Now, the contents of the Scripture which he was reading were these:

"He was brought as a sheep to the slaughter,
And as a lamb before its shearer [is] dumb,
So he opened not his mouth.
In his humiliation, his judgment was taken away;
But who shall declare his generation?
For his life is taken from the earth."

And the eunuch, answering, said to Philip:

"*I pray thee, about whom does the prophet say this? about himself or about some other?*"

Then Philip opened his mouth, and beginning from that Scripture, went on to preach to him Jesus. But as they were going along the road, they came on a certain water, and the eunuch said:

"*Behold, water! what hinders me to be baptized?*"

And he ordered the chariot to stand, and they went down both into the water, both Philip and the eunuch, and he baptized him. But when they came up out of the water, the Lord's Spirit caught away Philip, and the eunuch saw him no more. For he was going on his way rejoicing, but Philip was found at Azotus; and passing through he evangelized all the cities, until his arrival at Cæsarea.

XIV.

IT is only snatches which have been preserved to us from the overflowing Church life of the apostolic time; a single incident here and there, saved by one man's pen out of the great darkness of forgetfulness which has swallowed up the unwritten acts of all the apostles and of all their colleagues. We are able, for example, to follow a little longer the missionary footsteps of Philip, after his departure from Samaria; but what success the two greatest apostles had in that province, or how the mother Church in Jerusalem was meanwhile faring under the eyes of the Twelve, remains untold. Philip, too, is only one out of a crowd of scattered preachers, who, at that time, were all as busy as he in carrying the good news abroad over Palestine and beyond it; yet no name but his own lives in the history. The sad case of Simon, and the glad case of the African,[1] are only specimens out of the mission-work of a single labourer, and he is only a specimen of many missionaries. It ought to be remembered, however, that the recorded incidents are not selected for record simply as specimens. Other incidents might have served equally well for that use; no other incidents could have served so well the use to which the sacred writer puts them. His motive

[1] "An idyl out of the missionary history of the apostolic Church." Lechler in Lange *in loc.*

of selection can be inferred from his work. It was to illustrate the outward, heathenward, and westward drift of the Church's main progress during the first quarter of a century. He has aimed at showing how, through sheer stress of circumstances, as, for instance, by the violence of persecution, by a confluence of providential leadings, by the express orders of her Head, or by the gradual teaching of her officers, the Church, which began as a Judaic sect cradled within the temple, was urged, or driven, or led, out and forward, step by step, across one frontier line of nationality and of creed after another, till she found herself, almost in her own despite, the Catholic Church of mankind. The prohibition of preaching by the Sanhedrim, the Hellenism of Stephen, the dispersion of the brethren by Saul, and Philip's success in Samaria, have been so many distinct steps in this direction. The conversion of the eunuch is another step.

It was while Peter and John were leisurely travelling back to the mother city, preaching as they went, in village after village of that despised Samaria, which had embraced the glad news refused by Jerusalem, that Philip received a heavenly visitor.[1] We are told that one of Christ's angels, or messengers from the invisible, charged with an errand from the King, became visible to the evangelist, and, speaking the words of a man, bade him leave his work, to travel southwards by a certain road. We have already had occasion to observe how, during those days of the Church's infancy, her Lord's tutorship took a more direct form than it has since worn, and brought the

[1] See Alford *in loc.* on the imperfects and the force of δὲ in ver. 26. Cf. also Meyer *in loc.*

superhuman Overseer into more immediate contact with the human actors. Jesus was still dictating each fresh step in the progress of His cause by a mingled system of influence, one part of which, indeed, lay in natural circumstances and the inward play of men's thoughts about them, while another embraced the visible interference of celestial or super-earthly forces. It was only by degrees that what was supernatural was to die away, leaving only that which was natural behind. The lesson which we may suppose He desired by this means to write upon the heart of His Church is, that He is present in the natural not less than in the supernatural. Thus He works spiritual changes in men to-day, although no longer at the laying on of hands do tongues and ecstasies betray the presence of the Spirit. He guides the labours of true evangelists to-day, although no angel comes to bid them travel by a special road. What to us would be the value of any record full of mere idle marvels? Or what the better shall we be for such protrusions of the other world through the veil which screens it from vision, unless they teach us that there is, out of sight, behind this material world, another with which we and this life of ours do stand for ever in the closest and most vital relations? The Church ought no longer to need her Lord's messengers to be present to sense, because by this time the perpetual unseen action of the Lord ought to be always present to her faith. By an ordinary combination of circumstances, with a rational conscientiousness in the discovery of duty, men are still really led by God into " the south," where the way is " desert." Few can have thoughtfully observed their own lives, or those of their friends, without noticing instances quite as strange as this order must have appeared to Philip. Away from a position of promising usefulness, where a whole city lay waiting to be blessed, and the fruits of past labour seemed ready for the harvesting, God forced His servant. He drove him by providences not to be withstood into a lonely place, to pass some days there, in aimless and unwilling inaction. Nor could it be one whit an easier thing for Philip contentedly to abandon his field of work and go, perplexed and purposeless, whither that angel bade him, than it is for us to follow any disappointing providence. God's will was not less baffling or hard to obey, because an angel spoke it. Neither is it the less unmistakable or supreme because now no angel speaks it, but men are left to gather it from the events of life. What is life but a practice of trust in a silent and unseen Guide, Who explains nothing at the time, but leaves us to interpret His meaning only after we have seen the end? Lives without number are being lived all round us, which seem to have gone astray, through no fault of their own, from their very start; as if God had sent them early into a way which is desert and had left them there—misshapen, blighted lives, which have found no fit place, we think, to work in, nor any fit home to dwell in. Even such, if they seek God's guidance, are really led of Him; and, if true to duty, they shall be found, when the play is all played out, to have finished the work which He gave them to do.

It seems impossible with our present information to be quite sure by what route Philip was meant to go. Whether the words, "which is desert," are an insertion of the historian or a direction by the angel, there is no doubt that Philip himself understood the precise route from Jerusalem to Gaza which was intended. At present, however, not one of the four roads by which it seems to have been possible in the first century to travel betwixt these two points, is so distinguished above the rest by superior wasteness as to prefer an indubitable claim. Perhaps the most frequented tracks for ancient travellers going from Jerusalem towards Egypt, especially with wheeled vehicles, were those which first led right down from the hills by the usual route to Jaffa, and then turned sharply southward along the whole plain of Philistia. But then these roads traversed precisely the most highly cultivated and densely peopled district in all Palestine. On the other hand, the shortest cut was a nearly straight one, which seems to have struck diagonally across the hills to Eleutheropolis, and thence across the plain to Gaza. But even if this was passable to wheels in its mountainous parts, there remain such numerous traces of villages all along its course that it could hardly be styled desert. The use of that word by the Hebrews certainly did not imply barrenness, but it implied at least a sparse population, and a country more given up to pasture than under tillage. A rather early tradition placed the scene of the baptism at a spot some twenty Roman miles from Jerusalem on the way to Hebron; and at that very spot there remain to this day unusually large tanks of water by the roadside, fed by strong springs. This was one of the main thoroughfares of communication from the earliest times, as it is to-day, and bears to this hour the mark of ancient wheels; yet it might be fairly called "desert," since it traversed the backbone of the Judæan highlands, through an open, pastoral, and lonely district. The difficulty in this case lies in seeing how the foreigner's chariot could get across the rough country between Hebron and Gaza, a route almost unexplored by modern travellers, and certainly destitute of any important road. The usual course of travellers going down into Egypt *viâ* Hebron was not to diverge to Gaza at all, but to hold on southward along the great highway past Beersheba and the southern desert of Et Tih. In this uncertainty we must be content to leave the question for the present;[1] but if it is impossible to identify the place where Philip met the Eunuch, we have less difficulty with the far more important point of this stranger's position and previous training.

In the upper Nile valley, stretching south from the frontier of Egypt at Syene, as far as the point of junction of its two great confluents, the Blue and White Nile, lay a realm embracing what is now called Nubia and part of Abyssinia,[2] which had for its capital, at the time when our era opened, the island city of Meröe. During some four centuries it seems to have been ruled by a dynasty of queens, whose official name of Candace descended, like that of Pharaoh in Egypt, from one sovereign to another. Under the reigning queen of that title this man held the important office of chief treasurer. All over the East, from the very earliest times to this day, members of his unhappy class have been advanced by preference to responsible posts at the courts of tyrants; not only to the charge of the harem, or the tutorship of princes, but also to the

---

[1] It is possible that further light may be shed upon the point by the trigonometrical survey now going on at the charges of the Palestine Exploration Fund.   [2] Or perhaps, more correctly, of Sennaar.

most weighty offices of state, to the privy council of the sovereign, and even to the command of armies. It is this man's race, too, which has always furnished by far the largest number of such victims to oriental suspiciousness and the cruel exigencies of polygamy. Against vast hindrances this nameless African had come to know and worship Jehovah. He lived on the extreme frontier of civilisation. He belonged to a class excluded from the most humane influences of life, a class wont to be heartless, crafty, spiteful, and cowardly, to a proverb. In his own sphere he had attained what might have satisfied the ambition of most men. He had won power, wealth, and rank, three idols which do most of all to enslave or deaden the spiritual life. Why was he not at rest? Or, if still ill at ease, why did he seek relief elsewhere than in political intrigues? How, above all, had he risen within a barbarous pagan court to such purity and simple nobleness of character? It is more easy to imagine how a thirst after divine truth and spiritual life might be quickened or kept quick within him, through the words of the Old Testament, than to represent to oneself how a soul could be nursed into graciousness, and grow so gentle, transparent, docile, and lowly, within a palace at Meröe. Yet so it was. He comes before us as already one of Jesus' sheep, who were not of the Hebrew fold. That Septuagint version of the Scriptures, which, with all its defects, did right noble service by leavening every Greek-speaking land with the great thoughts of the old revelation, and so preparing the earth for the coming of its Christ, had found its way into the Eunuch's hands. Studying it in Queen Candace's court, he had learned there to worship one only living God, Who can be set forth by no goat-headed Ammon, no, nor Greek Apollo; Who is not to be pictured under material forms nor served with cruel rites; but to be sought in the secret devotion of the heart and pleased with the service of a righteous life. From vagrant Jews, who came to Meröe as they came to every place, he may even have learned a little more. At all events he plainly felt, as all simple and honest readers do, that there was a hidden deep of meaning within the sacred word—especially within the prophetic books—which no painful search of his could reach. Much of it was dark, because he was still ignorant; much more, because it was itself profound; but most of all, perhaps, because it wrapped up truth within a casket for which he possessed no key. Yet he was sure that truth lay there, since such plain texts as he could understand led him, while he pondered and obeyed them, into a life higher than that which men lived about him. He knew Jehovah's law to be perfect, for it converted his soul.[1] The serene trust in God, the lofty adoration, the pure, severe righteousness which breathed from the law and from the psalms, touched and moved his heart, and drew him above dishonour, above pride of rank and lust of power and envy of men and the petty discontents of a courtier. If that which lay open upon the page of this strange volume could do so much for the soul's life, what might not be hoped for, could only that treasure be unlocked which was hidden within its dark prophetic sections, or those mysterious promises be fulfilled which sparkled in its words? The glorious restlessness of a soul which has found, yet not fully found, God, which has drunk the waters of life, but not drunk enough, possessed him, and

---

[1] See Psa. xix. 7.

urged him from cares of office and the ease of luxury to a long and toilsome journey. Away down his river valley, and beyond the cities of Egypt, and across the sands, there lay the home of that favoured people whose God was now his God. Might it not be that, before the sacred shrine in the holy city, and from the learned priests who ministered to Jehovah there, would come a light to lighten the darkness of these ancient words, and fill his soul with peace? I take it to have been no thirst for barren learning which provoked him to so unusual an expedition. There are hearts that cannot be content so long as they think they can get nearer God, or know Him better, or have a clearer beam of favour from His face. The Eunuch's heart was one of these.

I fancy too that his heart must have been heavy when Philip accosted him by the way. He had turned his back on the holy city, and his face toward his distant heathen home, without having found what he came to seek. It might be some satisfaction to him (as it is now to us) to tread the streets of Jehovah's city; and his piety could hardly fail to burn within him in a more fervent flame when he worshipped, though from afar, before the place where God had dwelt, or sent up his praises from the outer court,[1] while trumpets blew loud anthems within and sweet incense rose with the smoke of lambs to the evening sky. Yet, after all, was he nearer God than he had been at Meroë? Had the priests or the scribes unlocked for him these mysterious oracles? This chapter of Isaiah, for example, so glorious dark, with included light piercing it everywhere, have they made it plainer to the understanding? or taught him who it is whose soul is to be made an

---

[1] A eunuch could be no more than a Proselyte of the Gate.

offering for sin? or what righteous "Servant of God" is to bear the iniquities of many? We know what a vain quest it was for a sin-pressed soul in those days to go seeking light from Caiaphas or Gamaliel. The pedantic scholarship of the Rabbis, the superciliousness of orthodox Pharisaism to an uncircumcised Ethiopian, the zeal of legalists who were too busy stamping out the heresy of the Nazarene to mind anything else; these were what he had found in the city of God. He must have turned his back on it with a heavy heart. Here, however, comes out the sweet and childlike disposition of the man. He goes back to his Bible. Not just to while away the tedium of a long march, for he has not yet left many miles behind him; but with such a touching longing after light as hopes against hope, he will recite again the mysterious words and ponder over the manuscript where truth lies hid. "There is then no man," he thinks, "to guide me, not even in Jerusalem. How can I understand the Scripture?" It is very noteworthy how the education of years, and all the slow processes through which this heathen had been divinely led to know Jehovah, to seek better knowledge of Him, and to miss finding it where he most expected it—combined to ripen him for that brief decisive hour in the wilderness of Judæa. One line of providence has brought Philip, only within the last two days, from Samaria; another line of providence has brought the Ethiopian, through many years, from idolatry to Judaism, from Meroë to Jerusalem, from the temple to the desert. Now these converging lines, of which the touch, the contact, is to be the birth of a Christian life, have met.[1]

[1] "Not in the temple of Jerusalem, but on the desert way to Gaza, was he to find the pearl of great price. Thus formerly the wise men from the East had to journey on from Jerusalem to Bethlehem to find the new-born Jesus." Gerok in Lange *in loc.*

THE ETHIOPIAN COURTIER. 281

I have felt justified in taking the Ethiopian's modest and serious question, "How can I, except some man should guide me?" along with his courteous invitation to the stranger to occupy a seat beside him in the chariot that he might instruct him, as indicating the state of preparation in which Philip found him. It betrays his sense of ignorance, and his desire, now grown next to hopeless, for light. This seems to explain his instantaneous reception of the truth. It needed no more than one full talk by the way, followed by a hasty wayside baptism, and he, who left Jerusalem hardly a Jew, entered Gaza wholly a Christian. Further, we can trace God's careful leading up to a swift result, in the particular section of his Greek Old Testament, which (as we say) the man chanced to read, in eastern fashion, half-chanting it aloud to himself, when the wayfarer drew near enough to overhear. The paragraph which opens with the thirteenth verse of the fifty-second chapter of Isaiah, and includes all the fifty-third, has always been felt, both by Jew and Christian, to be the supreme point of prophetic anticipation. That yearning after a Christ, Who, through service and suffering, should solve the problem of man's reconciliation to God, which runs throughout Hebrew revelation from Genesis to Malachi, giving weight to the whole history, and meaning to every type, attains its utmost distinctness in the section which the Eunuch read. Jehovah's Servant Israel, of whom the entire prophecy[1] treats, is in these fifteen verses held forth with such startling vividness of language, first in His lowliness and unmerited passion, then in His saving strength, that we, who read our best commentary on it in the Gospels, can hardly persuade ourselves that

[1] Isa. xl.–lxvi.

the words are prophecy, not history, or were not always as clear as they are now. For the first time in the interpretation of these precious words, prophecy and history met together when Philip and the Eunuch sat side by side. The Eunuch is the latest voice of the old economy, and one of its noblest, searching what the Spirit Who was in it did signify;[1] Philip is the clear, no longer parabolic, voice of the new, testifying what had been seen with men's eyes and handled by men's hands of the Word of Life.[2] The one economy is figured to us by this weary-hearted student, puzzling over dumb oracles, who, as he strains eager eyes for an answer, asks doubtfully, "Of whom speaketh the prophet?" The other is like a herald lightly girt for travel, whose mouth is quick to answer—to tell with joyful and assured words the story of Jesus, and preach to all men salvation through the Man Who died on the cross and rose out of the grave. As the messenger of the new, Philip held the very key which that student of the old had sought so long in vain. What wonder if, while an ardent loving disciple of Jesus ran over with kindling eye and deepening voice the strange story, grown so common now, yet no whit less touching or less tragical for use—how God's own Son became a babe and grew to work the homely works of a Man in Nazareth; how He spoke words from His Father and did His Father's works; how He was all love and grace and truth, the very light of God shining through the humblest, meekest, and sweetest of the sons of men; how some men loved Him above all, and some hated Him to death; what shame He bore, what bitter anguish for our sins, when the people rejected Him, and the Lord bruised Him, and on the dark cross

[1] 1 Pet. i. 11.   [2] 1 John i. 1.

His soul was poured out an offering for sin; but how at the third dawn God raised Him up to be a Saviour of the sinful, and by His knowledge to justify many because He had borne their iniquities:—what wonder, I say, if all this tale Philip had to tell while the chariot rolled heavily along the lonely Syrian road, rushed into the waiting heart which God had ripened to receive it, and lit up the darkness of years, and answered his unanswered questions, and stilled the fears, and more than realised the hopes, and filled up with a great gladness the mighty longings of his soul? This, then, was what God had had it in His heart to do for guilty, evil men. This had been the blessed hope which glimmered obscurely in the pages of the prophets. God is no longer afar off, to be sought for at Jerusalem; a God to be yearned after, longed for, guessed at, or hoped in—if perchance He will somehow, some day, have mercy. He is now a God-with-us, grown human and very near, because "numbered," as the prophet speaks, "with us transgressors;" a God sacrificed like a lamb for sin, dying all for love, yet living, too, to bless; a Man-God, God-Man, Who pours His whole heart out upon our heart, breathes His own breath into our spirit, lives in us, and draws us up to live with Him! One half envies the man who, in the ripeness of his manhood, after thirsting years, for the first time heard such things as these, and drank in the desert these waters of eternal life. "For," says Calvin here,[1] "what truer matter of joy can be invented than when the Lord doth not only set open to us the treasures of His mercy, but poureth out His heart into us (that I may so speak), and giveth Him-

---

[1] Commentary *in loc.* I quote from Beveridge's translation (in the Calvin Society's publications).

self in His Son, that we may want nothing to perfect felicity? The heavens begin to look clear and the earth beginneth to be quiet then; the conscience being then delivered from the doleful and horrible feelings of God's wrath, being loosed from the tyranny of Satan, escaping out of the darkness of death, beholdeth the light of life."

There is little more to be added. That verse of the Received Text which contains an express profession of the Eunuch's faith as a condition of baptism, is very probably to be rejected as an interpolation, inserted at an early date by some who felt the absence of such a formula to be a hazardous precedent for the Church. That the convert was so forward of his own accord to ask for the rite of initiation which sealed the pardon of his sins, and Philip so forward to grant it; that the Divine Guide, at whose call Philip had come to the Eunuch, should have so suddenly rapt him away when his work was done; and that the new-made Christian found in his faith and in the abiding unction of the Holy One such joy as made the loss of his human teacher a thing indifferent—are all touches which still further show how open God had beforehand made this stranger for His gospel, and what easy and abundant entrance it found into his heart. It is probably an idle guess which ascribes to him the first foundation of a Church in Abyssinia. At the same time, there are few who will refuse to see in this incident, with the early Church, a fulfilment of that psalm-word which says that "Ethiopia shall stretch out her hands unto God,"[1] or who can reflect without emotion on the providence which so early scattered far afield the good news from

---

[1] See Psa. lxviii. 31; early quoted by the Fathers.

heaven. Formally the door of faith had not yet been opened to the Gentiles. Yet here is at least one sporadic case, long before the angel was sent to Cornelius. Already the young kingdom of God begins to gather into itself the children of God scattered abroad.[1] How many such children of God were there, and in what strange places concealed from view, to whom, in that age even, not to say throughout the long ages of previous preparation, no Philip was sent and no Christ preached! There is a fear we may do less than justice to the "other sheep which are not of this fold." The Queen of Sheba very long before, and this Queen of Ethiopia's chamberlain — of how many more are these the types, to whom just so much of God's precious truth percolated, like water through the under-rocks, that they could contrive to drink and live, although it was never possible for them to move one step nearer Him, after Whom, through the dark heathen night and in the waste heathen lands, their souls sighed and cried for longing! How many such shall come from East and West to judge us, on whose face the sunshine of Christ's truth lies full, and whose very feet are laved, whether we will or no, by the streams of His grace? to condemn those of us who are too well content to possess the light for us ever to open our eyes to see it, nor care to stoop, that, throwing away the dust of earth which fills our grasping, busy hands, we may quicken our souls with the refreshment, and cleanse them in the purity of Christ's Holy Gospel?

[1] Compare Jesus' words in John x. 16, as well as John's in xi. 52.

XV.
Saul's Conversion.
ESTO DE LUPE OVIS.

Acts ix. 1–9.

Compare Acts xxii. 1–11, and xxvi. 9–20.

Revised Version.

Now Saul, still breathing threats and murder against the disciples of the Lord, went to the High Priest, and asked from him letters to Damascus to the synagogues, so that if he should find any who were of the Way, both men and women, he should bring them bound to Jerusalem. And in the journey it happened that he was approaching Damascus, when suddenly there shone about him a light out of heaven; and falling on the earth, he heard a voice saying to him:

"Saul, Saul, why persecutest thou Me?"

And he said: "Who art Thou, Lord?" Then He:

"I am Jesus Whom thou persecutest. But rise and go into the city, and it shall be told thee what thou must do."

Now the men who were journeying with him were standing speechless, hearing the voice indeed, but beholding no one. And Saul rose from the earth, and on his eyes being opened, he saw nothing; but, leading him by the hand, they led him into Damascus. And he was three days without sight, and did neither eat nor drink.

XV.

THAT blessed war of aggression which Jesus Christ wages upon the evil world is a war which is made to maintain itself. Christ's soldiers are His captured enemies. Every soul won from resistance to the cross is marked at once with the cross-badge, and sent into the field to win others. Of this the most notable instance in Christian history is the conversion of Saul. Jesus Christ never encountered a bitterer or an abler foe; Jesus Christ never won a mightier captain for His army of light. Our narrative has brought us to one of the great days of the Church. What happened that noon-day near Damascus was the most signal intervention in her affairs which Christ has effected since He went to heaven. It did more than any other event after Pentecost to determine the current and colour the future of Christianity. To one who reflects how much the theology of the New Testament and the later developments of doctrine in the Western Church have owed to this "Doctor of the Gentiles," the interest of the event may appear to be mainly a theological one. Again, when we fix our attention on the revolution which was wrought by it in Saul himself, and find that we can trace in his own letters, down to his latest, ineffaceable traces of this crisis, we might be forgiven if we made its biographical importance most prominent: especially since we have from his own lips two earlier narratives of what took place—the one spoken to a fanatical mob of Jews from the stairs of the castle of Antonia—the other recited in the palace at Cæsarea, before the brilliant court of King Agrippa. To the student of St. Paul's life, these original accounts of his conversion are of the first value. Here, however, it is neither the theological nor the biographical bearings of the incident which hold the chief place. The record of Luke is that of a Church historian, and all remoter or more personal interests are subordinated to that which is strictly historical. St. Luke is not writing a life of his master, Paul. He is writing a history of the steps by which Jesus Christ led His infant Church, from its birth at the coming of the Holy Ghost on a hundred and twenty disciples, till it had filled the Roman empire with organised Christian communities. This scope of his work the author never forgets, and we must never forget it. Now, to the current Church history of the time the vast importance of what occurred at Damascus lay in this, that it won for the Christian cause the man who was to be its first and greatest Gentile missionary. It was one of the preliminary steps towards the disentanglement of the Church from Judaism and the accomplishment of its catholic mission as a gospel for all men. Other steps succeeded; especially Peter's vision at Joppa, and the baptism of Cornelius.[1] These are to be presently related. Meanwhile, this conversion of Saul, the arch-inquisitor of Pharisaism, while it brought to the Church an immediate

---

[1] Note how Luke alone gives the visions by which Saul and Ananias were brought together; and note further how this runs parallel to the preparation of Peter and Cornelius to meet each other, in chap. x.

SAUL'S CONVERSION.

rest from persecution, prepared for the ultimate extension of a free, un-Hebraic gospel to the great world beyond. It was the winning for the young enterprise of a soldier, who by his Antiochian ministry was in a few years to found the first Christian Church in heathendom; whose mission trip to Pisidia was to raise the question of Gentile liberty settled at the Jerusalem Synod; whose second mission tour was to open to Christ the doors of Greece; whose third was destined, through his arrest as an apostate Jew and his appeal to Nero, to conduct him to the very centre and capital of the imperial heathen world.

This historical importance of the fact, that such a man suddenly abandoned the Pharisaic party who opposed the new sect, and became the Church's chief apostle and foremost preacher, amply justifies the detail with which St. Luke has related the entire story. Not only the apparition on the road, but the three days' blindness, and the visit of Ananias, all of which formed so many stages in the conversion, are reported at length. To the first of these stages, however, a quite special importance attaches itself. The immediate occasion of Saul's change of life was quite as exceptional as the change itself was eventful. This was not the ordinary case of a man led to believe in Jesus through the evidence of others, or through the testimony of the Church, or through the pressure of spiritual need. It was not even an extraordinary case to which there are few parallels; it was a unique case which has no parallel. The agent in the conversion of this man was not a mortal man, his fellow; it was the Lord Jesus Christ Himself. Christ directly called His misguided persecutor to Himself; He called him in person. For the apparition which confronted Saul on the Damascus road was no inward vision, such as afterwards appeared to Ananias, no dreamlike impression, as if the inquisitor saw what was not there bodily to be seen, or heard words which did not really stir the air. It was not a seeing and hearing only "in the Spirit," as when John the seer saw mystic sights in Patmos. It was (as I read the records) a veritable return of Him Who went up from the Mount of Olives, to show Himself once more in His risen humanity to the eyes, and speak with His own lips in the ears, of a mortal. Such a personal manifestation of Him Whom the heavens have received is, I suppose, solitary in Christian history. The evidence for it therefore is, as it needs to be, exceptionally strong. No event in the sacred narrative, of which, from its very nature, only one person could be directly cognizant, is historically better supported than this. Of course such a transaction cannot be compared, in respect of evidence, with public events, like the death or the resurrection of Jesus, to which many eye and ear witnesses could speak. Here there could be no eye or ear witness, but one. His evidence alone is at first hand, and it is explicit. It was upon this fact—that he had personally seen his risen Master, just as the other apostles saw Him—that Paul rested his claim to the privileges of the apostolate. "Am I not an apostle? ... Have I not seen Jesus Christ our Lord?"[1] "He was seen of James; then of all the apostles. And last of all He was seen of me also, as of one born out of due time."[2] Further, in reporting the words which he had heard from Ananias, when on the third day his sight returned, Paul cited them thus: "The God of our fathers hath chosen thee, that thou shouldest know His will, and see that Just

[1] 1 Cor. ix. 1.   [2] Ibid. xv. 7, 8.

One, and shouldest hear the voice of His mouth."[1] The evidence of Paul himself, thus confirmed by the vision of Ananias, was plainly accepted as conclusive by the Christian Church at the time; for it was only after Barnabas had declared to the older apostles at Jerusalem how the new convert "had seen the Lord in the way," that his apostolic claims received public recognition.[2]

Possibly it may be due to the emphasis so justly laid by the sacred records on this solitary appearance of the ascended Master, that very little has been told us of the internal history of the conversion. Its outward details we know; the great objective cause of it, the glorious One Whose face illumined, Whose voice thrilled into new life the soul of the Pharisee, has been left conspicuous—a figure of light—in the foreground. But we are not told, what we should have greatly liked to know, through what preparatory workings of soul the persecutor had been prepared for such a crisis, or what struggles accompanied the new birth of a nature so powerful as his, and filled up these three days of lonely and blind silence. As we follow the impatient traveller down to the moment when that sudden light prostrated him, and as we dwell upon those dark hours of secret thought through which he passed in the house of Judas, we can hardly help feeling it to be strange (though it may well be believed to be wise) that so little has been told us of the interior and spiritual history of this grandest of all conversions. Yet, let us check ourselves. Who can tell the spiritual processes of any conversion? Or why should we pry too curiously into that mysterious and sacred place, where, under cover of darkness, the Spirit of God broods over a soul whom He will

[1] Acts xxii. 14.   [2] Ibid. ix. 27.

renew of His great grace into the life and likeness of the Eternal Son?

At the same time, the general nature of the change which unexpectedly passed upon Saul, can be pretty well made out from what we know of the man, both before and after it.

Down to the moment when the glory smote him, this man was a Hebrew of the most extreme type.[1] A Benjamite of pure blood, and by birth a Pharisee, he had been educated in the chief rabbinical school of the holy city. In ardent study, in knowledge of patristic traditions, in zeal for the God of Israel and for His chosen race, in the strict observance of Pharisaic religion, he claims to have outstripped all his contemporary fellow-students under Gamaliel's tuition. With that intensity which was always his leading characteristic, this young Jew became a red-hot zealot for Judaism; this Pharisee followed Pharisaic prescriptions with the "most strait" observance. So far as punctilious keeping of Mosaic ritual and the customary piety of his time could go, his "righteousness, which was of the law, was blameless." Nor was this, in his case, as in the case of so many in his time, a solemn farce, cloaking secret immorality. This young man's soul was true, and it was bent on being righteous with its whole might. He thirsted after righteousness with a noble thirst which only very noble natures know. So far, therefore, as he knew or understood what would please God, he laboured in utter sincerity to please Him. But the law, as Judaism expounded it, was a very shallow thing, and the sort

[1] Compare the following: Phil. iii. 7; Gal. i. 14; Acts xxii. 3, xxvi. 5.

of righteousness which it required was quite within the reach of any man in earnest. Saul was singularly free by temperament from the lower appetites.[1] The currents of his nature ran towards a rigorous and proud morality. To such a man Pharisaic virtue was easy. He kept the letter of the law. He observed every detail of ritual. He shunned Gentile defilement. He boasted in his knowledge of God's will. He thanked God he was not as other men.[2] Such a school of morality, a morality of the letter and not of the spirit, is a very hotbed of pride. These were the days in which young Saul was "alive without the law," going about to establish his own blameless righteousness, and trusting to his own merits as a "gain," in which, beyond others,[3] he might safely boast.

It is easy to see that to such a man the preaching of repentance and faith in the cross of a crucified Deliverer from sin must have been gall and wormwood. The new sect insisted that Saul and his school had misread their Bibles and misunderstood God; that their boasted righteousness was nothing; that they had no less need to repent and confess their sins than other men; and that, so far from being favourites of heaven or children of God, they could only enter into God's kingdom by the help of One Whom they and their agents had persecuted unto death. To Saul, as an orthodox Jew, all this must have appeared to be flat blasphemy against Moses and the God of Moses. To Saul, as a self-satisfied and righteous Pharisee, it was like a personal insult. Accordingly, with his usual impetuosity, he flung himself into the work of stamping out a heresy which, on public and personal

[1] See 1 Cor. vii. 7.
[2] Compare again Rom. ii. 17 ff, x. 3, vii. 10; Phil. iii.
[3] Cf. his words, "I more," in Phil. iii. 4.

grounds alike, he had such good reason to hate. He led the inquisition after suspected persons. He voted, as we have seen, for the death of the arrested. He hunted the sect from town to town. He volunteered his services to the Sanhedrim as a commissioner to purge even Damascus from the taint of Nazaritism.

All this while I think it probable that Saul's mind was not quite at ease. It may be too much to say that he lashed himself into greater rage against the new "Way,"[1] or pushed his restless hostility to an extreme, just on purpose to crush down secret misgivings which began to stir in his bosom. Nor can we now discover how far the holy face of dying Stephen, lit up with the light of God, may have haunted and troubled the memory of the man who guarded the robes of the witnesses. But at least one can gather from those first suggestive words which Jesus spoke to him, while he lay prone, with muffled face, upon the road, that all had not been quite serene in the soul of the persecutor. Oxen do not kick back against the prickings of the ox-goad,[2] without feeling pain and restlessness. Jesus must have been before this trying to guide into the right "way" His furious and mistaken assailant. A few words heard in controversy with Stephen, it might be, or some meek victim's patience, a secret craving of Saul's own deepest heart, or a breath in quiet hour from the Spirit of God,—something must have stirred within this man, who appeared to other men so resolute, and

[1] His name for it at this time. See Acts ix. 2 (xiii. 10 ?), xvi. 17, xxii. 4, xxiv. 14. Cf. Luke's own use of the same expression in xviii. 25, 26, xix. 9, 23, xxiv. 22. The complete form is "God's way of salvation," as opposed to the Hebrew "way."

[2] The words, "It is hard for thee to kick against the pricks," are genuine in Paul's own account, Acts xxvi. 14, whence they have been improperly transferred to the Received Text of ix. 5.

who told himself that he was so unquestionably in the right, a suspicion or a fear that, possibly, after all, the Nazarenes might not be altogether wrong. Against such prickings Saul had kicked. Who, from his own experience, cannot understand Saul's case? To whom has it never happened that, when he felt well contented with his religious state, and pleased to think he was so near to heaven's favour, some ghastly doubt looked up of a sudden to trouble him,— some fear which refused to be reasoned away, that after all his standing might not turn out to be so very safe, or his religion so very perfect? Such occasional misgivings, promptly repelled, leave no trace behind, nor do they alter in the least the main purpose and course of a man's life. It is possible that Saul scarcely admitted to himself that he had misgivings. He certainly would have admitted them to no one else. His persecuting ardour burned none the less hot for them. Having caught sight of that scene, one of earth's loveliest, where the old delicious city of Damascus gleams white by its watercourses among green orchards, ravishing the eyes of the traveller weary with days of toilsome march across untilled wastes; having, I say, caught, a little before noon, his first glimpse of this, from the heights which bound upon the south the gem-like valley of the Abana, Saul pressed on, long past the usual hour for halt, pressed on beneath the fiercest midday sun, eager only to do the God of Israel service by cleansing so fair a bit of earth from those who were perverting the faith of Jehovah's chosen ones.

Suddenly, in a blaze of glory which drowned the sun at noon, the Man appeared Whom Saul believed to be a dead impostor. The shock which this apparition gave to his whole nature was as severe as it was sudden. Everything speaks of instantaneous and utter collapse. His physical frame felt it in being cast powerless to the earth, in the blinding of his eyes through excess of light, and in the feebleness under which for days he lay. It is to be traced also in those few and timid words which he was able to stammer out: "Who art Thou, Lord?" "What shall I do, Lord?" These are the words of one who is broken down, not in physical fright only, but by a blow which has snapped the strength of old pride on which all his former life rested, and thus for the moment crushed the man into the helplessness of a child. When we see him rise, staggering, groping, humbly letting his scared attendants guide him, confused and bewildered, to his lodgings, we have a picture in his outward of his inward state. The discovery of one single fact had undermined in a moment the whole foundation on which Saul had been building from his boyhood—was now working hard in his manhood. That fact was this—That the Nazarene is risen: is God! It took three whole days and nights of solitary mental struggle and spiritual agony before the strong man worked his way, by God's help, to the cordial acceptance of this fact, and of all that it meant for him; yet, from the very first instant on the road, he must have felt, at least, that it made his faith, his religion, his pride, his whole life, his very self, an utter and sheer mistake. If Jesus is the Lord, he, Saul, had always been hopelessly and fatally wrong. Nay, it may take more than three days' solitude, it may take years in Arabia, and a world of thinking, before he will quite recover himself, or build up a new life into such strength and compactness as the old one had. But at least the old is shattered at a blow, and for ever. It rises, it lives, no more. One look into a dead man's—what do I say?—into a living Man's face, has done that. Jesus lives, and Saul dies. Gamaliel's pupil, Sanhedrim inquisitor, blameless Pharisee, slayer of Stephen,—this old man is dead.

What those meditations were which filled up the three days before he recovered himself sufficiently to pray, we do not certainly know. I think we shall not greatly err, however, if we conceive the chief experience of these three days to have been the discovery of a spiritual law, which condemned his legal righteousness as (in his own words) "loss," and "dung."[1] Nor is it very hard to guess how this discovery might be made. Saul needed no man now to tell him that his way of pleasing God had been a hideous blunder, since it had led him to persecute God's Christ. But if such punctilious legal obedience as he had been straining after was proved to be consistent with the grossest possible breach of the law in its spirit, then Saul's dialectic was acute enough to see that it must be the spirit, and not the letter, of the law in which the secret of righteousness has to be sought. Nay, there was little need for dialectic. The spiritual sense of the man, purged now from pride and illumined by the Spirit of God, saw what false education and self-righteousness had hitherto kept him from seeing,—that "the law is spiritual." The moment that spiritual law of love to God and man, a law of heart-motives and not overt acts, came to him, sin revived, and he died.[2] Back through all his past life his memory must have gone ranging during that awful interval. Bit by bit what he had called "righteousness" became to his astonished soul ungodliness, pride,

[1] See Phil. iii. 8.   [2] Cf. Rom. vii. 9.

uncharity, sin; what he had called "gain" appeared utter loss. In the end, when the need of atoning blood, of divine forgiveness, and of a new spirit of life grew within his soul into clear consciousness, he began to look up out of his prostration and collapse. God began to reveal His Son in him. Hopeful desires formed themselves. His mind reverted for help to the names of those very disciples whom he had come to arrest. In a sweet vision he seemed to see one of these friends of Jesus come in to him, where he lay in his darkness, to give him light. Inner light, more even than the light of the eyes, his soul craved; and, grown meek now through all this prolonged spiritual struggle, behold, he prayed! He Whose first coming in person, by the way, had brought judgment with it, darkness, and feebleness, and almost death, came now, a second time, by the gentle words of His servant and the blessed sacraments of His Church. So coming, He brought light and peace and the hope of a new and better life.

I have said that no parallel, rarely any approximation, is to be found in later conversions to this of Saul. Yet in one inward, and in one outward respect, it has been often paralleled. Substantially it is repeated in the history of ten thousand souls. The same appalling discovery that the exterior observances of piety and virtue, which one took for righteousness before God, are no righteousness in His sight at all, but "filthy rags,"[1] unspiritual and unprofitable; this same discovery has been made times upon times since Paul made it. It is a common type of conversion among the well-trained, well-conducted of every Christian age. And though it is not

[1] Isa. lxiv. 6.

often that God's disclosure of it bursts upon any one with such a violent catastrophe as we have here, rending to its base a strong man's strength, yet it will be the wisdom of us all to search and see whether or not we have, in any fashion or at any time, made the Pauline discovery and learnt the Pauline lesson.

In another respect this story is not exceptional. One unexpected day has often revolutionised a life. We all live in the presence of spiritual forces which may at any moment get unlooked-for access to us. A stray word, a new acquaintance, the book we open, or some sudden disaster, may prove the very turning of our history. None can tell how events, which are diligently planned for quite other ends, may really be, in God's hands, leading us blindly up to the predestined moment which is to make all things for us new. Yet it is no man's business to remain an idle waiter on such critical moments of providence, since to all the question shall be at last put—"Why hast thou kicked against My goads?" It is in ordinary quiet hours, through every-day instruments, and within our own secret hearts, that for the most part God is now striving to prick men up to duty and guide them into the right way. Nor is there any room to expect that, if we stifle such interior suggestions of truth, or rebel against that guiding hand, Christ will ever meet us, as He met Paul, in a shape we cannot resist, to turn us by sheer force, as it were, from our mistaken path. We know enough, and we have reminders enough of what we know. Therefore let us hear His voice, which, if we will hear, we may; and yield to His touch, which, if we only choose, we shall feel.

XVI.
After Conversion.

DE OVE, PASTOR.

Acts ix. 10-30.   Compare Acts xxii. 12-21.

Revised Version.

But there was a certain disciple in Damascus, by name Ananias; and the Lord said to him in a vision, " Ananias ;" and he said, " Behold, I am here, Lord." And the Lord to him :

" Arise, go to the lane which is called ' Straight,' and seek in the house of Judas, Saul by name, of Tarsus. For behold, he is praying, and saw a man, Ananias by name, coming in and laying his hand on him, so that he might recover sight."

And Ananias answered :

" Lord, I heard from many about this man, what evils he did to Thy saints in Jerusalem; and here he hath authority from the chief priests to bind all who are callers upon Thy name."

But the Lord said to him .

" Go, for this man is to Me a vessel of election, for the purpose of bearing My name before both Gentiles and kings and children of Israel. For I [Myself] will show him what things he must suffer on account of My name."

So Ananias went away, and entered into the house, and laying his hands on him, said :

" Saul, brother, the Lord has sent me—Jesus Who appeared to thee in the way by which thou camest, so that thou mightst recover sight and be filled with the Holy Ghost."

And immediately there fell from his eyes as it were scales; and he recovered sight, and rose and was baptized, and having taken food was strengthened.

And he was with the disciples who were in Damascus some days, and immediately in the synagogues he proclaimed Jesus, that He is the Son of God. But all who heard were amazed, and said:

"Is not this he who wasted in Jerusalem the callers on this Name? and has come here for this purpose, that he might bring them bound to the chief priests?"

But Saul went on strengthening the more, and confounded the Jews who dwelt in Damascus, proving that this is the Christ. But when a good many days were fulfilled, the Jews plotted together to despatch him; but their plot became known to Saul. They were also watching the gates both day and night, so that they might despatch him; but his disciples took and let him down by night through the wall, lowering [him] in a basket. And when he arrived at Jerusalem, he attempted to join himself to the disciples, and they were all afraid of him, not believing that he was a disciple. But Barnabas took and brought him to the apostles, and related to them how in the way he saw the Lord, and that He spoke to him, and how in Damascus he had been bold in the name of Jesus. And he was with them going in and going out at Jerusalem. Being bold in the name of the Lord, he was both speaking and disputing with the Hellenists. But they were taking in hand to despatch him: and when the brethren were aware of that, they brought him down to Cæsarea, and sent him on to Tarsus.

XVI

SAUL was still lying blind and weak upon his bed, only the tumult of a spiritual convulsion, the inner struggles of a new birth, were over; so that he lay placid and humbled, praying not without hope. Lying thus, he was aware of some one's hands[1] laid gently on his head, and a kindly voice just over him said: "Brother Saul, the Lord sent me—Jesus, Who appeared to thee in the way as thou camest—that thou mightest receive back sight and be filled with the Holy Spirit." Opening his eyes, from which it seemed to him as if scales fell at that word,[2] they rested on the same face which he had just been contemplating in fancy in a pleasant vision that had come to him through the darkness; and Ananias, the messenger of the Lord, was at once no stranger, but a brother, welcome as an angel of God. The last face seen before noonday turned to midnight, had been the face of the wonderful Divine Man, Whom, in His saints, Saul had ignorantly persecuted. The first face seen, when sweet morning light revisited his eyes, was the face of one whom Jesus sent, or rather, in whom Jesus came, to save. If the Lord was present in the saints of His Church to suffer

---

[1] Or "hand." In ver. 12 the readings vary. Tischendorf prefers χεῖρα, but A, B, C, E, and Sin. have pl. In ver. 17 it is certainly plural.

[2] So we may take the ὡσεί. See Hackett on Acts, *in loc.*

with them, and in their persons to be scourged and slain, He was no less present in His Church members to work through them, and by their words to bless with comfort and peace the penitent persecutor. At the voice of a plain disciple, otherwise unknown to history, Jesus restored sight to the eyes which alone of mortal eyes had been permitted to look upon His glory. By the hands of the same disciple, Jesus imparted the gift of the Holy Ghost to a " chosen vessel," Who in spiritual gifts was not to be behind the very chiefest apostles. Ananias baptized St. Paul, as if to teach that the Church is instinct with life through all its true members, however lowly. Jesus, Who is everywhere in His body, pours His Spirit through its meanest parts. The least may be His organ of ministry to the greatest; or rather, no instrument is little when Christ's hand wields it, nor any soul mean whom Christ inhabits.

Baptism and the communication of the Spirit through imposition of hands were the usual rites by which a new convert passed into the full fellowship of the Church; and they meant exactly the same thing to Saul as to any other convert. He made the customary profession of faith, invoking the name of Jesus as his Lord,[1] and received the customary seal of the forgiveness of his sins.[2] There was only this peculiarity about the baptism of Saul, that it was administered at the express command of Jesus. In this, as in everything else connected with His apostle's call, the Master acted throughout in person. "Though Jesus Himself baptized not—but His disciple,"[3] yet it

---

[1] See Acts xxii. 16. The reading is αὐτοῦ; but the gloss, τοῦ κυρίου Ἰησοῦ, shows how the early Church understood it, and no doubt rightly. [2] Ibid. "wash away thy sins."
[3] Cf. John iv. 2.

was not on His own responsibility that Ananias ventured to number among the brethren a man who, two days before, had been their keenest foe. It was on the same warrant as Peter afterwards had to receive Cornelius—the express orders of the King. Thus, in those days, did the lately departed Chief continue to interpose His personal direction, when critical moments arrived in the administration of His young Church.

Yet while Saul's baptism meant the same as that of any other convert, it is very possible that he submitted to that solemn sacrament with a far deeper insight into its meaning than most of the early converts attained. Expressions in his letters[1] show what importance he attached to it at a later period. If we recall the experience through which he had just been passing, it will appear that even at the time it must have come to him charged with a world of spiritual significance. That it meant the washing away of the guilt of sin was plain; and it was a vast change for Saul the Pharisee to confess himself a guilty sinner, in need of washing. But the consciousness of sin with which Saul had been penetrated during these last three days, was not by any means exhausted in the simple recognition of the fact that he, like other men, had done things which he ought not to have done. It was not just through recalling isolated actions, by which he had literally transgressed a command of God, that Saul came to feel himself guilty. To some men, whose sinning has been of another type than his, the conviction of guilt does come in this way. Flagrant misdeeds, wilful and aggravated, and blacker than the rest of life, stand up before the consciences of such men to condemn them. Saul, however, had been

[1] See Rom. vi. 3–6; Gal. iii. 27; Col. ii. 12; Tit. iii. 5.

finding out, not so much that he had done sins, as that he was sin; that his very nature, not at its worst, but at its best, was flesh; that in it dwelt absolutely no good thing; that it was impossible for it to please God; that indeed its essence was enmity against God. He found that the more he had tried to serve God the less he had loved Him. Love alone, he now saw, could be the fulfilling of the real law, that law which is spiritual; whereas, in all his own attempts to keep the law, there had been no touch or breath of love: only pride, and fear, and dislike. He found that the more closely he apprehended the spirit in which a true son of God must serve his Father, the more unattainable became that filial spirit; since every attempt to drag himself, under the constraint of divine commands, to do what is commanded, only provoked him either to slavish dread or to rebellious resistance. All that was in him rose up and refused to be subject to the law of God, once it was perceived to be a law of love.

Now, where sin has been realised in this fashion as the very principle of one's unrenewed nature, nothing will satisfy the soul short of the destruction of that old man and the regeneration of a new. Propitiation through blood indeed there must be for the remission of sins that are past; "peace through the blood of the cross;"[1] and Saul was now for the first time grasping the "faithful saying" that "Christ Jesus came into the world to save sinners."[2] Yet even this will not meet the case unless the principle of the old life—the inward law of dislike to God and His will—be at the same time slain, and a new power of spiritual love and childlike obedience created within the soul. This, and nothing short of this, was what Saul

[1] See Rom. iii. 25; Col. i. 20. [2] 1 Tim. i. 15.

had begun to find in the cross of the Nazarene. In it his sin was condemned and slain. In it the law was visibly satisfied, magnified, and abolished. In it death even was put to death, and the sinner redeemed from the curse. But more than all these, in it his own enmity against God was slain. It is impossible to dislike any more a God Who is no longer threatening or commanding on pain of death, but Who, for His great love wherewith He loved us when we were dead in sins, has died for us, to justify us freely by His grace. The old carnal mind, which is not subject to the law of God, cannot survive this death of the Son of God. The cross kills it. Saul—the former carnal, self-righteous, God-disliking Saul—was crucified with Christ. Nevertheless he lived, because Christ lived. If the cross had proved fatal to his old self-righteous life, Jesus risen became the source of a new one. He will henceforth be a limb of Jesus. He will let Jesus animate him. He will lend himself to the service, he will become the slave of Him Who loved him and gave Himself for him. He will know nothing now—do nothing—boast of nothing—but what is done in him through the Son of God, by Whom, while ignorantly persecuting Him, he has been so suddenly and marvellously snatched in overabounding mercy from eternal death.

What a mighty revolution did it symbolise, that baptism at the hands of Ananias! From darkness to light —from death to life—from Satan to God! what words of contrast could then or afterwards describe the magnitude of a change which turned the whole nature of one of the strongest men God ever made, to run in precisely the opposite direction ; which made him love with passionate devotion One Whom he had been persecuting with fiercest hate; which transformed a Pharisee into a Saint; and prepared the man who was ravaging God's flock like a bloodthirsty wolf, to become a good shepherd, willing to lay down his life for the sheep. Surely it was out of the remembrance of his own life-crisis that Paul wrote these words to Corinth: "If any man be in Christ, he is a new creature: old things are passed away: behold, all things are become new."[1]

There was still, however, a great deal to come and go before Saul could be called ready for the special work to which God had destined him. Revolutions in spiritual history are often enough abrupt, rapid, and decisive, as this one was; yet are they almost always succeeded by a more slow and gradual development. In the words which the Lord addressed in vision to Ananias, and which were by him communicated to Saul,[2] it was foretold that he should bear witness to what he had seen of Christ's glory. This function he was not slow to begin to discharge at Damascus. But something had also been said of a mission to heathen nations, in the execution of which he was both to encounter serious perils and to testify for his Master before the face of kings. The destined dignity of the apostolate, and the exceptional character of his future work as the Apostle of the Gentiles, are plainly enough foreshadowed in these words of Christ at that early date. It is doubtful, however, how far Saul himself comprehended their significance at the time. It rather appears from

[1] 2 Cor. v. 17.
[2] See Acts ix. 15, where they are spoken by the Lord to Ananias, and in xxii. 14 repeated by Ananias to Saul. In xxvi. 16, they appear as if spoken immediately by the Lord to Saul on the road, the middle agent being dropped from the narrative.

the story, as if it was only after a pretty long period of probation and schooling that he was led up through various providences to the great task for which the Lord had destined him. One finds no evidence even of apostolic authority, certainly none of any ministry among Gentiles, until after Saul had been for some time settled at home in his native town. Yet we know, on his own undoubted evidence,[1] that three years had elapsed from the date of his conversion before he paid that first hasty visit to Jerusalem which ended in his being sent to Tarsus. Even if we understand these "three years," after the Hebrew manner of computation, as meaning only one entire year and part of two others, we get an interval longer by a good deal than the narrative of St. Luke would lead the reader to guess. Over this section of Paul's life, indeed, Luke hastens so cursorily that we are compelled to supplement his account from other sources. Why he does so I confess myself unable to decide. It could hardly be from ignorance that the sojourn in Arabia was passed by. Luke had been Paul's companion too long not to have heard of so singular and weighty a passage in his history. It certainly was not from ignorance that the vision in the temple was left out at this point, since it is related in a subsequent chapter.[2] I can only suppose that the various steps by which the future missionary-apostle was trained, through retirement, experience, and private revelations, for his lifework, did not appear to this writer and to Him Who guided the writing, to be needful for our understanding of the Church's history. Not the less is it our duty to make the most we can of what has been told, endeavouring, by comparison of other passages, to understand how the

---

[1] Gal. i. 18.   [2] Acts xxii. 17, ff.

Lord completed what He began on the Damascus road—the preparation of His " chosen vessel."

After a few days spent in quiet Christian intercourse with his new brethren, the little flock which he had come from Jerusalem to scatter, it was deemed advisable that Saul should publicly commit himself to the new cause by announcing in the synagogues the grounds of his conversion. He did so by proclaiming to his astonished countrymen that Jesus Whom he had come to persecute was certainly nothing less than the Son of God. This first preaching of Saul would seem to have been less controversial than it afterwards became. Perhaps it was literally not much more than a full recital of what he had seen and heard. What had taken place outside the city gate must have been known to the whole Jewish population, so far as the outward facts of it went, at least. The blaze of light, the inarticulate voice, the sudden blindness of the commissioner—every one had heard of these strange things from Saul's companions, and every one desired to know the explanation of them. By simply telling, on his faith as an honest man, how he had actually seen the crucified Teacher of Nazareth and heard Him speak, Saul could, in the first instance, preach Christ most effectually. It is no wonder that the Jews were struck dumb with utter wonder. Had any fanatical adherent of the new sect produced a tale of marvellous interviews with the dead Man Whom they worshipped, it would have been easy to set it down to a heated fancy. But when the rabid foe of the sect, the trusted emissary of the Sanhedrim, whose prepossessions ran no less violently against such a delusion than his shrewd and powerful intellect, seemed to secure him from it—when this man came forward to say that the dead Jesus was alive, that he had himself both seen and spoken with Him, and that the new sect was right in worshipping Him as Jehovah's Son, the Lord of Glory, it was not so easy to set such testimony aside. A plain unvarnished tale of personal experience in religion, even when that experience has nothing marvellous about it, will often arrest and impress persons who are incredulous of spiritual truth. Only, unless the hearer have an honest and willing heart, such impressions are likely to be very transient. Paul soon found that his countrymen began to listen to his narrative, with less astonishment indeed than at first, but with not a whit more faith in it. It is a very frequent trial to new converts, that what has struck them so sharply and seems to themselves unspeakably certain and precious, meets with indifference or scepticism from everybody else. To Saul this was only the first of a thousand trials of a like sort he was fated to meet with ere his work was done. On him, however, it seems to have had (what indeed it has on most robust and manly natures) a bracing influence. "He gathered strength the more." He dropped the merely personal testimony, which was losing whatever force it originally possessed, and out of the Old Testament writings, by collation of texts and force of reasoning, he sought next to shut up the intelligent Jews of Damascus to the conclusion that Jesus must be their promised Messiah. Utilising his rabbinical scholarship in a way he never expected, and borrowing those very arguments against which, when Stephen used them in the Cilician synagogue at Jerusalem, he had stoutly argued, Saul made his first essay in that Christian exegesis of prophecy in which he was afterwards to have such ample practice and surpassing success.

It may even have been this attempt to explain the Scriptures in harmony with his new creed, which first suggested to him a retirement from Damascus for purposes of study and reflection. At any rate, we know that he did withdraw into Arabia, and there are some things which make it probable that in Arabia he spent the greater portion of the first three years after his conversion. It would not need a long interval after his return to Damascus in fresh force, to stir up the Jews to that plot from which he escaped so narrowly; and one can better understand the suspicion of the Jerusalem Church on his arrival there, if, since his conversion, he had been for the most part living a retired life in an out-of-the-way place, than if he had already been for years a public preacher of the faith at Damascus. This would be the case, whether Saul was occupied with evangelistic work in Arabia, or only secluded himself for meditation and prayer. On that point we have nothing but probabilities to guide us, and each reader will lean in the direction to which his own temperament inclines him. If any very active and ardent disciple thinks so fiery a preacher as Saul could not keep silence for a year or two, that he might commune with his own heart and with God, I shall not dispute. At the same time, the parallel cases of Moses, Elijah, the Baptist, and (beyond all parallel) of the Lord Jesus Himself, together with the need which so many of God's most eminent servants in later times have felt, of long and sometimes of frequent retirement to those lonely retreats where the fire of spiritual enthusiasm can best be cherished into a glow through still heart-communings with the Eternal and His truth—all this persuades me to think that his steady zeal, which was to burn unconsumed for thirty years, no less than the profound and systematic knowledge of God's whole earlier and later revelation, which made St. Paul the teacher of the New Testament Church, was won in solitary study, prayer, and revelations from heaven, when, in the back wastes of Arabia, he nourished his mighty heart for the labours and sorrows of his ministry. The St. Paul whom we know in the later chapters of Acts, and in the marvellous epistles which follow in the canon, is a very altered man from the youthful and unchastened Saul whom we have up to this moment followed. One need hardly scruple to credit his so well authenticated, and yet so strangely concealed, sojourn in Arabia with a large share in that alteration. It may, to be sure, seem a superfluous training to some men, in an age so busy, social, and superficial as our own,—an age in which hardly any one ever is alone, or, if he be, deems it a calamity against which he must provide by paltry pastimes, or from which he must take refuge in sheer want of thought. To persons whose own character has run to shallowness through perpetual contact with many people and many things, or who never sat down to think alone for one good hour of any single thing which is worth thinking about, it may possibly appear absolute waste of time to send this "chosen vessel," like a hermit, into Arabia, while the world was waiting for its Christian message. For all that, there are only two ways of ripening to their best men of deep and wide natures, or rather one way to which two things belong, and these are solitude and thought. If the soul you propose to rear is to be, not great only, but great for God—which is the greatest of all—and be fit to do His highest work on earth, then must you add a third thing to these two, and say, solitude, thought, and prayer.

With a gospel which he had "neither received of man, nor been taught, but by the revelation of Jesus Christ,"[1] Saul returned at length to Damascus. Still the way was not yet clear for his special apostolic work. To the inward fitness of the man there were still to be joined the public authentication and destination of the apostle. He was as yet unknown to the Church, and the special sphere of his labour was unknown even to himself. No doubt Saul must by this time have been aware that he was to play a great part, and be a special messenger of his Master. Yet we find him waiting to be led, by the hand of Divine Providence, into that particular place where his work was to lie, just as we all, if we are honest servants of God, must learn His will for ourselves through the developments of His providence. He tried Damascus, but that field of labour was soon closed against him. From a Jewish plot of assassination, which was the more likely to succeed because it could use the military force of the Ethnarch, who happened at the moment to hold the city for an Arabian chieftain,[2] Saul escaped by night through a window which opened on the outside of the city wall.[3] It was the first of many "hairbreadth 'scapes." He went to Jerusalem. There no door seemed at first to open; for the disciples remembered his activity in persecution three years before, and were suspicious. Even when the kind offices of his friend Barnabas, the Cypriote, introduced him to Peter and James, the only apostles then in the Holy City, and when through their assurances

---

[1] Gal. i. 12. [2] 2 Cor. xi. 32.

[3] Either projecting over the wall on which it was built, as in illustration in Conybeare and Howson; or a window pierced through the city wall, as Hackett saw them in Damascus (Com. *in loc.*) and Thomson at Sidon (*Land and Book*, p. 97).

AFTER CONVERSION.

the Church consented to welcome him, the door thus opened was in a few days violently closed again. Saul had set his heart on repairing his former ravages, by preaching Christ where he had first made himself conspicuous by persecuting Christians, at the focus and headquarters of Jewish bigotry. Back therefore to the familiar synagogues, in which he had disputed with Stephen, he went, eager to take up Stephen's broken work. He seems to have hoped with the hopefulness of young and inexperienced zeal, that his testimony would count for something with those men by whose side he had in his ignorance fought against God. If ever an honest convert might expect to persuade his former friends, it was Saul. Before he had been more than a fortnight in Jerusalem, his old Hellenistic comrades were doing to him as he and they together had done to Stephen; "they were going about to slay him." It was not the danger to his life which made this trial so exceedingly bitter. It was the discovery that, after all, his words for his Master carried no weight, his ministry found no "free course." It was the disappointment of his cherished craving to win from death those very men among his misguided countrymen whom he himself had helped to misguide. He was depressed, baffled, perplexed. The Lord had bade him preach, and promised to use him for great ends. Yet in Damascus the Jews, in Jerusalem the Hellenists, refuse him and hate him. His words find no entrance; his work bears no fruit. The brethren were urging him to flee; but to what end? Where can he look for better hope of success? What would the Lord have him to do?

In this state of mind Saul had gone up to the familiar temple courts, to pray for light and guidance, when in a trance he received from the Lord Jesus a new indication of his appointed mission. In answer to his prayer, it seemed as if Jesus stood before him in the temple [1] and bade him do what the brethren urged, by quitting Jerusalem at once: "They will not receive thy testimony concerning Me." It proves how much Saul's heart was bent on succeeding with his work, in that before all other places, that in the teeth of so express an assurance, he ventured to urge reasons why his testimony might be expected to avail in Jerusalem. Just because they knew so well how he had imprisoned and beat the believers, what part, too, he had taken in the martyrdom of Stephen, Saul hoped that his own conversion might become the instrument of theirs. A second time, and more imperatively than before, came the hard word, "Depart." This time, however, there was graciously opened to the servant a clearer glimpse into the work towards which he was being blindly led or driven by the Master. "Depart," said the Lord, "for I will send thee far hence unto the Gentiles." So he arose and suffered the brethren to lead him forth quickly to Cæsarea, and thence, for greater safety, home to Tarsus. Thus doors were shut one after another, that at last the feet of the great Missionary might be ready to enter in at one undreamt-of door, which should by-and-by be opened: the door behind which there lay in unvisited darkness the mighty civilised peoples of the west—Greece and Rome and Gaul, and the hope of a new Christendom that should be, and the life of all the world.

[1] In the same place where Isaiah saw His glory (Isa. vi.; John xii. 41) so long before, and received his fruitless mission to prophesy to his unheeding countrymen, did the Messiah discharge Saul from that vain errand, and send him to more productive heathen fields.

AFTER CONVERSION.

While thus one messenger was being prepared of God, and kept in readiness at Tarsus, he who held the keys for Christ was elsewhere being led against his will to open the kingdom to the Gentiles at Cæsarea.

Dare we imagine that there is no Divinity Who shapes the ends of men? or shall we doubt whether the hands which hold the threads of earthly providence be after all those very hands which were "nailed for our advantage to the bitter tree"?

XVII.
An Apostolic Tour of Inspection.

Διεγείρω ὑμῶν ἐν ὑπομνήσει τὴν εἰλικρινὴ διάνοιαν μνησθῆναι τῶν προειρημένων ῥημάτων.

Acts ix. 31-43.

Revised Version.

Now then the church through the whole of Judæa and Galilee and Samaria had peace, being edified and walking in the fear of the Lord, and was multiplied by the exhortation of the Holy Ghost.

And it came to pass that Peter, passing through all [the saints], came down also to the saints who dwelt at Lydda, and found there a certain man, Æneas by name, who for eight years had lain on a mattress, being paralyzed. And Peter said to him:

"Æneas, Jesus the Christ healeth thee. Arise and make the bed for thyself."

And immediately he arose, and all the inhabitants of Lydda and the Saron [plain] saw him; who also turned to the Lord.

But in Joppa was a certain disciple, Tabitha by name, which being interpreted is called Dorcas. She was full of good works and alms, which she was accustomed to do. But it happened in those days that after falling sick she died; and having washed her, they laid her in an upper room. But Lydda being near to Joppa, the disciples who had heard that Peter was in that [town], sent two men to him, entreating: "Do not grudge to come on as far as to us." So Peter arose and went with them; whom on his arrival they led up to the upper room, and there stood beside him all the widows wailing and showing tunics and robes such as Dorcas used to make while she was with them. But having put them all forth, Peter bent his knees and prayed; and when he had turned to the body, he said: "Tabitha, arise." And she opened her eyes, and seeing Peter, sat up. Then giving her his hand, he raised her up, and when he had called the saints and the widows, he presented her alive. And it became known throughout the whole of Joppa, and many believed upon the Lord. And it came to pass that he stayed a good many days in Joppa with a certain Simon, a tanner.

XVII.

AT this point closes one long and important section of our narrative.[1] The raid upon the Church which began with the murder of the first deacon ended after the conversion of the chief persecutor. It has been seen how the persecution sprang out of the dislike felt by narrow conservative Judaism for the spiritual and catholic teaching of Stephen; how it led to the planting of a Church in Samaria, and the spread of evangelists throughout every province of Palestine; and how at last a greater successor to the dead Stephen was won in the person of Saul. From their own point of view, the traditional or Pharisaic faction had made little by that outbreak of hostility. The heresy which they thought to stamp out was only scattered far afield beyond any stamping-out of theirs. Under Providence, a vast stride had in reality been taken towards disengaging the new faith from the old. When the persecution closed, the Church stood on the eve of discovering God's great "mystery," that it was to be a Church not for Jews only, but for mankind. From this point of view, it was a gain to the new community to be driven out of orthodox communion by the Sanhedrim, for it was forced thereby to assume a more independent attitude and to know itself as

[1] Acts vi. 1–ix. 30.

something distinct from Judaism. It was no less a gain to have its converts dispersed against their will to every corner of Palestine and beyond it; to Cyprus, Antioch, and Damascus on the north, to Ethiopia on the south. And the best gain of all was the preparation in secret of a future apostle, adapted to Gentile and western peoples. At this point, accordingly, there opens a fresh section of St. Luke's narrative.[1]

The next event of primary moment was the conversion of Cornelius; but the importance of that event in the development of Church history was so great, that it is worth the historian's while not only to relate its occurrence with extreme minuteness, but also to show how it was providentially brought about, and to what results it led. Peter's tour of visitation, with the circumstances which led him to Joppa; the separate preparation of both the apostle and the centurion through heavenly visions; the particulars of their meeting; the manner of the Gentile's conversion and baptism; as well as the full recapitulation of all this which Peter gave in self-defence to the Jerusalem Church—everything is related with an almost excessive circumstantiality, in marked contrast with Luke's usual rapid manner. Everything, however, is meant to bear upon the great fact. The preceding narrative has brought matters to this point, that there remains nothing more to do but formally to open the door of the Church to uncircumcised heathen. For this the Church stands ready. The new wine ferments within the old skin of Mosaism, and an ampler vessel must be found for it. Christ's following is already more than a Jewish sect; it

[1] The long paragraph which begins at chap. ix. 31, ends only with the 18th verse of chap. xi.

is a Jewish Church. But Christ's Church cannot be for ever a Church of Jews only. The next step is the admission of non-Jewish members. Here, therefore, the history of the purely Hebrew Church is virtually at an end. The interest of the story is about to pass away from that elder branch of Christendom. A new, long, and as yet inexhausted era of religious history is about to open. Easily as a careless reader may pass without thought from the thirtieth to the thirty-first verse of Luke's ninth chapter, he is really turning over one of those great leaves which mark the opening of another chapter in human history.

It was while Peter was engaged in visiting certain scattered groups of converts which were already to be found in the maritime plain of Sharon that he was first brought into contact with the Roman officer at Cæsarea. Probably, therefore, that visitation was introduced into St. Luke's narrative primarily to show how Peter came to be found in his vicinity at the sea-coast town of Joppa. If any circumstances could appear accidental to a devout eye, these surely could not which led an apostle, without knowing it, to the spot where, with his back to Jerusalem and his face to the western world, he was destined to break down for ever a wall of privilege which for at least two thousand years had confined God's grace within a single family line. No chance-laid train, but a call from heaven, had originally brought the Chaldean shepherd to Mamre, that the world's blessing might be shut up within his own circumcised body and that of his son. So now, when the long restriction was about to be withdrawn, and the jealously imprisoned blessing to be set free to overflow the world, it could be nothing less than the visible hand of God which made all things converge and meet at one predestined moment. First, rest from persecution suggested to Peter a quiet visitation of the scattered brethren. Then the cure of Eneas, talked of all over the plain of Sharon, made Peter's presence and power known in Joppa, and possibly in Cæsarea. At the same juncture, the death of Dorcas suggested to the bereaved Church at Joppa to send for the apostle. Once there, the fame of her restoration opened a door of usefulness, which detained him on the coast till, through the falling-in of a separate line of events, the messengers of Cornelius found him in the tanner's house.

Besides this direct value of the introductory narrative, however, it possesses a secondary interest. Rather, an interest which may have been only secondary in the writer's thought has become to his modern readers the more interesting of the two. We get here our last glimpse into the state of the purely Hebrew Church in Palestine. From the venerable mother Church whose centre was in the holy city, the history is about to pass away. Antioch is to become a more fertile mother of Churches and the true focus of Christian life. But before the interest is shifted, the historian dwells on this progress of the great Jewish apostle from the city to the coast, that we may see how pleasant and pure was the religious life which grew up within the remnant of Israel, saved according to the election of grace.[1] The Jerusalem Church of the earliest days, the Church on which the Holy Ghost first descended, the Church where brotherly love almost solved the problem of social inequality, the Church which was defended by

[1] Rom. xi. 5.

AN APOSTOLIC TOUR OF INSPECTION. 333

the eloquence and watered by the blood of Stephen, had now become, thanks to its persecutors, the Church[1] of Palestine. It owned congregations in every province; in Galilee and in Samaria, as well as in Judæa. It counted saints even in the smaller townships like Lydda and Joppa. Neither persecution nor extension had dimmed its characteristic graces. It continued to be as holy as ever in its walk, and not less full of the comfort of the Spirit. It abounded still in charity to the poor. It was gladdened by the mighty works of Christ's apostles. It was almost as closely knit in the unity of a family, as in those early days when its members sat down at one board within the walls of one holy city.

Luke's description of the Palestine Church during that interval of peace of which Peter took advantage for his visit of superintendence, tells of singular spiritual prosperity. The Church had rest from war. It was "built up," or edified.[2] This word has passed into the peculiar vocabulary of Christendom, always in the same sense of inward growth in the spiritual life through the cultivation and expression of Christian feeling. Probably its primary reference in this passage was to the resumption of those frequent assemblies of disciples for common prayer

[1] The reading in ver. 31 is ἐκκλησία, and the singular is maintained throughout. The plural of the word does not occur till xv. 41; though the idea of a plurality of Churches lies in κατ' ἐκκλησίαν, in xiv. 23.

[2] The standing metaphor of St. Paul for progress in Christian life may have been borrowed by him from our Lord's own use of an expression in one of the Psalms. See Psa. cxviii. 22, quoted in Matt. xxi. 42 and parallels (cf. Jesus' words, Matt. xvi. 18). Consult Bruder for Paul's frequent use of the word and its derivatives. Here it seems to be imitated from St. Paul, by his scholar Luke. But the image is not foreign to St. Peter either: see Acts iv. 11, where he also follows Jesus' use of Psa. cxviii., and with this compare 1 Pet. ii. 5-7.

and the Holy Sacrament which persecution had made for a time impossible or perilous. At any rate the private life of these Hebrew brethren answered to their social devoutness. The Church "walked in the fear of the Lord." Towards their new Lord, Jesus Christ, as the Son of God, the disciples directed that reverential ethical "fear" of Jehovah in which Hebrew piety had always been accustomed to find the very root and secret of all religion. To a godly Jew of the best time and of the best type, to fear Jehovah was the beginning of sacred wisdom and the fountain of spiritual life. By it men learned to hate and forsake evil. It prolonged men's days. It brought them riches, honour, and happy life.[1] The consistent Christian conduct of these Palestine believers was coloured by this that they had inherited a grave and awful regard for the divine authority, such as had deepened almost into sternness the moral character of their most religious ancestors. Only it was in the dear and familiar face of Jesus of Nazareth that they had now learned to recognise the Jehovah of their fathers. God was become nearer and kindlier than before, yet no whit less venerable for utter sanctity. No wonder such a Church grew. The proved constancy of these brethren under persecution, together with their reverent and righteous lives in days of quietness, might well attract their neighbours to the faith. It was not this, however, but another force which mainly added to the membership of the Church. "It was multiplied by the exhortation of the Holy Ghost." The Paraclete did His predicted work of convicting the world of sin, and regenerating the souls of men through the

---

[1] Cf. Job xxviii. 28; Psa. cxi. 10; Prov. i. 7, xiv. 27, and xix. 23. See also Prov. viii. 13, x. 27, xvi. 6, xxii. 4; Psa. xix. 9.

preaching of the gospel. The word which converts is ever that word of exhortation growing into a word of comfort,[1] which only the Holy Ghost Himself can give to the preacher. When men feel that it is God Who addresses them in the message of salvation, then the Church's witness to her Lord becomes an aggressive, converting, and conquering word. So the Church of Palestine throve and grew, having peace.

Out of Peter's journey of apostolic inspection,[2] only two incidents have been preserved, one at Lydda and one at Joppa. It is plain, however, that his tour may have embraced a considerable tract of country before he arrived at Lydda. That town lay only some eighteen miles from the capital on the direct road to Cæsarea; but it could not have been his first halt, for we are told that he arrived there while he was passing through among all the saints.[3]

[1] Both these ideas must be held fast in the παράκλησις from which the Holy Spirit borrows His most characteristic New Testament title.

[2] It is much to be desired that we could say with confidence whether this journey of Peter preceded or followed Saul's visit to him at Jerusalem. With our present chronological data, I fear we cannot hope to settle that question. That it comes after Saul's visit to Jerusalem (ver. 26-30) in the narrative proves of itself nothing. A new paragraph has here begun; and it would be quite in Luke's manner, if, after following the career of Saul, without interruption, till his return home to Tarsus, he should now fall back to take up matters which had been elsewhere happening in the meantime. If it was the cruel attempt of the Emperor Caligula to coerce the conscience of the Jewish people, which gave the Sanhedrim something else to do than, in its turn, persecute the Nazarenes, then this peace must have fallen before the year 41, which was the year of Caligula's death. This, however, is only a guess; and even this, were it certain, would still leave the date of Saul's conversion nearly as uncertain as ever.

[3] We have to supply τῶν ἁγίων in ver. 32, and not, as in the authorised version, τῶν τόπων. The καὶ and the general construction require this.

It is probable enough that he had already visited the central highlands, or even Samaria and Galilee, before he turned back to overtake the coast plain. There, however, the interest of his tour culminated. Between the limestone hills which form the backbone of Palestine, and the Mediterranean Sea, stretches from north to south a long, rich, fat, and in ancient times well-peopled plain. Only at two points of the sea-board is this continuous flat of deep loam broken by a sudden spur of rock. The one is at Carmel, the other at Joppa. The portion of coast plain which lies betwixt these two was called as here "the Sharon;"[1] the city of Cæsarea being about midway between the two extremities of it: while the part lying to the south of Joppa as far as Gaza, bears in Holy Writ another name which our version has not preserved but translated, the name of "Shephelah." Like Sharon, that word means simply, "plain." It is the plain of Philistia. Now, almost due inland from the low rock on which the conspicuous and unmistakable port-town of Joppa has stood so long, is this small town of Lydda (now Lud), girdled with olives. It stands quite near the base of the hill-country where you drop down upon the plain through the passes of Benjamin.

If Lydda was the first of all the thick-set villages of the flat country to be visited by Peter, as it well might be, then it is easy to see how the fame of a miracle done there upon a confirmed paralytic, would naturally spread from one rural hamlet to another across the ten unbroken miles to Joppa, and along the main Roman road as far northward as Cæsarea or farther. Its effect upon the population is pithily described as both extensive and

[1] "Or Saron." Ver. 35, τὸν Σάρωνα.

AN APOSTOLIC TOUR OF INSPECTION. 337

deep.[1] For us it is difficult to realise the part which miracle-working appears to have played in the early diffusion of the gospel. Not only does it seem to moderns as if hardly any miracle could be so well authenticated as really to be accepted by the public at large; one fails no less to realise that state of mind in which a person could be led through any spiritual or moral revolution, even by a miracle which he did accept. The first of these difficulties is lightened indeed when we duly estimate how unlike were the views of a first century Jew to those of a nineteenth century Englishman on this matter of the supernatural. The Jew was prepared to expect divine communications, and he expected no divine communication without a visible or tangible miracle. His national history was full of such interpositions; the hopes of his race demanded their recurrence. Our Lord accordingly found no scepticism among the people as to the reality of His wonders. Whatever party spite might allege as to their source, in respect of their actual occurrence He found easy credence and an appetite for them only too gross. But the second point is more difficult. What relation is there between crediting the bare fact of a miracle and being morally converted to genuine penitence or trust? Here the experience of our Lord's ministry affords us no assistance. He did not win followers through wonder-working. He won popularity, not success. He drew crowds but not hearts. Yet in the case of this man Eneas at Lydda, a general conversion of the agricultural population in the Sharon plain is stated to have been the immediate result—a conversion so general that Luke can

[1] Acts ix. 35.

employ a popular hyperbole and say, they "all turned to the Lord." The explanation of this unusual success lay, as I am disposed to think, in the circumstances of the plain-population. So far as we are informed, our Lord had never visited that district. Whatever the people may have known of Him in other ways, they were less hardened against His claims by previous familiarity with and rejection of them, than either the Galileans or the Judæans. It was like virgin soil therefore, and recent evangelism by such scattered disciples as Philip, who resided at Cæsarea,[1] had already prepared the ground. Before Peter's visit many among the devout country people must have been aware of the tenets of the new sect and predisposed to accept Jesus as Messiah, who had not yet decided to join the little nuclei of converts meeting here and there for worship. On such susceptible villagers the falling of this single spark sufficed to set the country in a blaze.

However this may be, it was the knowledge of Jesus' great favour shown to Eneas through the word of Peter, which brought the apostle a pressing invitation from the saints at Joppa. On the humble little Church in that town there had come in those days a serious loss. Acute observers of moral changes in history have remarked how Christianity suddenly shifted the supreme type of character from the masculine to the feminine virtues. In the pagan world, "virtue" itself meant simply manfulness. It was the combination in the perfect Man Himself of all those graces which formerly had been deemed womanish or weak, such graces as humility, meekness,

[1] See Acts viii. 40, xxi. 8.

tenderness, and serving charity, with that stately group of virtues which made up the antique ideal—foresight, fortitude, justice, and self-control:[1] it was this combination in Jesus which rectified the judgment of humanity and restored to us a symmetrical image of character. To effect such a rectification, however, it was needful to lift into special prominence the hitherto despised graces of feminity. Manliness in Jesus is everywhere taken for granted; womanliness in its best sense is made conspicuous. The cross of the Man of Sorrows confutes the ancient preferences of the world. It is the glorification of self-sacrifice, of gentleness, of endurance, and of meek forgiveness. One immediate result of this was not only to foster a fuller development of all such beauties of character as belong most eminently to womanhood, the quiet and lowly spirit, chaste modesty, and silent loving patience; but also to give scope within the Christian Church for the true functions of woman. With the birth of Christian beneficence came the recognition of woman's work. Shut out from office in the State, woman found for the first time within the Church a sheltered and becoming sphere for all truly womanlike services. While Jesus yet lived, she found her sphere in ministering to His personal comforts.[2] After He was gone, she found it still in ministering to Christ in the persons of His poor ones.[3] Doing it to them for His sake, she still was able to do it unto Him. At least two female orders can be traced in the obscure arrangements of the primitive Church: the order of deaconesses and the order of widows; of which the one

---

[1] The four cardinal virtues: prudentia, fortitudo, temperantia, and justitia.   [2] Luke viii. 2, 3; Mark xv. 41.
[3] "Christo in pauperibus." Cf. Matt. xxv. 40, and John xii. 8.

organised, and the other rewarded, the Christian labours of faithful women.[1]

To that small congregation at Joppa belongs the honour of having contributed the first female name to the records of Christian service. She, whom the people called, both in their homely Aramaic and in their Greek speech, by the name of "the Gazelle," because that loveliest of Syrian animals was from early times, to the amatory poets of the East, a favourite emblem of a beautiful woman,[2] has fitly bequeathed her name of Dorcas to express, not the gift of personal beauty in her sex, but the Christian ornament of meek and gracious charity. Dorcas was no deaconess; the age of Church organisation had not yet come; but whatever she was, maid or widow, she had learned of Jesus Christ her Lord His best lesson,[3] and was enough of a woman to discover how she could most fitly practise it. By quiet feminine handiwork it was her wont[4] to work for Christ. Among the desolate and friendless of her own sex she found suitable objects for her unobtrusive aid.

Her death was to the saints of Joppa a common grief. It brought out for the first time how much she had been to them. It was not the widows only who missed their benefactress, but the whole congregation lost one who was to them a "living epistle" of Jesus Christ. They seem to have conceived some hope that the loss might not prove

[1] See Rom. xvi. 1 (Greek); 1 Tim. v. 9, ff.

[2] טבירא = δορκας. Same name, in form צְבִיָה, occurs in 2 Kings xii. 1, and 1 Chron. viii. 9, of different persons. Cf. amatory allusions in Song of Solomon ii. 9, 17, iv. 5, vii. 3; Prov. v. 19. The grounds of the comparison lie in the delicate grace of form, the large deep soft dark eye, and perhaps the light springing movements of the creature.

[3] She is called μαθητρία, a word of late Greek, only here used in N. T.   [4] Cf. the imperfect, in ver. 39.

a final one. Was not Christ's chief apostle within a dozen miles of them, and had not Jesus just been showing on the paralysed limbs of Eneas that, though absent, He could still work as in the years when He lived with men? Might not a courteous but urgent message bring into the midst of themselves the organ of divine life and power? and might not the Lord hear in pity His bereaved saints? It is hardly to be supposed that Peter accompanied the deputation back to Joppa with any certain knowledge what it might please his Master to do for the mourning Church. But when he stood beside the dead in the centre of that touching group who wailed in the upper chamber, and pointed to the very clothes they were wearing[1] as evidences of the greatness of their loss, he felt shut up at least to carry to his Master the petition of His people. Having imitated the behaviour of Jesus in the house of Jairus,[2] by putting them all forth, he imitated the behaviour of Elijah in an upper room at Zarephath,[3] by crying unto the Lord. As he had said to Eneas, "Jesus Christ healeth thee," so now he begged Jesus Christ to revive dead Dorcas: for it is Jesus Christ — the Master — Who alone saves autocratically at His choice; Peter, and all other servants, only ministerially, as their divine Lord enables them. Still, therefore, it is the very life of Jesus, poured through His Christian members, which giveth life to the world. While Peter prayed alone in the awful silence of death, that incommunicable secret assurance of faith[4] in which must have always lain the authority of any man

[1] This is conveyed in ver. 39 by the middle voice, $\epsilon\pi\iota\delta\epsilon\iota\kappa\nu\upsilon\mu\epsilon\nu\alpha\iota$. See Meyer *in loc.* (*note*).
[2] Matt. ix. 25.   [3] See 1 Kings xvii. 19-22.
[4] Cf. the $\pi\tilde{\alpha}\sigma\alpha\nu\ \tau\dot{\eta}\nu\ \pi\iota\sigma\tau\iota\nu\ \ddot{\omega}\sigma\tau\epsilon\ \ddot{o}\rho\eta\ \mu\epsilon\theta\iota\sigma\tau\acute{\alpha}\nu\epsilon\iota\nu$, of which Paul speaks in 1 Cor. xiii. 2.

to attempt a miracle, possessed his soul, and enabled him with calmness to do, what, without it, only insanity could have done — to speak to the cold corpse these words, "Tabitha, arise."

This is the second recorded death within the Christian community. In Jerusalem, a young man, a public officer of the Church, and a foremost witness to Jesus in high places, died beneath the stones of his enemies. At Joppa, a lonely unobtrusive woman expired in the quiet of her own sick room. Both in Stephen and in Dorcas the life of Christ was seen to vanquish death. That was not death, as men count dying, to "fall asleep" with the face of Jesus full in sight, and His voice of welcome already beginning to be heard. Neither is this death, as men have hitherto known it, when dead Dorcas quietly opens eyes which seemed to have shut for ever, to find an apostle kneeling by her bed. Henceforth it is not Christian to fear a foe which our Lord Christ hath so plainly bound. Let it be remembered, too, that Stephen's victory was a better one than that of Dorcas; and Stephen's is the victory which may be ours. It has not been granted to many of the saints to return, and calmly to resume, like her, their wonted tasks of earthly ministration. It would be no kindness if it were. To depart, in St. Paul's judgment, is far better. Whereas to all saints who seek the grace of faith for dying need, it will be granted to fall asleep as Stephen did in the serenity of Christian hope, and to pass like him from the shadows of the valley to the face of God.

The restoration of Dorcas to her weeping widows, through so rare and signal an act of power, was probably a seal set of purpose by the Lord on that new department of charitable labour within His Church which Dorcas had made so much her own. To the Church, rather than to Dorcas, was the kindness done, when one who was so "needful" was suffered to "abide" a little longer in the flesh."[1] The widows were comforted; all Christian ages have learnt how the Master values the humble and retiring industry of devout women when it clothes Christ's poor by its own needle; while through a splendid demonstration of what divine strength lay concealed behind the diviner charity of Christ's ministering Church, many souls in Joppa and elsewhere "believed in the Lord."

[1] Cf. Phil. i. 22-26.

XVIII.
Cornelius.

I WILL GIVE UNTO THEE THE KEYS OF THE KINGDOM OF HEAVEN.

THAT THE OFFERING UP OF THE GENTILES MIGHT BE ACCEPTABLE, BEING SANCTIFIED BY THE HOLY GHOST.

Acts x. 1-48.

Revised Version.

Now, a certain man in Cæsarea, by name Cornelius, a centurion of the cohort called the Italian, devout and fearing God with his whole house, giving also many alms to the people and praying to God continually, saw in a vision plainly somewhere about the ninth hour of the day, an angel of God coming in to him and saying to him: "Cornelius." And he gazing at him and becoming alarmed, said: "What is it, Lord?" But he said to him:

"Thy prayers and thine alms came up for a memorial before God. And now send men to Joppa, and fetch a certain Simon, who is surnamed Peter. He is lodging with one Simon a tanner, whose house is by the sea."

And when the angel who was speaking to him departed, he called two of the domestics and a devout soldier of those who waited on him, and having related all things to them, sent them to Joppa.

Now on the morrow, as these were journeying and drawing near to the city, Peter went up on the roof to pray about the sixth hour. But he became hungry and wished to eat; and while they were making ready, there fell on him an ecstasy, and he beheld the heaven opened and a certain vessel like a great sheet descending, let down by four corners upon the earth, in which were all the quadrupeds and reptiles of the earth and birds of the heaven. And there came a voice to him:

"*Rise, Peter, slay and eat.*"

But Peter said:

"*By no means, Lord, for never did I eat anything common and unclean.*" And a voice again the second time to him:

"*What God cleansed, make not thou common.*"

Now this happened thrice, and immediately the vessel was taken up into heaven.

But while Peter was at a loss in his own mind [lit., in himself] what the vision might be which he had seen, behold, the men who had been sent from Cornelius had made inquiry for the house of Simon, and stood at the gate; and having called, were asking if Simon who is surnamed Peter were lodging there. So while Peter was meditating about the vision, the Spirit said to him:

"*Behold, [three] men [are] seeking thee. But rise, get thee down and go with them, doubting nothing; because I have sent them.*"

So Peter went down to the men and said:

"*Behold, I am he whom ye seek. What is the cause for which ye are come?*" And they said:

"*Cornelius a centurion, a man just and fearing God, borne witness to also by the whole nation of the Jews, received a response from a holy angel to send for thee to his house and to hear things from thee.*"

Having therefore called them in, he lodged them.

Now on the morrow, he rose up and went forth with them; and certain of those brethren who were of Joppa went with him; and the next day they entered into Cæsarea. Now Cornelius was expecting them, having called together his kinsmen and intimate friends; and when it came to pass that Peter was entering, Cornelius met him, and falling at his feet, worshipped. But Peter raised him, saying: "Stand up: I also am myself a man." And conversing with him, he entered, and found many come together, and said to them:

"You [well] know how unlawful it is for a man who is a Jew to associate with or come near to one of a different race; and to me God showed that no man is to be called common or unclean; wherefore also without gainsaying I came when I was sent for. I ask, therefore, for what reason ye sent for me?"

And Cornelius said:

"Four days ago, until this hour was I [fasting, and] at the ninth hour praying in my house, and behold a man stood before me in bright clothing, and said: 'Cornelius, thy prayer was heard and thine alms were remembered before God. Send therefore to Joppa, and call hither Simon who is surnamed Peter. He is lodging in the house of Simon a tanner, by the sea [who when he is come shall speak to thee].' At once therefore I sent to thee, and thou didst well to come. Now therefore, all we are present before God to hear all the things which are prescribed to thee by God."

Then Peter opening his mouth, said:

"Of a truth I perceive that 'God is no respecter of persons,' but in every nation he who feareth Him and worketh righteousness is accepted with Him. The word which He sent to the children of Israel, preaching peace through Jesus Christ (He is all men's Lord);— ye know the matter which was spoken of throughout the whole of Judæa, beginning from Galilee after the baptism which John proclaimed—Jesus Who was from Nazareth; how God anointed Him with the Holy Spirit and power; Who went about doing good and healing all that were over-mastered by the devil, because God was with Him. And we [are] witnesses of all things which He did, both in the country of the Jews and [in] Jerusalem: Whom also they slew by hanging upon a stake. Him God raised on the third day, and granted that He became manifest, not to the whole people, but to witnesses who had been chosen before by God, to us who ate with [Him] and drank with Him after His resurrection from the dead. And He charged us to proclaim to the people and to bear witness that it is He Who was ordained by God, Judge of living and dead. To Him all the prophets bear witness, that every one who believes in Him receives remission of sins through His name."

While Peter was yet speaking these things, there fell the Holy Spirit upon all who were hearing the Word. And the believers of the circumcision, as many as came with Peter, were amazed, because upon the Gentiles also was poured out the free-gift of the Holy Spirit. For they were hearing them speaking with tongues and magnifying God. Then answered Peter:

" Is any one able to forbid the water, that these should not be baptized, who have received the Holy Spirit as we also [did]?"

So he directed them to be baptized in the name of the Lord.

Then they prayed him to remain some days.

XVIII.

AT length we reach a moment in the history of the Church second only to the day of Pentecost for the magnitude of its results.

The reception of the first Gentile into Christian fellowship forms a tale with three parts or scenes, through which the action moves as in a drama towards its dénouement. Each of these has a day to itself. The first takes place at Cæsarea, about the hour of three in the afternoon, within the chamber of Cornelius. The second is in Joppa, at noon of the next day, on the roof of Simon the tanner's house. The third falls two days later. Again we are at Cæsarea, within the centurion's quarters, and again the hour is three in the afternoon. The first and second lead up to the third, but the first has its share also in preparing for the second. Throughout this progress we trace the successive propulsions of a Divine Hand. In the opening scene, a heavenly messenger gives the first movement to the action by bidding the soldier send for the apostle. In the next, a vision from heaven prepares the apostle for the soldier's message. In each of these the human subject is alone at a still hour of prayer, and he alone is witness to the Hand which guides to its result. In the third, however, when the issues for which both these two have been preparatory are ripe for their accomplishment, then what has been secretly wrought breaks into open light, and in the presence of a house full of witnesses the same Divine Hand crowns and seals its work.

I.

Cæsarea and Joppa, lying some thirty miles apart, were at that time the two seaport towns of Palestine. The one was the ancient Jewish harbour, the other the new and more splendid Roman port. Joppa is as old at least as the conquest of the land by Joshua,[1] and reappears at intervals in Hebrew history as the great gate to all comers by the sea. Through it arrived the pine and cedar from Lebanon, with which Solomon fitted up the first, and Ezra the second temple.[2] From it Jonah sailed in his flight to the west.[3] It was the single landing-place, and a very bad one, on the whole of that harbourless shore which bounded Israel on the westward, and which served, by the fact of its being harbourless, to cut Israel off from maritime enterprise, as well as from contact with maritime nations. When the Jews began, shortly before our Lord's birth, to have more close and friendly relations with western peoples, the want was felt of a new coast city, with greater western luxury about it and a safer port. This want the magnificent energy and profusion of Herod the Great supplied. He created an artificial harbour of refuge, guarded from the south and west by enormous breakwaters; and he built a city of palaces, furnished with every convenience for the luxurious life of the Greco-Roman world.[4] Greeks and Jews contended whether the new city, at once seaport and metropolis,

[1] Josh. xix. 46.　　[2] 2 Chron. ii. 16; Ezra. iii. 7.　　[3] Jonah i. 3.
[4] Cf. here Josephus, *Antiq.* xv. 9. 6, and *B. J.* i. 21. 5-8.

should be considered more Jewish or more Greek.[1] In fact, however, it was essentially Roman. Its very object was to mark the tie of amity between its founder and the Roman State. Its name of Cæsarea Sebaste was a compliment to the first Roman emperor. The building which, amid a crowd of theatres, baths, and temples, rose highest, and the white stone of which gleamed farthest across the Mediterranean, was a shrine to the honour of Rome and of its emperor. Cæsarea seemed a ready-made Roman capital; and when, after Herod's death, Palestine was annexed to the Roman province of Syria, his great coast city received the court of the Roman procurator, and its barracks sheltered the Roman troops.

Here then was quartered the regiment, or cohort, in which Cornelius was a subordinate officer. Three legions the Romans usually kept in Judæa, numbering in all some 35,000 men,[2] and these were recruited from the population of the province. On the other hand, the cohort to which Cornelius[3] was attached, probably received its name of the "Italian" because its ranks were made up exclusively of home-born Italians. It may have been a company of the Pretorian Guards,[4] or it may have been a corps of Italian volunteers :[5] at all events this officer, who bore the name of one of the most noble Roman clans, must have been a Roman by blood and birth.

The New Testament literature abundantly proves how

[1] So Greek was its population, that in the synagogues the Old Testament was read in the Septuagint version.

[2] Known to have been the 5th, 10th, and 15th. See Conybeare and Howson, ii. 341, ff.

[3] A centurio was over $\frac{1}{6}$th of a cohort = $\frac{1}{2}$ maniple.

[4] Josephus speaks of five such at Cæsarea—one called Augustan. See *B. J.* iii. 4. 2.   [5] So Wieseler, *Chron. d. Ap. Zeitalters*, p. 389.

extensively Jewish influence had paved the way among Gentile nations for the coming of Christianity. This was one task assigned to the peculiar people of Jehovah, which had not been left undone. Of course, orthodox Jews believed that for a heathen God could entertain no favour, until the heathen became by circumcision an adopted member of the select family of Abraham. Therefore they compassed sea and land (as Jesus said) to make one proselyte.[1] In spite of the sternness, rigour, and, in some aspects, repulsiveness of the Mosaic code as read by later Pharisaism, they succeeded. Some men, and far more women, all over the pagan world fully embraced Judaism. But the influence of the Jewish faith was much wider than this.[2] Many earnest and thoughtful men, disgusted with traditional polytheism and its worn-out myths, yet finding no peace to their souls, either in the fashionable scepticism of the time or in its abominable license, turned with curious interest to that solitary antique faith which still stood erect, self-confident even to arrogance, and pure even to severity, in an age which had dissolved or corrupted every other religion. The worship of Jehovah was to be found in the cities of every civilised land. No intelligent and travelled man could have escaped some knowledge of it. Its synagogues stood open. Its sacred books circulated in Greek.

---

[1] Matt. xxiii. 15.

[2] On the question so much debated, whether Cornelius was or was not a Proselyte of the Gate, it seems probable that this class of proselytes was a later arrangement of the Rabbis (if it ever existed, save on paper), but that it fixed what had been floating and unformed before—viz., the position of such foreigners as are here described, who drew more or less near to the worship of Jehovah and the customs of Israel, without committing themselves by formal conversion to Judaism. See Plumptre, in Smith's *Dict. of the Bible.*

Its emissaries and devotees went everywhere. Though it founded no formal missions, it proselytised with ardour; while its unlikeness to every other religion, its self-containedness and spirituality, its proud exclusiveness, its glorious hopes, were of themselves enough to attract the eyes of many. A gentleman from the west, possessed of some culture, and stationed for years in a Jewish city, had the best possible opportunity for studying the religion and the literature of the Jews. If such a man happened at the same time to be serious in his search for light and frank in his acceptance of it, he was likely to draw very close indeed to the foreign faith which he found around him. Cornelius, like another centurion in the Gospel,[1] is an example of the best type of such men. He had not only gone the length of discarding his ancestral idols and the ceremonies of the State religion; he even worshipped God after the fashion usual among the Hebrews. We find him fasting all day till three o'clock, observing the stated hours for daily prayer, and liberal in giving alms to the Jews[2] of Cæsarea; alms, prayers, and fasts being (as we see from the Sermon on the Mount)[3] the three cardinal points of popular Hebrew piety. Nor can there be any question as to the sincerity of this soldier's faith in God, and devout spiritual life; for he evinced it by his upright and humble behaviour. His domestics and his orderly describe him as a "just man," of "good report among the Jews." The terms on which he stood with the slaves[4] of his household show him to have been a considerate and gentle master. Nor is this all.

[1] Luke vii. 1, ff.
[2] Τῷ λαῷ, in ver. 2 = to the [chosen] people of the Jews.
[3] Matt. vi. 1–18.
[4] Not δοῦλος is used in ver. 7, but the humaner word οἰκέτης.

It seems indubitable that he was at this very time in deep spiritual anxiety, craving clearer light from God. He knew of the coming and preaching and wonders of the holy Man of Galilee. He could not fail to have heard of a new sect that everywhere declared this Man to be the promised Saviour. The neighbouring country was at the moment ringing with Peter's name. In his own town there dwelt a deacon and evangelist of the Church.[1] But these new revelations from the Jehovah of Israel, Who had (it was said) visited His people at last to raise up for them an horn of salvation,[2] were revelations of mercy for the elected and covenanted nation, the circumcised sons of Abraham. For himself, a Gentile foreigner, was there any word of hope and peace from the one great God of heaven? Will God hear his prayers, or accept his offerings? Or must he, after all, if he would have life, forsake his nationality, his profession and his friends, to enter by the straight door of circumcision into that narrow alien fold of Judaism?

There can be little doubt that over this question the honest heart of the centurion was struggling when he resolved to devote the whole morning of one quiet day to fasting and prayer in his own chamber. For when, at the hour of vespers, there came in to him a visitor in shining apparel, who roused him from his prostrate posture with the word "Cornelius," the first answer he received to his startled and reverential question—"What is it, Lord?" was this, "Thy prayer is heard."[3] What

---

[1] Philip. See Acts xxi. 8.   [2] See Zacharias' hymn, Luke i. 68, ff.

[3] So in Cornelius's own account of the interview in ver. 31, it is in the singular: σου ἡ προσευχή. St. Luke, on the other hand (ver. 4), gives it in the plural. His petitions were many, but they had one specific scope.

that prayer was, which the blameless and charitable life of the Roman caused God to remember, we gather from God's answer to it; and the answer is this: "Send men to Joppa, and call for Simon, who shall tell thee words whereby thou shalt be saved."[1]

Scattered all round the wide shores of the Mediterranean and beyond it, there were at that day multitudes of souls whom Jesus called His "other sheep," who were not of the Jewish fold,[2] whom also He desired to gather. Very various as must have been their degrees of preparation for the gospel, of present faith and light, or of readiness to hear His voice, yet the Shepherd's eye rested upon them all. Their prayers were heard. The day, long sighed for by sages and godly souls through that night in which God "winked at" the ignorance of men,[3] the day of hope for all nations, was dawning. The light which had already risen on Israel was moving westward to rise upon the Gentiles, and become the light of the world. Nor could any better representative of western heathendom be found than this Roman soldier—type of Rome's all conquering world-might and latest product of a long-growing civilisation, which was soon to give place to another. He was ready. To him, first of heathens, God, by plain voice and vision of a celestial messenger, spoke words of acceptance; and the heart of Cornelius—a prompt and honest and obedient heart—was open to the word of the great Captain. "Immediately, therefore, he sent for Peter."

---

[1] The three reports which we have of these words of the angel are all different. In chap. x. 6, the words, "He shall tell thee what thou oughtest to do," are to be rejected from the text. In chap. x. 32 it is simply, "Who, when he cometh, shall speak unto thee." This implies, however, that Peter would speak God's answer to his prayer. And so Peter understood it when he less exactly reported it in chap. xi. 14.

[2] John x. 16.   [3] Acts xvii. 30.

II.

Peter, on the other hand, a day's journey off, in Joppa, was not ready. The Gentiles of that age were prompter to enter the Church, than was the Church to open its doors. Although no more than thirty miles lay between these two representative men; although he who held the keys had come down, led by God, to the very forepost of Israelitish territory, whence, as from a watchtower, he looked right west across the Gentile sea towards the Gentile lands; yet in spirit that spokesman and doorkeeper of the Jewish Church stood at a great gulf's distance from the foremost Gentile who was knocking so patiently at the Church's gate. To Peter, of course, as to every other Jew, it was quite a familiar idea that the Gentiles should come one day to worship God and believe in His Messiah; but it had never yet occurred to him, or to almost any other Jew, that this could happen unless by the Gentiles first becoming Jews. By training, Peter was a Jew of the intensely national school. In spite of their faith in Christ, he and the bulk of Palestine believers had remained, up to this point, Jews still. To such men the division which God had set up betwixt the two portions of mankind did not seem at that time a temporary party-wall (as St. Paul afterwards described it [1]), intended to be taken down after it had served its purpose, in order that wider room might be made for both in one new temple. It was a fence of permanent and hopeless exclusion for all beyond, of permanent inclusion for all within. God had, as they believed, limited His grace for ever to the covenant of circumcision. All men who had not been brought near by that covenant and consecrated

[1] Eph. ii. 14.

by its rites, were unclean and profane. It followed that the Church, or assembly of such as believed in Jesus Christ, could not be a wider communion than the followers of Moses, but a narrower. It formed a lesser fold inside the fold of Judaism. It was a more retired and safe shrine, to which you could only pass through the fore-court of the law. Any man might, it was felt, get into the fellowship of Jesus, and all men, it was hoped, would some day do so; still, to the great world of uncircumcised heathen sinners, access could lie only through that preliminary apparatus of cleansing which God had prepared in the Abrahamic covenant and the Mosaic ritual.

To rectify this mistake was the design of Peter's vision on the housetop. It was the day after Cornelius sent off his messengers: two household slaves and one orderly, all of them men who sympathised with their master's religious convictions, and knew the purport of their mission. These three Italians, having walked a portion of the distance after three o'clock on the evening before, were now, at noon of the next day, coming pretty near to Joppa. They had not loitered, for it is a ride of eleven hours to the modern traveller,[1] and they were on foot. Noon was an hour of prayer; and Peter had chosen for his oratory the flat housetop,[2] which, at the hottest time of day, would be as quiet and still a spot as could be had. It was a spot, too, most apt to awaken thoughts of God's great line of demarcation betwixt chosen Jew and uncovenanted heathen. Before him, as he knelt, lay the land of Abraham and of the promise. From his rock to which the town's white houses clung silent in the heat, he could look over green

---

[1] See Porter, in Murray's *Handbook*, ii. 364.
[2] See ver. 9: ἐπὶ τὸ δῶμα = "upon the house."

groves of orange-trees at its foot, to the broad well-cropped plain across which he had journeyed, till his eyes rested on the fainter line of Benjamin's hills. There, behind the hills, unseen save by fancy, stood the holy city, to whose familiar temple he still with the pious usage of his people turned his face to pray. On the right hand and the left, stretched to south and north the yellow streak of blown sand, which, then as now, must have marked the line of coast. He was on the furthest verge of sacred soil. Behind him was nothing but the sea; not the sheltered tiny lake of his fishing days, but the Great Sea, mysterious, cruel in its brightness, oppressive for its vastness, beyond whose far horizon lay the strange foreign world of the uncircumcised—the unknown and dreadful lands from which came the infidel and the conqueror. If, in such a place, any natural thoughts awoke in Peter touching the limits of his nation's fold and the lost sheep who were not of the House of Israel, they were interrupted by a very commonplace and prosaic craving. It is improbable that noon was a usual meal-hour, so that Peter's hunger probably had some special occasion. Yet to this slight and casual circumstance the whole revelation attached itself. He was hungry, and while the household of his namesake the tanner prepared food below, he on the roof, fresh from prayer and meditation, was overtaken in an ecstasy.[1] He was awake, like Cornelius the day before, and, like Cornelius, he was fasting; but, unlike Cornelius, who retained his senses unoppressed, Peter was absorbed out of consciousness of external facts, through the unusual power of spiritual impressions. Being lifted above his ordinary thinking, he lay open to whatever super-sensuous

[1] Ἐγένετο ἐπ' αὐτόν ἔκστασις.

communications might anyhow reach his spirit. The divine teaching came in the form of a vision. The sky above appeared to divide, that down from its secret glowing depths of blue might come a thing, which wore the look of a vast linen cloth, gathered up at its four corners into four ends,¹ by which it was, as it were, suspended from the sky. Slowly this thing came down,² till, as it neared the apostle,³ he could see over its rim, and in it was the appearance, which grew plainer as he gazed, of innumerable living things of every kind that walks, or creeps, or flies, as if all animals known to Peter in his Syrian home had somehow been collected in one vast crowd. Clean and unclean creatures, it struck him, were mixed promiscuously together. While he gazed, a voice seemed to say beside him, " Rise, Peter, kill and eat : " and to the unseen, unknown Speaker, Peter made characteristic, energetic, and very Jewish answer—" By no means, Lord, for common or unclean thing never entered into my mouth." ⁴ The words which replied upon these of Peter—the second utterance of the mysterious Voice—formed the key words of the whole vision, and are precisely identical in both the reports which we possess :—" What God did cleanse, make thou not common." It remains uncertain whether only these pregnant words were repeated three times, or (which seems less likely) the whole conversation ; but after the third repetition, suddenly the gathered sheet with all its

---

¹ Ἀρχαί can hardly refer to "rope ends" here (Alford), or to the corners of the open sky (Wieseler). The reference to the four quarters, which even Alford admits, is also doubtful.

² Cf. the imperfect καταβαῖνον, in ver. 11, with εὐθὺς ἀνελήμφθη, in ver. 16.   ³ See ἦλθεν ἄχρι ἐμοῦ, xi. 5.

⁴ Cf. chap. x. 14 with xi. 8. Peter's own version is the more vivid and energetic.

varied life seemed to be drawn quickly back into the sky by some invisible Hand.

Taken by itself, this vision might hardly have been quite intelligible to Peter. It might on reflection have indicated no more to him than some approaching change in the laws which regulated food. But the providence of God soon helped him to a clue. He was still meditating on the meaning of what he had seen, when he heard the three strangers approach the outer gate of the entrance court, and call to know if one Peter were lodging there. Hurrying down the outside stair, which led from the roof to the court without passing through the house, Peter himself met and admitted the men. In the light of their message and the dealings of God with their master, Peter felt instinctively that he was meant to read the true lesson of his ecstasy. So read, it was not hard to interpret it aright. He saw that in the abolition of that symbolical distinction bewixt clean animals and unclean, betwixt what might and might not be eaten, there was also enclosed the abolition of all such unreal distinctions as had hitherto divided before the face of God the Gentile from the Hebrew.

It could hardly fail to strike a thoughtful Jew that the distinction drawn between different species of animals in the eleventh chapter of Leviticus,[1] whatever foundation for it might be discoverable in nature, was closely connected at least with that segregation of Israel from all other peoples to be alone holy to Jehovah, which is really the vital nerve of the entire civil legislation of Moses. For one thing, the distinction could not be merely a dietetic one. The law embraced more than the use of, or

[1] Recapitulated in Deut. xiv. 3–21.

the abstinence from, certain beasts as food. Unclean animals were unclean to touch as well as to eat. Not when alive, indeed, for that would have made ordinary existence intolerable; but whatever or whoever (certain cases excepted) touched the dead body of a prohibited animal, became ceremonially unclean. Dishes were to be broken, if breakable, and if not, to be steeped in water, which had contained any portion of such carcases or been touched by them. The avoidance of such contact with these creatures was enforced in the most solemn manner by the special sanctity which as God's people belonged to Israel: "Ye shall not make yourselves abominable with any creeping thing that creepeth, neither shall ye make yourselves unclean with them, that ye should be defiled thereby. For I am Jehovah your God: ye shall therefore sanctify yourselves, and ye shall be holy: for I am holy."[1] Besides, it was obvious that the distinction of meats was then, as it is to this day, a very powerful instrument for keeping Jew and Gentile apart in social intercourse. Like innumerable other laws discouraging contact with foreigners, this difficulty about food made it practically most inconvenient for any Hebrew to live on terms of ordinary friendship with a Gentile. Table companionship was, as it still is with strict Jews, a thing next to impracticable. After the Jews came into hostile contact with other nations, carefulness on this head became almost a sacramental badge of loyalty to Jehovah's covenant and the exclusive prerogatives of their race. The refusal of Daniel and his companions to defile themselves with the "meat" provided by the King of Assyria,[2] is, perhaps, not an instance to the point, for these royal "dainties"

---

[1] Lev. xi. 43, 44.   [2] Dan. i.

were probably not flesh, but baked meats which had been presented before an idol. But in the horrible persecution of the Jews under Antiochus, "men chose rather to die that they might not be defiled with meats, and profane the holy covenant;" and the refusal to eat swine's flesh took its place beside circumcision and Sabbath-keeping as a test of martyrdom for the faith of Jehovah.[1]

It is clear, therefore, how the uncleanness of Gentile food and the uncleanness of Gentiles themselves came to be so inseparably associated in Hebrew thought, that the one was the incessant reminder and index of the other. Peter's vision, in which God expressly abolished the one, was thus a suitable preface to the outpouring of His Holy Spirit on Cornelius, by which He was about to abolish the other. Even before Peter had seen that most eloquent of all demonstrations that divine grace is not limited by physical boundaries of race, or bound to ceremonial purifications, he had by reflecting on vision and providence together, under the Spirit's teaching, gathered the drift of the revelation made to him. God showed him before he reached Cæsarea that " he should not call any man (as little as any beast) profane or unclean." I can hardly imagine that St. Peter needed any special teaching to free him from that vulgar and uncharitable prejudice of his race, which despised every Gentile as inferior, and shunned him as outcast of God. It was quite another thing to see that God had seen fit to cancel a distinction between men which He had Himself established, and which He had made it the very business of His people to respect. Neither Peter nor any other man had a right to set aside the compulsory condition of cir-

[1] See 1 Macc. i. 63; 2 Macc. vi. 6–18, vii. 1.

cumcision and ceremonial observance until it pleased God to set it aside. If it did please Heaven now to throw down that ancient restriction, and open the doors of its favour to men of every race without a shadow of preference, then this new law of the kingdom must be revealed as unmistakably as the old law had been.

In this vision, therefore, interpreted to Peter by the Holy Ghost, Gentile Christians may read the charter of their gospel freedom. We owe it to the revelation of that noontide at Joppa that we are Christians and yet not Jews; bound no longer by the ceremonial which pressed upon ancient saints like a yoke; encircled no longer by artificial distinctions of clean and unclean; but Christ's freemen in a world where to the pure heart all things are pure, and all men are equal before God. To persons who have been born and bred in an atmosphere of Western and of Christian thought, it may seem as if it were no very wonderful discovery to make that God will forgive men who are not circumcised as readily as men who are. We have drifted so far away from the time at which this idea was novel that it fails to strike us as surprising. Yet it is that very "mystery" of which St. Paul became later the guardian and administrator, for which he contended his life long, in which he found the kernel of Christian liberty, and over which he so frequently chants doxologies of thankfulness—"the mystery which in other ages was not made known unto the sons of men as it is now revealed unto His holy apostles and prophets by the Spirit—that the Gentiles should be fellow-heirs, and of the same body, and partakers of His promise in Christ by the gospel." [1]

[1] Eph. iii. 5, 6. Cf. ver. 9, 10, also i. 9–14, ii. 11–22; Col. i. 25–27; Rom. xi. *pass.*, xvi. 25–27.

It is to the atonement of our blessed Lord and Saviour Jesus Christ that the non-Jewish world (according to St. Paul) owes this reconciliation. We were far off; now are we "made nigh by the blood of Christ." We were aliens from the commonwealth of Israel; He hath broken down the middle wall of partition. We were hated by the privileged Jew and him we hated, till Jesus abolished in His flesh that enmity which sprang from the law of commandments contained in ordinances. We were without God in the world, but Christ reconciled us to God in one body by the cross. The strangers and foreigners are now fellow-citizens with the saints; they are of the household of God. Moreover, if it is Jesus' priestly death which has made all this possible for unclean men, it is Jesus' kingly rule which brought it about. Not the servants, but the Master, must we thank for it. To Paul He revealed it in secret: to Peter, by a vision. Step by step, through symbol and through providence, by the opening of men's minds and by visits of angels, by force of facts and His own direct downpouring of the Holy Ghost, He Who reigns and loves us all for whom He died, did force upon the reluctant Church of these first days the conviction that the road to Christ does not lie by Moses alone, no, nor by Abraham; but that Christ's kingly City of Refuge and Peace "lieth four-square,"[1] with gates wide and high, always open, to face each quarter of the globe; so that the penitent pilgrim, whether he follow in that Italian soldier's steps, or draw near from any farther-off shore or province of great dark heathendom, may have no roundabout journey, past Sinai and Moriah, to reach the portal; but may approach by a straight path, and enter right in, to find sweet welcome from the King.

[1] See Rev. xxi. 10-17.

III.

The event, for which the preceding steps had been a preparation, took place on the third day after the vision of Cornelius, on the second after that of Peter. The scene shifts back to the officer's quarters in the barracks at Cæsarea. The good centurion had calculated quite correctly the length of time likely to be consumed by the journey of his messengers and their return. He allowed one night for rest at Joppa, as well as for Peter to make his arrangements to accompany them; and because the distance exceeded an average day's march, he supposed the party to have spent another night on the road. This delay was made all the more requisite by a circumstance which Cornelius could not anticipate. Conscious that the divine summons to Cæsarea and his vision on the housetop must be precursors of some very momentous transaction, by which the future relations of Jew and Gentile within the Church were to be affected, Peter adopted the precaution of taking witnesses along with him. No fewer than six [1] of the believing Jews of Joppa were selected to be his companions, in order that their evidence might afterwards confirm to the whole Jewish Church whatever indications of His will the Lord should vouchsafe. The party, thus increased to the number of ten, did not actually reach Cæsarea till towards three o'clock [2] in the afternoon of the second day. By that time Cornelius was fully expecting them.

[1] See Acts xi. 12.

[2] So I understand the difficult and disputed words of Cornelius in ver. 30. Μέχρι ταύτης τῆς ὥρας seems to imply that he was then speaking at about the same hour of the day as that to which his fast, four days before, had extended. But the prayer which was interrupted by the angelic apparition must have followed immediately on that fast, and it took place at the ninth hour.

It was probably not the first occasion on which his house had been the rendezvous for a number of serious Roman inquirers. This centurion was in all probability the centre of a circle, partly made up of relatives and partly of intimate friends, who shared to a certain extent his own religious sentiments. To them he had in the mean time made it known how God had been pleased to promise him that, through the words of a Jewish teacher from Joppa, those difficulties respecting Judaism and the new Nazarene sect over which they had often prayed together would be resolved, and satisfaction given to that deep craving after peace of soul which they had so long sought in vain to appease. Cornelius had evidently taken God's promise of a teacher not at all in the sense of a private favour granted to himself for his own peculiar desert, but as a common grace, in which it was meant that his friends were to share. So it had been arranged that they should meet that day within his rooms to await the messenger of God. It is significant of the state of things prevailing among more thoughtful heathens in the first century, that, at one garrison town, so many [1] persons should have been found, all of whom were sufficiently, if not all equally, ripe to welcome, on its first announcement, the glad tidings of Jesus Christ.

The centurion met the apostle at the outer gate of his quarters. That he prostrated himself at the feet of his visitor, could not mean in a Roman, what it might have meant in an Oriental, a simple obeisance of courtesy. It was really in some sort an act of religious reverence, and for this heathen, nothing could be more natural. To heathen habits of feeling, the worship which belonged to

[1] Cf. πολλούς, in ver. 27.

the immortal gods, belonged also in an inferior degree to a crowd of subordinate but semi-divine beings, deified men, or local and tutelar divinities. It spread itself abroad, in a still laxer form, over everything which was at all connected with the State religion, its idols, its temples, or its priests; and at Rome itself, religious rites had just begun a few years before to be paid to the Head of the State[1] as the quasi-divine representative upon earth of celestial rule. The strict barriers, therefore, which among Jews confined religious adoration in every form and degree to the one true God alone, were utterly foreign to pagan habits of thought. This man only obeyed an instinct which every Gentile would have owned, when he prostrated himself before one whom he had been told by a heavenly messenger to regard as a special agent and oracle of the Supreme God. The decision with which Peter at once repelled such exaggerated reverence marks the strong contrast between Hebrew and heathen feeling.[2] To the Jew, there stretched an infinite and bridgeless gulf betwixt Him Who is alone God, adorable for ever, and all other beings who, as dependent creatures, are like nothing before Him, and vanity. This gulf paganism had striven to fill up with whole species of imaginary personages, somewhat less than the supreme deity, but a good deal more divine than man; in consequence of which the sentiment of adoration was broken down, and the stern awful sense of divine sanctity or separateness was enfeebled, till worship became a graduated system of more or less respectful observances. It is

---

[1] See Alford, *in loc.*, citing Suetonius (*Octav.* 52).

[2] Cf. with ver. 26 the words of the angel to St. John, in Rev. xxii. 8, 9.

needless to add how much nobler as well as more true was the Hebrew than the pagan view. Such a horror of idolatry as feared to divert from the one Jehovah to any created being the least particle of that religious reverence which the Jealous One had challenged for His own, was one of the most important lessons taught to the world through the House of Israel. It early happened to the Gentile Churches of East and West to suffer this rigid monotheism which they had learned from Palestine to be corrupted by the inveterate pagan proclivities of their members.[1] From this source there rapidly sprang adoration of saints, picture and image worship, and the veneration of the relics of martyrs; till in the seventh century multitudes in the East revolted from a Christianity which had become little better than baptized polytheism, and flung themselves back upon the more rigorous monotheism and the more spiritual worship of Mahommed. It were a happy thing for Christendom if all its Churches even yet understood these early words of him whom the great Latin Church has selected for its favourite patron and reputed founder: "Stand up: I myself also am a man."

This state of superstitious awe in which the Roman approached St. Peter was most unfavourable to the frank or intelligent reception of a message so simple and human in its form as the gospel. But the friendly conversation in which it was remarked that Peter engaged his host as he accompanied him to the guest room,[2] with the outspoken and manly explanation which he there gave

[1] Especially after A.D. 325, when the Church was deluged with half-converted, conforming heathen.

[2] See ver. 27, συνομιλῶν αὐτῷ (i. e., with Cornelius) εἰσῆλθεν (into the room: the former εἰσελθεῖν, ver. 25, refers to his entrance into the court by the outer gateway).

to the assembled guests, put Cornelius entirely at his ease, and brought him back to his habitual attitude of quiet thoughtful inquiry. This stranger, though heralded by a celestial apparition and bearing words from God, was yet — not only a "man" — but quite a plain and ordinary Jew, with a provincial accent,[1] and attended by companions whose social standing was equally humble. His look wore nothing celestial to overbear the imagination of the soldier. He was not even above the prevailing social prejudices of his countrymen, for his first words, uttered with the abruptness which belonged to his impulsive character, were an apology for having ventured to disregard the usages of his nation. No law of God forbade to the Jew all intercourse whatever with Gentiles, only it had grown by this time to be the rule in circumspect Jewish society, as we learn from Latin writers,[2] and the later regulations of the Talmud fixed it as a sacred duty. These Gentiles, quartered in a Jewish town, knew very well what the practice of devout Hebrews was;[3] and Peter was frank enough to admit that for his own part[4] nothing but a special revelation from heaven could have induced him to depart from it. By the vision at Joppa, by inward spiritual direction, and by the force of events, God had now made it clear to His servant that no man was henceforth to be treated as profane or unclean. The distinction among mankind, on which

---

[1] Matt. xxvi. 73.

[2] See in Alford, *in loc.*, passages from Juvenal and Tacitus. The passage in *Josephus c. Apion*, ii. 29, has doubtful force here. Cf., however, John xix. 28. The case in Josephus, *Antiq.* xx. 2. 4, is therefore exceptional.

[3] Cf. the emphatic ὑμεῖς ἐπίστασθε, in ver. 28.

[4] Compare the καμοί, in ver. 28, with διό, in ver. 29.

Hebrew usage rested, was at last so far abolished that the Gentiles had been by the blood of Christ made clean enough for Jewish touch; even as the ancient distinction of meats, which before kept them apart, had been abolished, so that Peter could sit now at Cornelius's table with an untarnished conscience. It was for this reason, as he explained, that he had come when sent for, without one word of objection or of scruple, and he begged to know why they had sent for him.

The composed account which Cornelius thereupon gave of his vision four days before, and the polite terms of welcome[1] in which he expressed the readiness of himself and his friends to hear God's message, reflect the simple, transparent character of the man. In tone they form a contrast to the energetic, almost vehement, rapidity of Peter in the discourse which followed. The moment was come for the apostle to deliver the message with which his Divine Master had charged him, and the soul of the man kindled with his blessed burden. He brought glad tidings to these longing souls; and the first words in which he is reported to have opened his testimony are so impetuous, so defiant of construction, that they have been the despair of grammarians.[2] Yet before he even begins to preach the gospel, he gives most emphatic expression to the great lesson which this whole series of events had been teaching to himself. Before him sat an audience such as he had never previously preached Christ to. The narrative of Cornelius and the waiting faces of his friends have crowned that sequence of proofs by which God had

[1] The phrase, σύ τε καλῶς ἐποίησας, ver. 33, is not a compliment to Peter, but a courteous form of welcome.

[2] On the construction in ver. 36-38, the reader may consult Meyer, Alford, Olshausen, &c., *in loc.*, and Winer, *Gram.* (6th ed.), p. 507.

been conducting him, whether he would or not, to a conclusion grand enough to thrill him with agitation. That God respected no man's person, was a doctrine he had read indeed often enough in Holy Scripture,[1] and, in the letter of it, knew by heart. But never till now had he realised its import or dreamed how wide its application was. Never had he seen that this impartiality of God, which passes by external differences to deal only with what is moral and spiritual in men, places all just and pious souls of whatever nationality on the same platform before God's grace, and makes them equally fit on that ground alone to receive the kingdom of God's dear Son. Peter had heard his Master say, in that amazing sermon preached at Capernaum,[2] that the one condition of any man's coming unto Him was a certain secret inward drawing of the soul by the Father in heaven; and that whosoever came, being thus taught and drawn of God, He should in no wise cast out. He had also heard Jesus declare in the temple[3] that the moral and religious preparation required for the reception of His gospel, lay in that tractableness of will which desires with a child's docility to do God's will. Still Peter had never before realised that such words possessed spiritual width enough to take in uncircumcised, as well as circumcised, men: so that every one throughout God's world who was of the truth should hear Christ's voice.[4] Now he saw it. Here were men, pure Gentiles, who yet, through God's mysterious grace, feared God and wrought righteousness; in whom the moral and spiritual conditions of acceptance into the kingdom were complete,

---

[1] See, *e. g.*, Deut. x. 17, and 2 Chron. xix. 7.
Cf. John vi. 37, 44, 45.   [3] Ibid. vii. 17.   [4] See Ibid. xviii. 37.

although the external physical conditions he had supposed needful were wholly wanting. These men God Himself had so far recognised as fit candidates for mercy, that to them as they were God had sent him to declare the glad tidings of peace.

No question is raised here, either in Peter's mind or by his words, as to God's acceptance of men like Cornelius without their believing on Jesus Christ. The acceptableness he is thinking and speaking of is acceptableness simply as persons to whom the gospel of Christ may fitly be sent and with success preached. Further than this we are not at liberty to press his language. That most fascinating mystery, over which charitable hearts will always hang, of the position which such men as Cornelius would occupy were they never to hear the name of Jesus or be baptized into His Church; that unanswered question, touching the hopes of the honest-minded heathen, who, having not the law, do by nature the things contained in the law,[1] walking after such light as they possess, is left by this Scripture in the same darkness as by every other Scripture. Devout and reverent thinkers may allow to themselves such secret thoughts as are consistent with a due submission to the justice and sovereignty of God; but the Church, which can speak in her public testimony only where God has spoken, must here be silent. That only which has been revealed, is matter of faith.

Yet let no one deem it a trivial discovery which St. Peter made at Cæsarea. That God bids all ready and waiting and willing souls alike welcome to His blessed evangel, and without reference to their antecedents or

[1] Rom. ii. 14.

their advantages or their conventional recommendations, has flung wide to them the doors of His free grace, was then and is now the very glory of the kingdom of Christ. Here is no question asked, but, Are you inwardly prepared to receive the gospel? A heart made good and honest by the grace of God, a will to do His will, a fear of God and effort after justice, an ear that waits to hear, a lowly spirit that prays for light—these are the conditions of acceptance. It is true, such a person has still need to be told of Jesus Christ Who reconciled us to the Father; since, besides His, there is no other name given under heaven whereby we must be saved.[1] Only such a person is very welcome to Christ, indeed is already not far from Him. He hears at once the voice of Christ Who seeks him, and comes at once to Christ's light, when the light of Christ only comes to him.[2]

So much of his intended sermon as Peter had delivered when he was gloriously interrupted,[3] falls into three parts. The first is an historical retrospect of facts which, having happened within a few years before and in their immediate neighbourhood, were already known to his audience. The second is the testimony of an eye-witness to one stupendous fact, not yet certainly known to the hearers, which filled up with light and meaning all the preceding history. The third is an authoritative proclamation on behalf of God of the way to pardon at His judgment-seat through His exalted Son, Jesus Christ. The whole speech thus moves through the same cycle of ideas as are found in all other speeches of St. Peter. It

Compare Acts iv. 12.   [2] John x. 16, iii. 21.
This appears from ἐν δὲ τῷ ἄρξασθαί με λαλεῖν, of xi. 15.

wears the same threefold character of an historical review, an apostolic witness, and an evangelist's proclamation of peace.

In the first place, Peter rapidly recalled certain notorious facts connected with the ministry of the Nazareth Teacher, that ministry which began in the adjacent province of Galilee after John's baptism, and was terminated by Jesus' own violent death at Jerusalem. People who lived in Cæsarea could not help knowing that rumour which a few years before had gone abroad [1] and convulsed society in Palestine; how, after receiving, as was said, at His baptism in Jordan the unction of the Holy Ghost which marked Him out for the Christ, Jesus had traversed the whole land as a teacher and a wonder-worker; how, as a minister of God specially to the circumcision [2] (though He was at the same time "Lord of all men," Jew and Gentile alike; as Peter parenthetically interjects), He had preached to the children of Israel God's gospel of peace [3] through Himself as their Messiah; how He proved that He was not alone in this nor "spoke of Himself," [4] but had "God with Him," by beneficent works of healing, wrought everywhere on such of His unhappy countrymen as evil spirits had afflicted with sore troubles, especially those over whom Satan had, as it were, tyrannised, [5] mastering even their wills; finally, how a Man Who thus carried about with Him, in some pregnant, though as yet

[1] This seems to be the meaning of τὸ γενόμενον ῥῆμα, in ver. 37.
[2] Cf. Paul in Rom. xv. 8.
[3] Ἐυαγγελιζομένος εἰρήνην, ver. 36.
[4] John viii. 16, 29, xiv. 10, vii. 17, viii. 28.
[5] Cf. καταδυναστευομένους, in ver. 38, only found elsewhere in Jas. ii. 6. See similar language of spiritual possession in St. Paul, 2 Tim. ii. 26.

indefinite, sense, the special presence of God,[1] had been violently put to death by crucifixion.

So much they already knew by common rumour. What they could not yet know was that the Crucified had since come to life again. The evidence of this (Peter said) had not been given publicly to the nation which had rejected Him. It was kept for chosen witnesses previously selected[2] of God for that end when Jesus called them to apostleship. Yet, since this fact was one which made all the rest weighty, and transformed the biography of the Nazarene into a gospel for mankind, therefore to these chosen witnesses the evidence had been made absolutely complete. They not only saw Him; they ate with Him;[3] they drank with Him. Proof the most searching and indubitable had been afforded them in order that their words might certify the world. "And we," said Peter, in name of his absent colleagues, "we are they who ate and drank with Him after He rose from the dead."

Thus far the preacher sketched in outline the historical basis on which the gospel reposes. To us, both these classes of facts, those which were patent to Jesus' contemporaries, and those of which the Twelve were witnesses at first hand, are become matters of remote history, borne down to us on the credible authority of certain written documents. We cannot, as Cornelius could, cross-

---

[1] Peter's words here, ὁ Θεὸς ἦν μετ' αὐτοῦ, seem purposely guarded. They express the conclusion to which any candid observer ought to have arrived at the date of Jesus' crucifixion. His resurrection led, of course, to more than that. The reference here to Jesus' works, as proofs that He was sustained by the power of God, is in striking harmony with much of Jesus' own in the fourth Gospel.

[2] Προκεχειροτονημένοις, in ver. 41, is a ἅπ. λεγ.

[3] See Luke xxiv. 40-43; c. John xxi. 13. His use of *liquid* food is not expressly stated in the Gospels.

examine a man who had eaten with the risen Christ; nor can we, as he, by a week's tour among the highlands of Galilee might have done, investigate what it was this Man taught, and what were the works He was said to do. Under this disadvantage must lie every generation except that first one. Yet the first-hand evidence has been preserved to us with such freshness and abundance in those collected pamphlets which we call the New Testament, as substantially to defy criticism and to satisfy with quite reasonable certainty a candid historian. More than this we have no right to ask. Less than this we could not trust to; for it is on this substructure of plain fact that we must place, just as Peter did, the stupendous doctrines of Christ's gospel.[1] These doctrines, as recited by that primitive preacher, are mainly two: the one that God has made Jesus of Nazareth to be the Judge at last of all men, living or dead, Jew or Gentile; the other, that the road to pardon and justification at the bar of this Judge lies through faith in Himself. The elevation of a Person Who appeared at a given period in human history to the throne of divine justice, so that in His hands, through which men drove nails, shall yet lie the everlasting doom of every living soul, is not so much a doctrine as a revealed fact. It is one of those facts, however, which wraps within its bosom a world of teaching. The divine dignity of the Man thus entrusted with the supreme task of Deity, the innocence and sacrificial worth of His passion, with the vital moment of each other man's relation to this single Man; these are all implications involved in that

[1] It is noticeable that Peter speaks of his message as a thing Jesus commanded him to preach. This command was probably on a different occasion from any recorded in the Gospels—different from Matt. xxviii. 29, or Acts i. 8.

fact and carried along with it. Further, it is because Jesus is to judge that He can now save. Absolution from sin, like condemnation for it, lies in His hand. It comes through His name. It comes to the men who trust Him for it. It lies open and free to trusting souls of any land or race. Finally, it is in this Saviour Judge and His pardon of sin that we must find the focus, the burning centre, of the earlier Old Testament revelation, preparing for or foretelling grace to men—the centre, in fact, of all earlier training or drawing of human hearts to wait in darkness for a light to arise: "To Him give all the prophets witness."

To this point only Peter had arrived, purposing to amplify and urge his message; but for prepared hearts few words are needful. Men who are waiting for God leap before the preacher. The inspiration of the Holy Ghost makes speech superfluous. The advent on these heathens in its highest form of that peculiar spiritual influence which is characteristic of the Christian Church—I mean of the Holy Ghost as the Spirit not only of new birth, but also of the assurance of sonship to God—is an event which has no parallel save Pentecost. This was the Pentecost of the Gentiles. Suddenly, just as at Jerusalem, on the whole assembly of worshippers, with some visible, unmistakable signs, if not with rush of wind or tongue of flame, there fell the Holy Ghost. Again, too, as at Jerusalem, the tongues of the heathen men were filled with strange and unknown words of exultation, and aloud, in the heat of a holy rapture, each one broke into the praises of the God of salvation. It was not possible for Peter and the Church then, it is not possible for us now, to mistake the divine purpose in this repetition at Cæsarea of what had occurred in Jerusalem. God would put the alien and so long "unclean" nations on a platform no less high than that of the Jewish mother Church. He would authenticate by as solemn a baptism from heaven their admission into the household and kingdom of His Son. "What God hath cleansed," said the voice in the vision, "that call not thou common." The marvel of Cæsarea repeated the warning. God did cleanse heathendom in the person of Cornelius and his fellows, and Peter dared no longer call heathen men common. It was this perfect parallel between God's gift of His Spirit to these Romans and the gift of His Spirit " at the beginning," which Peter employed, both at the time and afterwards,[1] as a conclusive proof that God meant, under the new gospel economy, to treat the circumcised and the uncircumcised alike. Those words in which the Lord Jesus, on the eve of His ascension, had promised to the first little company of friends who clung regretfully about Him, that He would soon baptise them with that Spirit-baptism of which John's had been a figure, flashed through Peter's mind when he saw the memorable scene of the upper chamber renewed in the barrack-room.[2] This, too, was a fulfilment of that promise. This, too, was the true baptismal blessing, the actual reception of men into the Church of Christ. Cornelius and the rest are not circumcised; but they are indubitably disciples by the best right, and in the fullest communion with the Head, since they have been introduced into fellowship by Christ's own hand, and sealed with Christ's own seal. "Who can forbid the water,[3] where He has not withheld the Spirit?"

[1] Immediately after at Jerusalem, Acts xi. 15–17, and in the Synod later, chap. xv. 7–9.   [2] See Acts xi. 16, c. i. 5.
[3] Note the article in τὸ ὕδωρ, ver. 47, parallel to τὸ πνεῦμα.

Wherever, therefore, we find the fruits of the Holy Spirit of Christ, there, on the authority of an apostle, we are bound to recognise the Church of Christ.[1] Churches which unchurch communions of believing and holy men, because their ecclesiastical order is not valid, nor their episcopal descent continuous, appear, on these principles, to be guilty, not only of folly, but of schism. They misunderstand, and then they rend, the spiritual body of Christ. But if hierarchism and high-churchism accord ill with the transactions at Cæsarea, it fares little better with the ultra-spiritualism of those who despise church order, or deem of no account the due administration of the holy sacraments. Never, save on that solitary occasion, did the special gift of the Holy Ghost precede the baptism of a convert. Even on that occasion the exceptional presence of the thing signified did not render superfluous the observance of the sign. God is not bound even to His own order; nor can baptism possess any magical virtue to confer what God conferred without it. Yet the Church even then followed in the steps of her Lord, ratifying by her outward act what He had already done by inward grace. To administer the sacraments, indeed, was not in that primitive age the highest office of Christian ministers. Following the same rule as St. Paul observed,[2] Peter left it to the six brethren from Joppa to complete by baptism the formal reception into church-fellowship of these first Gentile converts. Baptised they were, however, with the baptism of water, confessing their sins and invoking the name of the Lord Jesus.

Thus was consummated the first formal or official

[1] *Ubi Christus, ibi ecclesia.*   [2] 1 Cor. i. 14-17.

recognition that the law of Moses and the older rites of Abrahamic Judaism were, as conditions of life and rules of duty, for ever abolished in the Christian Church. Of the far-reaching theological issues of that day's transaction, we shall find the clearest, no less than the most authoritative, exposition, in these words by the most theological of the apostles:[1]—

"For now, the righteousness of God, to which both the law and the prophets had so long borne witness, has been made manifest, quite apart from the law; that righteousness of God, which comes through trust in Jesus Christ to all those who do trust Him, whether Jew or Gentile. For now there is no longer any difference; since we have all alike sinned and fallen short of the moral likeness of God our Father; so are we all alike justified gratuitously by His free grace through the one atonement made for all in Christ Jesus. Him God has set before us all at last as a propitiatory sacrifice through faith that rests in His blood. Thus, too, is the righteousness of God at last made evident. In His forbearance it pleased God of old to pass over in silence the sinful acts of men in times gone by; but now in this present age He has set Christ before us all to make His righteousness plain—how He can be just and yet justify the child of faith. . . . . God is no God for Jews only. He is the God also of the Gentiles: one and the same God, Who will justify circumcised and uncircumcised men alike, through their faith."

[1] Rom. iii. 21–30. I have used the freedom to modify the Authorised Version, and slightly to paraphrase the text, in the hope of giving greater freshness to the sense of the original.

XIX.

Peter Reports to the Church.

μηδ' ὡς κατακυριεύοντες τῶν κλήρων.

Acts xi. 1-18.

Revised Version.

Now the apostles and the brethren who were throughout Judæa heard that the Gentiles also had received the Word of God. And when Peter went up to Jerusalem they of the circumcision were contending with him, saying: "Thou didst go in to men uncircumcised, and didst eat with them." But Peter began and set forth to them from the beginning, saying:

"I was in the city of Joppa praying, and saw in an ecstasy a vision, a certain vessel descending like a great sheet let down by four corners out of heaven, and it came even to me; into which when I gazed, I observed and saw the quadrupeds of the earth, and the wild beasts and the reptiles, and the birds of heaven. I also heard a voice saying to me: 'Rise, Peter, slay and eat.' But I said: 'By no means, Lord, for common or unclean thing never entered into my mouth.' But the voice answered a second time out of heaven: 'What God cleansed, make not thou common.' Now this happened thrice, and all were drawn up again into heaven. And behold, at once three men stood there by the house in which I was, sent from Cæsarea to me. And the Spirit bade me go with them. But there went with me also these six brethren, and we entered into the *house of the man, and he reported to us how he had seen the angel in his house, standing and saying to him: 'Send to Joppa and call for Simon who is surnamed Peter, who shall speak things to thee in which thou shalt be saved, and thy whole house.' But on my beginning to speak, there fell the Holy Ghost on them, as also on us at the beginning: and I remembered the Lord's word, how He said: 'John indeed baptized with water, but ye shall be baptized in the Holy Ghost.' If therefore God gave to them the like free-gift as to us also, who believed on the Lord Jesus Christ, who was I, able to hinder God?"*

Now, when they heard these things, they held their peace, and were glorifying God, saying: " Then to the Gentiles also did God give the repentance unto life!"

XIX.

THE importance of the centurion's baptism rested, not simply on its being the issue of a series of divine interpositions which led up to it, but quite as much on its being instantly recognised and accepted by the Church as the commencement of a new era. Its recognition by the Church, however, hinged on its having been manifestly brought about by the hand of God. Hence, Peter's narrative of those divine revelations and interpositions by which the Lord had Himself fitted everything together so as to leave no doubt of His will, was necessary before the Church could welcome with joy the new and altered conditions of Church membership.

News of what had occurred at Cæsarea reached Jerusalem before St. Peter. He does not appear to have sent any report to his colleagues at head-quarters, nor did he go up to the capital until he had first spent some days with the new converts. Still it is natural to conjecture that his return would be somewhat hastened by the unexpected turn things had taken. He could scarcely feel free to complete his round of visitation at leisure, as if nothing of importance had happened. He took with him to the capital those six believing Jews of Joppa whom he had brought with him to Cæsarea, which looks as if he returned straight from Cæsarea to Jerusalem without any further visitation of Churches, under some expectation that he might need to explain or vindicate what he had done. Meanwhile, during the days he remained with Cornelius, imperfect rumours of these strange events had reached, not only Jerusalem, but also the believers who lived in the landward districts of Judæa and were in immediate dependence upon the mother Church in the city. That mother Church was still watched over by more than one apostle besides Peter himself. James the son of Zebedee had not yet received the grace of martyrdom. In all likelihood, James the son of Alphæus was already the recognised resident head of the Jerusalem congregations. Others, of whom history is silent, may have still exercised their office within the original territory of Judæa. All these, with the brethren throughout the province,[1] heard that the Gentiles also had received the word of God, the gospel message of life in Jesus Christ. From the terms of Luke's narrative we gather some notion of the rumour which reached them. Cæsarea, not Joppa, was the source from which it came. Therefore they knew little or nothing about Peter's vision and the chain of circumstances by which he had been prepared to treat Gentiles as no longer unclean. They knew of Cornelius [2] and of the angelic visitant whom God had sent to him.[3] Whether or not the more spiritual side of his conversion was reported, or the advent of the Holy Spirit on him and his friends in wonderful manifestation, they were at least told that Peter had sanctioned the administration of

[1] Cf. κατὰ τὴν Ἰουδαίαν, in ver. 1.
[2] Cf. τοῦ ἀνδρός, in ver. 12, which, while sinking his name, assumes that the man had been heard of by them.
[3] Cf. the art. in ver. 13, τὸν ἄγγελον.

baptism to men who had not first submitted to circumcision, and had entered into domestic table fellowship, possibly into holy eucharistic fellowship,[1] with them. Even as thus imperfectly reported, the event was felt to be one of the highest possible moment. That persons who stood wholly without the pale of the chosen people and the ancient covenant should have the gospel preached to them at all, should receive it gladly, and should profess so much faith in Jesus, that an apostle could judge them fit for baptism—this alone meant an immense deal. For if to Cornelius and his comrades the message of the kingdom could come, why not to other Romans outside Palestine? Why not to all heathens throughout the world? A vision began to open up of expansion and progress, which, to homebred Jews, nursed in Hebrew exclusiveness, would seem next to bewildering. Nor could the news, in one aspect of it, appear to hearts that loved Jesus a thing to be regretted. Joy at the diffusion of the Saviour's precious name, and at the making glad of human souls through forgiveness of sins by His blood, could not fail to be the first instinct of every genuine disciple. Only the circumstances under which the thing was reported to have occurred, looked, at first sight, so suspicious, that joy was crossed or checked by uncertainty and alarm. What they knew as yet was no more than the naked fact, and even that put in its worst light, that Peter had broken through all rule by treating uncircumcised men, both ecclesiastically and socially, as if they were circumcised. Why he had done so, or by what steps he had been led to make so serious an innovation, they did not know. Therefore they hardly knew whether to be glad

[1] Can the συνέφαγες, in ver. 3, mean this?

or vexed. For heathens to receive the word of life was one thing; for the Church to receive heathens off-hand, without the usual legal purifying, was a very different thing.

Thus matters stood when Peter reached Jerusalem. It is not easy to be sure how the affair came up for discussion. Luke says that Peter delivered his explanatory report at a time when "they of the circumcision" were disputing or contending with him;[1] but it is hard to ascertain what such a phrase as "they of the circumcision" can mean, when applied to that period of the Church. By the time St. Luke wrote, the phrase had indeed become usual to denote primarily the whole number of Jewish, as opposed to Gentile, Christians, and then specially the party which urged the observance of Jewish ritual. But at the earlier time of which he was writing, such a phrase could not have been in use in either sense. No Judaizing party yet existed, and as all the converts were Jews, it was not needful to distinguish Jewish converts by any specific name. By applying, then, this later phrase to the early Church, does St. Luke intend to describe the whole body of believers, who were all of course, in the literal sense of the words, "men of the circumcision"? or does he designate that portion only of the believers who afterwards came to form a Judaizing party? I incline to the latter alternative. It appears to me hardly likely to have been the entire company of the "apostles and brethren" who set themselves in open opposition to Peter's conduct. In that case it would have been more natural for the writer, who had just named them in the preceding sentence, to refer to them by a pronoun—When Peter was gone up to Jerusalem *they*

[1] διεκρίνοντο, ver. 2.

were contending with him. More probably, the difficulty which all more or less felt came to speech in the mouths of a certain section of the Church. The strong Jewish prejudice in favour of Mosaic law, which a few years later was to work such wide-spread mischief, as all St. Paul's letters show, must have already lain latent in the minds of many baptized Jews. No occasion had till now arisen to stir that prejudice into activity, but these recent events at Cæsarea did form such an occasion. Those brethren who were sure to feel most aggrieved by Peter's laxity, and to resent it most warmly, were precisely the very brethren who at a later day, when Gentile liberty had come to be a question hotly contested, consolidated themselves into an avowed and active party. Nothing could be more natural than that the dissatisfaction with Peter's action, which to some extent every Jew in the mother Church may have shared, should first break out into open displeased remonstrance from that class of Jews who were the most conservative, the most national, the most bigoted, and the most zealous for law and custom. Jews of this type were more numerous in Jerusalem than anywhere else. At a later period they proved strong enough to overbear even Peter's firmness.[1] And if Luke desired to indicate them, he could scarcely avoid using the familiar term which, when he wrote, described the corresponding church-party of his time. It is true they were not yet a party "of the circumcision," but they were the men out of whom such a party was soon to grow; and their action that day was really the earliest open exhibition of those opinions which the circumcision-party came ultimately to embody.[2]

[1] Gal. ii. 12.   [2] So Calvin (in loc.) and Lange (Bibel Werk).

This view is supported by the language ascribed to these complainants. Had it been his fellow-apostles who desired from St. Peter an account of what had passed at Cæsarea, the great spiritual transaction of the reception of Christ by heathens, and of heathens by Christ in baptism, would surely have formed the matter of inquiry; whereas the point in Peter's conduct over which his questioners wrangled was the subordinate detail of "eating" with the uncircumcised. In social intercourse at the house of Cornelius, he had disregarded, not a law of Moses, but a traditional usage of orthodox Jews, and this they make the head and front of his offending. Nor would the official heads of the Church have been likely to edge their reproaches against a foremost apostle with any word of contempt cast at the Gentiles; yet the phrase used by the objectors for the new Roman converts (though rendered softly in our Authorised Version, "men uncircumcised") is in fact an untranslatable expression of rude and displeased contempt.[1]

By whomsoever put, Peter met the question with a calm and careful narrative of facts. It can hardly fail to startle those who know how his name has since been used in Christendom to cover the most unbounded claims of Church authority, that we should here find this first of apostles reduced to justify his apostolic action before an assembly of his brethren. Yet this is in perfect accord with the whole New Testament. The apostolic Church is never represented as a close oligarchy, much less as an empire with an infallible head. Not even apostolic office confers autocratic power. Not even miraculous gifts of inspiration are held to secure practical infallibility.

[1] πρὸς ἄνδρας ἀκροβυστίαν ἔχοντας, ver. 3.

The grace and wisdom of Jesus Christ reside exclusively in no man or college of men, but in that "Body" of Jesus Christ which is the assembly of all the faithful. Before that assembly of the faithful[1] it is that the "Prince of the Apostles" is content to plead. If any man might have carried matters within the Church with a high hand, surely it was this Rock-Man, to whom Jesus had given the keys; and if ever he had an excuse for being peremptory or self-assertive, it was at the moment when, led by the voice of his Master, he had just set open to the whole heathen world the gates of the kingdom of God. Yet to his brethren, even to brethren whose tone was unpleasant and disputatious, he felt bound to offer a most careful explanation, to fortify his statement by the evidence of witnesses, and to appeal to their own reason in justification of his conduct. Peter, not less than Paul, might have fairly said: "We do not preach ourselves, but Christ Jesus as the Lord, and ourselves as only your servants for Jesus' sake."[2]

The narrative which St. Peter gave passed lightly over facts which his hearers already knew, to relate in detail those previous revelations to himself which had prepared him for the reception of Cornelius. Having in a previous chapter considered the events at Joppa, it is not necessary to repeat them here. Only it is worth remark how Peter connected together his significant vision of the clean and unclean beasts with the coincident arrival of the Roman messengers and the inward monition of the Holy Ghost,[3] as a threefold cord, of which each strand was severally spun by a celestial Hand, and which drew him

---

[1] As we see here, and more fully in the fifteenth chapter of Acts.
[2] See 2 Cor. iv. 5, in the original.   [3] Ver. 9-12.

with a force he dared not withstand to the new work God had waiting for him at Cæsarea. So far the incident had been purely personal, and rested on his sole testimony. At this point there entered the corroborative evidence of the six brethren. They knew as well as he what took place in the centurion's house. On the uncircumcised Romans they too had seen the Holy Ghost descend in manner and in measure as at Pentecost upon the waiting apostles. On this final and decisive fact Peter reared his brief but very conclusive argument. While he actually stood in the soldier's chamber and saw the afflatus inspire his heathen hearers, there had occurred to his recollection his Master's mighty promise to baptise His disciples with that Divine Spirit of Whom water-baptism was only the symbol and pledge. That promise he now recalled to the brethren's minds. This second effusion of the predicted Spirit he recognises as precisely identical in character with the former one at Pentecost—a fulfilment of the Master's promise not less signal. And from the "like gift," given by the same Heart-searcher, he infers a like spiritual condition in the receivers. They too must have found forgiveness and acceptance with God. Nay more, it was Peter's conviction that on himself and the rest of the original disciple-band, God had bestowed this free gift of His Spirit in excellent measure simply because they had believed on the Lord Jesus Christ.[1] It was neither their Jewish birth, nor their circumcision, nor anything peculiar to their external position, which formed the ground of their baptism at Pentecost. It was simply

---

[1] This is implied in the words of ver. 17, which thus become of very great importance: αὐτοῖς . . . ὡς καὶ ἡμῖν πιστεύσασιν ἐπὶ τὸν κύριον κτλ.

their faith in Jesus. To Gentiles therefore who believed had now come the very same "free gift" of God, as once on Jews who believed, on purpose to prove that, in this cardinal matter of favour with God and reception of the promised Spirit of life in Christ, "neither circumcision availeth anything, nor uncircumcision, but faith."[1] "Since God (says he) gave to them the identical free gift which He also gave to us who were believers on the Lord Jesus Christ, what was I, that I could withstand God?" In these few words, spoken at so early a date by the lips of St. Peter, there lies, shut up as in a seed, the whole doctrine of free grace and justification by faith alone, which in after years it became the work of St. Paul's life to develop and defend. No better commentary on these words can anywhere be found than the later language of his "beloved brother Paul:"—"We, Jews by nature and not sinners of the Gentiles, yet knowing that a man is not justified by works of law, but through faith of Jesus Christ, even we did believe on Christ Jesus, in order that we might be justified by faith and not by works of law; for by works of law shall no flesh be justified."[2]

This is language which Paul addressed to Peter in the city of Antioch. Years had come and gone since first Peter defended himself before a company of brethren at Jerusalem for the offence of eating with Gentiles. A second time he was arraigned before a company of brethren at Antioch, but it was for the opposite offence of refusing to eat with Gentiles. In Jerusalem, fresh from the wonderful vision of Joppa and the more wonderful revival of Cæsarea, Peter was strong in his apostolic conviction that God was treating all men alike, and had "made clean by

[1] Gal. v. 6.   [2] Gal. ii. 15, 16. From the Greek text of Tischendorf.

faith" alone the hearts both of Jew and Gentile.[1] To place on Gentile necks a Jewish yoke seemed then to him nothing short of "withstanding" and "tempting" God.[2] Before his manly speech the incipient misgivings of Hebrew prejudice were for the moment silenced. The enthusiasm of the Jewish converts over this new-won freedom, and their happy consciousness of a wider brotherhood, broke forth in general praise. It seemed at that promising dawn as if the new-comers out of heathendom might be suffered without jealousy—or even welcomed with joy—to sit down at the table of the kingdom with the children of Abraham, to eat one bread of God and drink one cup of salvation. It might have been hoped then that the Church, knowing no more distinctions of race or privilege, would pass without strife or schism from its old subordination to Mosaic law into the spiritual freedom of Christ, from the swaddling-clothes of its childhood to the rights of its majority. Did not the whole Judæan Church hold its peace from objections at the explanations of St. Peter, and give continuous glory to God Who to the Gentiles also had granted repentance unto life? Alas! so fair a promise was doomed to be early overcast. The rise of a separate Gentile Church at Antioch not long after came to be viewed with rivalry, not, it is true, by the chiefs of the Judæan mother Church, yet by a large and influential section of its stricter members. A synod at Jerusalem could decide the question, but it could not compose the strife. By the time Paul met Peter face to face in Antioch, the pressure of ultra-Hebrew feeling in the Jerusalem Church had waxed so strong, that before it Peter himself wavered and gave way. In a moment of feebleness he actually pre-

[1] Acts xv. 9.   [2] Cf. xi. 17, c. xv. 10.

tended to disown the truth which God had first taught him on Simon's housetop, and consecrated for ever in the centurion's room; pretended to respect distinctions which he, foremost of all men, had been honoured to declare abolished within the Church of Christ. The sterner stuff of which Paul was made withstood that pressure of partisan bigotry to which Peter yielded. Paul, not Peter, is the rock which, by God's grace, turned aside for ever from the Gentile Churches a current which would otherwise have swept Christianity into Mosaic legalism and Hebrew exclusiveness. Yet in their convictions the two apostles were absolutely at one. All suspicion of any real antagonism which might be drawn from Peter's unhappy inconsistency at Antioch is rebutted by his noble words spoken long before in Jerusalem. The language in which he summed up to his brethren the net result of the whole series of divine acts and providential coincidences which had led to his action in Cæsarea, is actually the earliest appearance in Church history of what is termed by pre-eminence, from its chief teacher and most steady champion, the Pauline doctrine of free and impartial grace for all men through faith alone.

The limitation which for so many centuries confined the light of revelation and the saving favour of God to the members of one small and strictly-guarded tribe of Syrian Shemites, was a limitation which must for ever have shut out us and our fathers. So long as the road to the true Light of men led only through the narrow portals of Solomon's temple, the uncircumcised world lay in hopeless darkness. Heaven was inaccessible, save from one privileged and sacred spot of earth. Even under this limitation, men owed it to God's goodness that heaven was accessible at all. No compulsion, save that of His own free love, lay upon our Father to widen the area of His grace. In His wise pleasure He had elected Israel; in His wise pleasure He might have let the election stand. But the very election itself contemplated from the first ultimate catholicity. Israel was made a guarded focus of light just that it might one day enlighten the Gentiles. Happy had they all known their calling of God, as their best prophets and seers knew it, the Jews might have enjoyed the conscious honour and blessedness of being the teachers of mankind, freely handing round to every other nation the truths which had been taught and the life which had been given to themselves. It was their national selfishness which grew proud over the exclusive possession of blessings which it ought to have been their nobler pride to make the common heritage of men. What God gave to mankind they strove to keep to their tribes. Thus it came that, violently and with ruin to themselves, the grace of life had to tear itself away from their grip, in order to overspread the globe; and this curse was fulfilled in their national experience: "He that will save his life shall lose it." Yet it was by the hands of Jews, after all, that the grace of God was first conveyed to a Gentile home in Cæsarea; by the lips of Jews that thanks for that grace were first rendered to God at Jerusalem. Nay, through the remote instrumentality of Jewish missionaries, are we ourselves become the heirs and fellows of that earliest band of uncircumcised children of God which clustered round a Roman officer in the Cæsarean barracks.

XX.

The Church of Antioch.

εὐχαριστοῦμεν σοι ὅτι τὸ ὄνομα τοῦ χριστοῦ σου ἐπικέκληται ἐφ' ἡμᾶς.
Liturgy of S. Clement.

Acts xi. 19-26.

Revised Version.

Now then, they who were scattered from the trouble which arose on account of Stephen, passed through as far as Phœnicia and Cyprus and Antioch, speaking the Word to none except to Jews only. But some of them were men of Cyprus and Cyrene, who coming to Antioch began to speak to the Greeks [also], preaching the Lord Jesus. And the Lord's hand was with them, and a great number who believed turned to the Lord. But the report about them came to the ears of the Church which was in Jerusalem, and they sent out Barnabas to pass through as far as Antioch. Who when he came and saw the grace which was of God, rejoiced and exhorted all with the purpose of their heart to cleave to the Lord; for he was a good man, and full of the Holy Ghost and of faith. And a considerable multitude was added to the Lord. But he went out to Tarsus to seek out Saul, and when he had found [him] brought [him] to Antioch. And it came to pass that for a whole year they assembled in the Church and taught a considerable multitude, and that the disciples were first called "Christians" in Antioch.

XX.

SO long as an historian is called on to narrate events which have succeeded each other on the same field of action, his story may run on in continuous chronological order. But where several series of events have occurred about the same time, in different places, his narrative will cease to be rigidly chronological. One set of connected incidents must be related together till the narrative has reached some natural pause. Then the narrator has to go back upon an earlier date, to take up events which have meanwhile been transpiring elsewhere. The earlier half of the book of Acts is a narrative of this latter sort. At least, it becomes such a narrative after the death of Stephen. That great occurrence set in motion more than one line of Christian activity at various points within and beyond the limits of Palestine. Already we have followed three distinct narratives which sprang out of it. First came Philip's successful mission to Samaria. Then followed Saul's inquisitorial expedition to Damascus, with the wonderful change which ensued. Lastly, we have considered St. Peter's visitation of the persecuted congregations on the coast-plain after the Church found rest again, and the divine reception of uncircumcised Romans at Cæsarea to which it led. In proceeding now to relate the next great forward step taken in the self-development and propagation of our Christian faith, by the founding of a Gentile Church at Antioch, the historian has once more to fall back, for his point of departure, upon the scattering of the Jerusalem Church on the death of her first martyr.[1] This was another and a still more remote line of Church extension, due to the same dispersion. Samaria, Damascus, Cæsarea, and Antioch were thus four centres of independent movements; but how far the movements were synchronous or successive it is impossible now to determine. It is quite possible that Saul may have been spending part of his three years in Arabia and Damascus when St. Peter was receiving Cornelius into the Church at Cæsarea. It is very probable that the conversion of Cornelius was not even known at Antioch when the first-fruits of heathendom began to be congregated there. The two or three years which preceded, and the two or three which followed A. D. 40, formed a time of restless progress and prodigious change for the new faith. Cut off from orthodox Judaism by the sentence which condemned Stephen, it was beating in every direction against the bars of Hebrew exclusiveness, and finding out by experiments in various lands how wide was the field which its Head had destined it to occupy. Of all the doors by which it found admission to the Greco-Roman west, the readiest and the widest was Antioch.

Our inspired account of the founding of the mother Church of heathendom is disappointingly brief, but it is extremely interesting. When the trouble which arose about Stephen burst asunder the Judæan Church after

[1] See Acts xi. 19, alluding to viii. 4.

years of silent growth, and projected its members as exiles and fugitives over the whole of Syria, one band of dispersed believers took the northern road through Samaria to that strip of fertile coast lying along the Levant for some hundred and twenty miles to the north of Tyre, which went under the name of Phœnicia. Dispersion made every believer a missionary. Whether outspoken by temperament, or the reverse, no disciple of Jesus who found himself among fellow Jews who had never heard His name, or did not yet receive Him as Messiah, could feel at liberty to conceal his new convictions. He must proclaim his Lord as the promised hope and salvation of his countrymen. Each adherent of the new creed thus became of necessity a propagandist, and the testimony of faith spread the faith. Now, the Phœnician coast towns maintained a lively commercial intercourse with the great Levantine island of Cyprus opposite. Cyprus, again, had equally close business relations with the mouth of the Orontes as with the harbourless Phœnician coast, and the mouth of the Orontes was the port for Antioch. By such natural stages, following the routes of trade, the gospel passed from port to port, one Jew trader conveying the tidings to his fellow, and the scattered Jerusalemites carrying it everywhere, till it found for itself a foothold within the great Syrian capital, the wealthy, corrupt meeting-place of West with East.

Antioch was at that time one of the three leading centres of civilization. Rome as an apex, Antioch and Alexandria as base angles, may be said to have formed a triangle embracing the commercial and political power of the world. Of these three, Antioch was the first to receive the gospel of Christ. At the outset, here as elsewhere, it was only in the synagogues and amongst the Jews, large colonies of whom were settled in the city, that Christ was preached. But after a while, how long after we do not know, a fresh band of ardent promulgators of the Cross came over from Cyprus, Hellenistic Jews, who were themselves natives of that island or of Cyrene, and who introduced, whether of design or through that leading by circumstances which men call chance, the daring innovation of speaking about Jesus to the Greek population as well as to the Hebrew. These new-comers were by no means leaders or missionaries or official members of the Church. They were plain traders, full only of the love of the Lord Jesus. If they had committed a mistake in speaking of Him to Gentiles, it could not have compromised the Church; but their bold love guided them more truly than the timid prejudices of the apostles. That they had not gone beyond the mind of their Master, was soon made plain by the extraordinary success which at once attended the experiment. It is a striking fact, needful to be known if we would understand the planting of the Church, that, at that prepared and chosen moment in the world's history, the Jew was the only man who had any strong religious convictions. Him oppression and change had made only more tenacious of his ancestral faith and of everything which separated him from other people. But the Gentile population, especially in great cities and seaport towns, was restlessly sceptical, trying many religions without believing in any. It cost the Gentile, therefore, far less than it did the Jew, to lend an ear to the new gospel which began to be spoken about: it cost him far less to embrace it. Within the Jewish quarter in the city of Antioch, fewer conversions had followed; but once the news spread to the heathen, a great number, even in dissolute, gay, and abandoned Antioch, turned from Apollo, and the unnameable pollutions of his foul Daphne groves, to be cleansed in the precious blood of God's dear Son. The hand of Him Whom they preached as the Lord of all men was with these foreign evangelists. That inward mysterious might of the Holy Ghost sent by Jesus Christ, which makes preaching effectual at His pleasure, made their preaching effectual. It is not a bad test by which to judge of any new or doubtful plan for spreading the gospel, which the more active and venturesome spirits in the Church may start, to ask whether the hand of the Lord Jesus be visibly with it. Success, when it really means the highest of all success, becomes its own apology. That cannot be bad mission-work which saves a multitude of souls.

It was this reputed success of the new movement which drew attention to it at head-quarters. It was its unauthorised novelty of procedure which exposed it to suspicion. A cautious and conservative mother Church in Jerusalem, still the head and seat of undivided ecclesiastical authority, heard, not with aversion but with doubt, what Greek-speaking brethren were doing in the Syrian capital. It was resolved to send down a commissioner to inquire. At the same time, the choice which the Church made of an agent is sufficient to show that this step was taken in no unfriendly or narrow spirit. Of all prominent men known to us in the earliest Church, Barnabas is the man who was most likely to look kindly on the proceedings of the lay preachers at Antioch. Himself a Hellenist and a Cypriote like themselves, he had been early distinguished for his warm-hearted liberality and his power of impressive exhortation. It might well be that he still shared the mistake of the whole Church, in believing Judaism to be the only regular porch to Christianity, and went down to Antioch with some misgivings as to what he should find there. But no man in the Church was less suspicious than he, of a more open spirit, or more generous instincts. The body which sent down such a commissioner had clearly not prejudged the case, and the result justified its choice. "He was a good man, and full of the Holy Ghost and of faith," says Luke; and because he was so, he rejoiced when he had seen the grace of God in the new converts from heathenism. Any one who has ever been privileged to witness a widespread quickening in the religious life of a community, or to come close to any large number of people who have simultaneously and recently received the good news of salvation as a new thing, and, for them, most certainly a true thing, will not forget the unmistakable and inimitable stamp of divine gladness set upon men's faces, or the sweet, simple affection with which brothers and sisters in Jesus greet one another, the tender sense of new-pardoned guilt, the devout susceptibility to the divine Word, the frank personal clinging to Jesus as to One quite near, the elevation above their usual carefulness and each petty vexation of daily life, which are the beautiful marks of such a time. All this Barnabas had seen some years before. He had been present in Jerusalem when the first unction of holy joy came from the Lord in heaven. He was himself one of those who had been carried away most completely with the enthusiastic love of those early days. Now, at Antioch, in a heathen city, in the very stew of pagan uncleanness, he found himself to his surprise in the midst of the same wonderful young life in God. The very same fresh child-like sense of reconciliation and peace, and the same pure, devout joy, were filling the new-born Gentile Church which had at first filled the new-born Hebrew Church. He recognized the grace of God in Jesus Christ, and was glad. Misgivings about Gentile unfitness or the uncleanness of uncircumcised men, could not live in such an atmosphere. The life was the life of Christ; the air was the air of heaven.

In virtue of his personal character, as well as of his commission, Barnabas would at once assume a leading place in the direction of the young society. He seems also to have seen at once what was required. A crowd of persons who, only a few months or weeks before, had been worshippers of impure idols, were now disciples of Jesus. The number of neophytes who pressed to baptism daily increased. The fervid expansive zeal of the brethren was still drawing large accessions from their heathen neighbours. What the Church most wanted now was not fresh missionaries; it was instruction, confirmation, and upbuilding. In the case even of well-taught Jews at the capital of Judaism, who had enjoyed the preparation of the old economy and were acquainted with its sacred books, the apostles had found daily instruction requisite for the establishment of new converts.[1] How much more needful was it for men bred in utter ignorance and in gross idolatry! Besides, the Antiochians were a clever, but giddy and fickle people, fond of change, and demoralized by the exciting amusements of their gay capital. Barnabas accordingly bent all that power of fervent exhor-

[1] Cf. Acts ii. 42.

tation from which he drew his surname upon the task of consolidating the hastily gathered congregation. "He exhorted them all that with purpose of heart they would cleave to the Lord Jesus." He did better than that. He did the best thing for the cause of Christ in Antioch, and in all the West, when he called to his side in this arduous work his far greater friend from Tarsus. Here, again, the selection of Barnabas as the delegate from Jerusalem turned out most providential. It is doubtful whether any other man in the Church would have recognised that the hour had come for Saul, and that Saul was the man for the hour. Ever since he knew the miraculous circumstances of Saul's conversion, Barnabas seems to have watched his career as one who foresaw to what great things God had destined him. He was probably aware that, once and again, the Lord Jesus had expressly indicated the heathen world as the true sphere of Saul's labours. He at least knew that, by twice conspiring against his life, once at Damascus and once at Jerusalem, the Jews had shut against the ex-inquisitor the door of access to themselves. Since Saul's hasty flight from the holy city, when his friends sent him down for safety to the obscurity of his native town, it may well have appeared to Barnabas a puzzling circumstance that a man so exceptionally gifted, so divinely summoned, and so fit for the widest usefulness, should be virtually imprisoned and silenced at Tarsus. We cannot indeed suppose that Saul's mouth was altogether shut from speaking of his Lord where he had opportunity; yet it is certain that at Tarsus he could not find a very large Jewish population within reach, and it was only to Jews he was as yet called to minister. Some of his relatives had already been disciples for years;[1] and, as he quietly wrought at tent-making in his paternal home, he may have succeeded in turning to the faith of the Crucified others of his own family, or of his compatriots who had been the companions of his boyhood at the synagogue school. Still, for a man so ardent, ambitious, and energetic, such limited activity as this was comparative idleness: it seemed a poor result to have reached through special revelations and apparitions from heaven. But God's plans unfold themselves in God's own time. To the devout heart of Barnabas it was given to see, in this new opening at Antioch, the call for which Christ's servant had been kept waiting in Tarsus. He went "to Tarsus to seek Saul, and, when he had found him, he brought him to Antioch."

At the pleasant task of instructing newly-baptized converts from paganism, the two friends laboured happily together for a twelvemonth. It is not said that they themselves evangelized. Their work was pastoral, not missionary, lying inside the infant Church. The number of catechumens who passed through their hands must have been very considerable, and the result of such systematic and thorough training could not fail to be a steady congregation, well knit together, and tolerably organized. In the bulk of it, it was a congregation of Gentiles; of persons who were not only Greek in speech and culture, but born heathens, uninitiated into Mosaism by circumcision, and ignorant even of Jewish usages. It is true that its two chief pastors were pure Jews, its earliest evangelists had been Jews, and the list of its prophets given a little later contains only one non-Hebrew name.[2] Still, the rank and file of its membership was drawn from the

[1] Rom. xvi. 7.   [2] See Acts xiii. 1. Lucius is not a Hebrew name.

worshippers of Apollo—not from the followers of Moses. They had never undergone the process which made men proselytes to Judaism. This was a fact the importance of which can hardly be overstated. Christ's Church grew up out of the bosom of an exclusive and jealously-guarded people, but at Antioch for the first time it came to stand clear of national limits. In that memorable year (A.D. 43 or 44), Christianity shook itself loose from the restraints of Mosaism. It took, no doubt, a long while before its freedom could be vindicated and secured; still the earliest practical assertion of it, an assertion unchallenged for the moment, took place in the year when Saul and Barnabas presided together over the new-born communion of Syrians in the Syrian metropolis. For many a long year after, Christianity wore a double form. It gathered round two head-centres, not one—a Hebrew centre at Jerusalem, a Gentile centre at Antioch. Only by slow degrees did the younger Church, like the son in the patriarch's family, become first the rival, and then the supplanter, of the elder.

The establishment of this great fact, of a Church independent of the synagogue and the temple, was signalized by the coining of a name. So long as those who believed that Jesus was the Messiah were all Jews, and continued to frequent Jewish worship and observe Jewish rites, so long they were undistinguished by the general public from other Jewish sects. Within the strange enclosure of Judaism, it was well known that various subdivisions of that religion found a place. This new "way" of worship might be only a fresh variety added to the catalogue. But when a quite separate society came to be formed outside the Jewish religion, which was seen to embrace Gen-

THE CHURCH OF ANTIOCH. 413

tiles as such, and to impose on its converts no Hebrew peculiarities, it became needful for sake of convenience to distinguish it by a separate name. The heathen population of Antioch had little difficulty in inventing one. I find no reason to suppose that "Christian" was at first a nickname or a term of reproach. It is true that it was never, in apostolic times, accepted or used by the disciples themselves; and when Christians began to be persecuted, the word very naturally became a badge of discredit, a popular term of abuse.[1] In its first use, however, it may quite well have been no more than a serviceable and harmless designation. The one characteristic tenet of the new religionists was that Jesus was the Divine Saviour of mankind, and this they expressed by translating into Greek the old Hebrew title of Messiah, the "Anointed" or "Consecrated One." They constantly called Him "Christ," because, to call Him "Christ," was by a single word to express their whole faith in Him;[2] and their heathen neighbours, taking this recurring title for a proper name, formed from it (in the regular Latin way) the party name of "Christianoi," Christians. It was some time before the Church learned to glory in the name which strangers had given her, so far as to give her Lord thanks that His name was named upon her.[3] In the meanwhile she continued to call her members only "disciples," "brethren," or "saints."[4] Ultimately, however, the Antiochian term passed over all Christendom. It has

[1] Cf. 1 Pet. iv. 16.
[2] Hence the monogram formed by the two first letters of the Greek word "Christ" (☧) came to be—what it still is—the most widespread symbol of our faith.
[3] See the Clementine Liturgy, quoted by Conybeare and Howson, and elsewhere. [4] Cf. the Apostolic Epp. *passim*.

long been the most honourable name a man can carry. It is itself enough to convict or to abash the man who wears it with an evil life.

As Western Christians, we are the spiritual descendants of these first Syrian converts. Ultimately, we may trace our ecclesiastical pedigree to the Church of Pentecost, but the line comes through Antioch. It was Antioch which soon afterwards began to be the focus of missionary enterprise for the whole of the heathen West. From it were sent forth those missions which evangelized in succession Asia Minor, Greece, Italy, Spain, Gaul, and Britain. It proved itself a prolific parent of Gentile Churches. Yet it owed its own origin to the unauthorized and experimental labours of a handful of Cypriote Jews. No apostle's hand planted the infant Church, no formal mission agency broke ground in heathendom. To sporadic lay Christians, trying to do good where business led them, and driven by love for souls to attempt new modes of spreading Jesus' name, belongs the honour of opening to Christ's gospel the door of all the mighty heathen West. It is better so. It suits better the genius of a free and spiritual faith, the least encumbered of all faiths with priestly orders, ritual, or privilege, in which life is everything and form the least of all things, that it should burst the barriers of the old economy by a sheer explosion of spiritual life. The new wine fermented till the old skin cracked; then both Asia and Europe drank of the wine of God's salvation. Surely the European Churches stand condemned by the conditions of their own birth, if they suffer this self-propagating life to be stifled up with hierarchical or official trammels; if they refuse to let the glad tidings overflow and pour themselves abroad upon sinful souls through the lips of any brother, or through the channel of any novel yet unforbidden agency. The Churches of to-day are not less free than the first Church was to adapt their methods to the unexampled conditions of our modern populations. They are no more entitled than it was to look coldly on fresh movements of Christian zeal on which it may please the Lord to set His own seal of success. If we share the lively joy in Christ which lifted up His brethren of old, or the same warm and courageous love for our unchristian neighbours, there will hardly be a single member in our Churches who will not find openings to speak for Christ. The good news will be for ever finding vents. Grace and salvation will percolate through a thousand little acts and words, till it reaches here and there some heart that only waits to be reached. To modern Christians has been given the same Word as to the Cyprian disciples. Antioch appeared in their eyes a city more hopeless to tell upon for good than London or Paris in ours. They were very few ; we are many. Only they had, what we too much lack, faith in the hand of Christ; and they had what we lack still more, an impulsive love that cannot keep still. So they spoke to the Greeks also ; and the little effort grew, till in Apollo's grove of laurel a Christian Church supplanted Apollo's shrine, and Antioch became one of Christendom's ecclesiastical capitals and the venerable mother of the Christianity of Europe.

XXI.
Fruit from the Gentiles.
I CAME TO BRING ALMS TO MY NATION, AND OFFERINGS.

Acts xi. 27–xii. 4.

Revised Version.

But in those days prophets came down from Jerusalem to Antioch. And one of them, Agabus by name, stood up and signified through the Spirit that a great dearth was about to take place throughout the whole inhabited earth; which came to pass under Claudius. So the disciples, according as every one was able, resolved each of them to send [something] by way of ministry to the brethren dwelling in Judæa; which also they did, sending [it] to the presbyters through the hand of Barnabas and Saul.

But about that time Herod the king laid hands on certain of the [members] of the Church to ill-treat them. And he took off James the brother of John with the sword; and seeing that it was agreeable to the Jews, he proceeded to apprehend Peter also—it was [the] days of the unleavened bread—whom when he had arrested he put into prison, delivering [him] to four quaternions of soldiers to guard him, intending after the Passover to bring him out to the people.

XXI.

THE relation of the new Church at Antioch to the old Church in Judæa was sure to become, sooner or later, a delicate point. It was remarked in the preceding chapter that Antioch became "first the rival and then the supplanter" of Jerusalem. For the first years, however, of their joint existence, there was no word of either rivalry or supplanting. The relation of the two Churches was that beautiful one which St. Paul, writing years afterwards under parallel circumstances, described in these words: "If the Gentiles have been made partakers of their spiritual things, their duty is also to minister unto them in carnal things."[1] Without ceasing to be "Gentiles," Antiochian Greeks had become equal sharers with their Jewish brethren in "spiritual things," which until now had been the exclusive patrimony and privilege of the Jew. Israel's Jehovah was now their God as well. His Anointed was their Saviour. They were fellow-heirs and fellow-citizens with the ancient Israel. It was a becoming acknowledgment of the vast debt under which all the world must ever lie to the Jew, but it was no repayment of it, when rich Antioch sent bread to poor and starving Judæa. It was the first fragrant and pleasant fruit[2] of a love which it had been well if no later strife had ever turned into resentment.

[1] Rom. xv. 27. Cf. 2 Cor. ix. 12–15.
Cf. Paul in Rom. xv. 28, " When I have sealed to them this *fruit.*"

This then was the earliest relation of the two Christian centres. Jerusalem sent "prophets" to Antioch; to Jerusalem Antioch sent back corn. One of the prophets was named Agabus. Once again in the history [1] does this man appear, and then also he appears as a predictor by symbol,[2] not by word only, of future disasters. This is the more noticeable that prediction was by no means the usual or characteristic function of the prophetic order in the apostolic Church. They were men whom God's Holy Spirit gifted with persuasive and impassioned speech, combined with insight into spiritual truth; so that in the Christian assemblies they poured forth addresses which searched the heart, kindled the devotion, or stung the conscience of the hearer. We have lost the name long ago; the thing in substance has never failed in the Church of Christ. The public prediction of Agabus [3] had, on this occasion, a very immediate and practical design. He foretold an impending dearth in Judæa, that the Church might make provision for it, and on the hint they acted. The whole reign of Claudius was marked by public disasters, dearth and earthquakes, at many points throughout the empire. No single year of scarcity, indeed, affected the entire inhabited world which lay in peace beneath his sceptre. But in the opening years of his reign it was Italy which suffered from failure of crops; in the fourth year, Palestine; in the eighth or ninth, Greece; in the eleventh, Italy again. Thus, from time to time, in this land or in that, God was laying upon the nations His evil rod of famine. The special occasion to

---

[1] Acts xxi. 10.   [2] Cf. ἐσήμανεν, in ver. 28.
[3] Cf. ἀναστας, ver. 28, which shows that it was in the public meeting for worship.

which the prophecy of Agabus pointed, seems to have been the great distress in Judæa during the year A.D. 45 and after it. We are here on sure chronological ground. We know that in that and succeeding seasons the want of food was so great, that many deaths by starvation occurred in Jerusalem, and great exertions were made for the relief of the population. A new convert to Judaism, of high rank, visiting that city for worship, was so struck with its condition that she sent to Alexandria and Cyprus for supplies. I refer to the Queen of Adiabene, whose son also, when he was "informed of the famine, sent great sums of money to the principal men in Jerusalem."[1] On such occasions it was usual for the foreign synagogues of wealthy Jews settled abroad to remit aid to their brethren in the Holy Land, as at this hour numbers of indigent Jews in Jerusalem are sustained by the charity of their compatriots scattered over Europe. The Church at Antioch, however, did not contribute through the synagogue of Antioch. In the separate assistance despatched to the disciples of Jesus by a congregation of Greek Christians, there lies the first express historical recognition of the fact that Church and Synagogue had parted company; that to be a follower of the Nazarene cut off a son of Abraham from the charities of his own people; and that henceforth the tie of fellow-Christian was to prove a stronger bond betwixt Jew and Gentile than any older bond which bound Jew to Jew or Gentile to Gentile. A new force had plainly entered humanity. A new name, the name of Christian, had been uttered, and it had already begun to dissolve ancient unities, to reconcile ancient feuds, and to construct on the ruins of race-hatreds

[1] See Josephus, *Antiq.* xx. 2. 5.

and national distinctions a spiritual and catholic society, whose watchword is one crucified Lord, and whose cement is one Spirit of love.

It seems, I think, certain that, thanks to divine forewarning, the Christians were beforehand with their charity. Matters only reached their worst some two seasons later, when the good queen and her son came to the relief. But the supplies destined for the poor believers of Judæa were already in the hands of the Church authorities at Jerusalem in the course of the summer of A.D. 44. This is evident from the fact that the visit of the commissioners who carried it to Judæa happened about the same time as Peter's imprisonment and Herod's death.[1] Now Peter was imprisoned in April, and Herod died in August. Somewhere, therefore, in the spring or summer of that year the generous offering of the young Syrian Church was handed over to the presbytery[2] of Jerusalem, for future use in the impending time of need. Antiochian Christians were most prompt to credit God's warning, and to come to the aid of the mother Church. They even gave handsomely to others when as yet they could not be sure that the famine would not press grievously upon themselves. The signs employed by Agabus indicated no limits to the visitation, and Syrian crops might fail as likely as not just when Judæan crops failed.

---

[1] I adhere to the order in Luke as here chronological. The mission (xi. 30) synchronizes with the commencement of persecution (xii. 1, κατ' ἐκεῖνον τόν καιρὸν). Then follow the events of xii. 1-24, extending to the 6th August. After that, Barnabas and Saul return, notwithstanding (δὲ) that the gospel was making special progress in Judæa in consequence of these events (xii. 24, 25).

[2] The οἱ πρεσβυτέροι must have acted as a body in receiving a sum of money.

FRUIT FROM THE GENTILES. 425

Besides, at that very time their own city was lying in partial ruin from a recent earthquake, which must have told heavily upon numbers of its population. All this enables us to appreciate the hearty cheerful generosity which inspired these new converts. However sore a famine coming at the heels of an earthquake might prove for Antioch, Antioch owned resources which Judæa had not. Antioch had capital, commerce, and docks; the rich grain countries of Cyprus and Egypt lay open to its ships; no failure of crops could mean to it what it must mean to poor isolated agricultural Judæa—simple starvation. Besides, had it not received from Judæa those spiritual blessings of salvation which had made the Christians glad? Was it not their duty to minister back again to Judæa in carnal things?

It is true to this day that Christianity plants in genuine Christian hearts a brotherhood which can cross the barriers of nationality and of speech. When the spirit of reformation, for example, revived the primitive faith throughout Europe, the newly-reformed Churches of Germany, Switzerland, France, Holland, and England, were at once brought into close and friendly relations. They exchanged famous teachers, they sheltered one another's confessors, they shared each other's fortune, they leagued their political influence for their common good. It even seemed at one time as if revived Christianity might have welded the reformed nations into that for which now men begin to sigh, a permanent federation of friendly commonwealths. The Evangelical Churches of our own day (such as the Wesleyan Connexion and the Presbyterian Churches of Scotland and America) have shown a similar readiness to succour feeble and struggling congregations of Evangelical Protestants in Roman Catholic lands, as in France, in Bohemia, in Italy, and in Spain. Such, however, are only slight examples of a force which ought to fuse all Christendom into one spiritual brotherhood. If ever that decaying virtue called patriotism is to lose itself in a larger or more cosmopolitan charity, it must be on a Christian, not (as some noble spirits are vainly dreaming) on a communistic or democratic basis. Socialism has no lord of the conscience to substitute for Jesus Christ. Where the conscience owns no lord, there can be no real loyalty; and without loyalty to the Chief, love for the brotherhood can be at best a sentiment, not a principle. It is sad to see how many of the best hearts in Europe are to-day groping after the foundations of a new civil order, in which all men shall be brothers and no man shall wrong his fellow's rights, while yet they cast off the very name of Him in Whom alone these two principles of love and order, of freedom and authority, meet and kiss. But there is something sadder still to see. It is a Christian Church so rent into rival morsels by theological and sectarian animosity, that, instead of practically demonstrating to the distracted peoples where to seek for the true secret of human brotherhood, it rather repels from Christ and from His faith those whose hearts are most passionate for peace and fellowship. No man who judges Christianity only by the existing Churches of Christ, take them all in all throughout Christendom, can rest on them his hopes for the unification of the world into a federation of equal, free, and peaceful men, mutually respecting each other's rights. The ecclesiastical organisations of Christendom have caricatured the divine idea of the kingdom of God. The spirit of schism is the

FRUIT FROM THE GENTILES.

cause of our torn and helpless and un-Christlike Christianity—that spirit which puts orthodoxy into the place of faith, ritual in the room of love, and substitutes its *esprit de corps*—its own petty self-conceit—for the catholic fraternity of Jesus Christ. In a return of the Churches to true catholicity—which means a practical recognition of one another as fellow-members in that one Body, which is Christ—lies the return of strength to the Church. Then, when Jerusalem shall not envy Antioch nor Antioch vex Jerusalem, when Churches that are poor in this world are rich in faith,[1] and those that are rich in this world are "ready to distribute, willing to communicate,"[2] when visible Churches are felt to be knit together by invisible bonds of love and helpfulness—then, if ever, will men learn that to be a Christian is to be free of a universal, because spiritual commonwealth, all whose citizens are one, all equal and all loving.

The Gentile Church made its gift more precious by sending it through its most honoured members. Saul and Barnabas were its chief pastors—its twin strength and ornament. By their hand was its offering conveyed to the "elders."[3] It is notable that just before we part from the mother Hebrew Church of Judæa do we hear for the first time, and in quite a casual fashion, of its being ruled by presbyters. This official name, the most venerable and biblical of ecclesiastical designations, frequently recurs in later documents, at first associated with the apostles in connection with the synod at Jerusalem,[4] afterwards with deacons, or alone, in the Churches of

[1] Jas. ii. 5.   [2] 1 Tim. vi. 18.   [3] See Acts xi. 30
[4] Cf. Acts xv. 2, 4, 6, 22, 23, xvi. 4, also xxi. 18.

Ephesus,[1] Crete,[2] Philippi,[3] and the congregations of dispersed Hebrews[4] throughout Asia Minor. Here it occurs for the first time, but without a word of comment, as though every reader of the history would know as a matter of course that the Jerusalem Church had its presbyters. That the Jerusalem Church had almoners or deacons, Luke's readers have been already informed ; and if that office had not already fallen into abeyance on the very spot where it arose and won its first palm, it would be the deacons' duty, when the time came, to disburse the liberality of Antioch. Yet it was to the elders, as official representatives and heads of the Church, that the capital sum was formally transferred by the commissioners; not to the apostles, whose function was catholic rather than local; not even to James the Less, whose relation to the Judæan Church appears to have been specially close ;[5] not to the deacons, whose duties were administrative only; but to the presbyters or elders. The origin of an office and a name, around which so much later controversy has raged, remains untold.[6]

The two commissioners found the mother Church in the holy city entering on a dark and perilous time. A good many years[7] had passed since it enjoyed rest from the former persecution which arose about Stephen. Of

[1] See 1 Tim. *passim* (specially i. 3). Cf. Eph. vi. 21 (Greek).
[2] Tit. i. 5 (though in this letter deacons are not named).
  Phil. i. 1, though the parallel name, ἐπίσκοποι, is here used.
[4] Cf. Jas. i. 1, c. v. 14; and 1 Pet i. 1, c. v. 1.
[5] See Acts xii. 17, and xxi. 18.
[6] Its occurrence, however, first in the Jerusalem, or pure Hebrew Church, may be held to tell, *quantum valeat*, in favour of its having been originally borrowed from the usage of the synagogue.
[7] Neander (*Pflanzung u. Leitung*) thinks about eight years. It depends on the uncertain chronology of Stephen's death.

its progress during the interval we know nothing. The mention of "elders" alone indicates that its organisation may meanwhile have been developed. The renewal of persecution suggests that possibly it was aggressive or prominent. The galaxy of apostles clustered at its head ought to have kept it spiritual and ardent. More than this it is impossible to discover. At any rate, the Lord saw fit to renew its time of trial. A second time blood was spilt for Christ. This persecution had a quite different origin from the last. Then, it was the Sanhedrim which moved; the occasion was a theological controversy, the excuse was a charge of blasphemy. Now, it was merely a political move on the part of a crafty prince who had reason to court popularity with the conservative, orthodox, or national party. Herod Agrippa the First was a born Jew, but bred, like other young princes of tributary dynasties, at the imperial court in Rome. After a life of vicissitude and intrigue he had, some years before, been set up as a puppet-ruler over the northern divisions of Palestine. The accession of Claudius brought him further promotion. Judæa was added to his dominions, and once more, as in the days of his grandfather Herod the Great, all Palestine owned a single native king. Herod Agrippa had inherited, along with his grandfather's splendid extravagance, his grandfather's crafty policy. While he built theatres and held games, to gratify the Grecianized part of his subjects, he affected zeal for the national faith, to conciliate the strict Pharisaic faction. Little as he can have cared for the laws or worship of his ancestors, he spent much of his time in Jerusalem, repaired its walls, diligently attended the daily sacrifice, was scrupulous in the observance of ceremonial rites, and so far succeeded as to win from the Jewish historian of the time a better reputation than he deserved.¹ It seems to have been in pursuance of this policy that the king, with that unscrupulous violence which characterised the Herodian house, began to assail the Church. His measures were tentative and gradual, like the steps of a man who acts on policy, not conviction. To begin with, he arrested, and probably scourged, certain unnamed but no doubt active and prominent members of the new sect.² Encouraged by the success of this experiment, he ventured on a more decided blow. James the son of Zebedee was not only one of the Twelve, but one of the innermost Three, and from his vehement character³ is certain to have made himself conspicuous. Some handle he may possibly have given to the king through his fiery words, but even if he had his execution was a strong step to hazard. It is very singular that St. Luke, who narrates many occurrences with great minuteness, chronicles the martyrdom of the first apostle who fell for the faith without a syllable of explanation or detail. In two words only, with a swiftness like the descending sword-stroke of the headsman, does he record at once and dismiss the tragedy. To us it may be allowed to recall Who it was Who foretold to James in the day of his ambition that he should indeed drink of his Master's cup, and be baptized with a like bloody baptism.⁴ In a way he little dreamt of, was he to pass from the block to that throne in the kingdom for which he had

---

¹ See Josephus, *Antiq.* xix. 7. 3, and elsewhere.
² This is the meaning of ἐπίβαλεν . . . τὰς χεῖρας κακῶσάι τινας κτλ. See Meyer, *in loc.*
³ He was one of the *υἱοὶ βροντῆς,* Mark iii. 17. Cf. Luke ix. 54.
⁴ Matt. xx. 23.

ignorantly begged, and discover by experience the meaning of that deep saying of his Master—"Whosoever will lose his life for My sake shall find it."[1]

It seems to have been at first questionable how this unjust beheading of a prominent citizen by the new king would be taken by the Jewish authorities. Mere pride of citizenship might have led them to resent an act of illegal violence. Yet so bitter had now become the enmity of the Sanhedrim against the disciples, that that court could witness its own jurisdiction overridden by a despot, the tool of a foreign power,[2] not only without resistance, but even with applause, so long as tyranny sought its victims among the saints. Even Herod was welcome if he would rid them of the Nazarenes. The approbation with which his first step had been received must have been quite undisguised, since he at once followed it up by the arrest of the leading man in the Church. To seize and imprison Peter was to strike at the head of the community —its boldest spokesman, its most active superintendent, its foremost representative. That Peter was all this is plain from the part he played in the preceding history. A reflection, too, of the importance which both sides attached to this seizure, may be seen on the one hand in the unusual precautions[3] taken to guard against escape, as if the king feared a rescue might be attempted; and on the other hand in the continuous, night-long meetings of the brethren to beg for the special interposition of their

[1] Matt. xvi. 25.
[2] Beheading was a Roman, not a Jewish mode of execution; so that it was done without a sentence of the Sanhedrim—done as his uncle had done to John the Baptist.
[3] The four soldiers appointed for each watch; and the being chained to a soldier by both hands, not, as was customary, by one only.

celestial Chief Himself. I must reserve for another chapter the singular deliverance which Jesus granted on the supplication of His saints, and the designed contrast in which the sacred historian has set the two narratives of the apostle's liberation and the tyrant's death. Here it is only with the perturbed condition in which the deputies from Antioch found the Church that we have to do. I see no good reason to doubt that Saul and Barnabas may have been in Jerusalem when the Church was praying for Peter.[1] The season was Passover, and they would naturally hasten to reach the holy city in time for that solemnity, to whose sacred associations St. Paul at least long continued to be attached.[2] A dark and heavy Passover it proved to be. But many of those who met on the night succeeding it in Mary's house had seen a heavier and a darker. They had seen the Passover on whose eve the great Lamb of God had been offered up a sacrifice for our sins. They had watched and wept through those long and weary nights when He lay fast asleep, not like Peter, in the king's prison, but in the deeper prison-house of the King of Terrors. Through two nights of unexampled gloom and despair had they watched then, with too little hope left in them even for prayer. Now there could come to them no more such nights of blank and

---

[1] The guess (see Meyer, *in loc.*) that they first visited the landward congregations, in order to avoid the wrath of Herod, seems to be without all probability, and assumes an independence in the separate congregations of which there is no evidence. Jerusalem dominated Judæa too much for such men not to proceed at once to the sacred capital as head-quarters. If they set out from Antioch about the same time (xii. 1) as Herod made his first move against the Church, they might well be in Jerusalem before the end of the days of unleavened bread.

[2] See Acts xx. 16, c. xviii. 21. Cf. 1 Cor. v. 7, 8.

utter grief. How could they forget that the seals and guards even of that dungeon of the grave had not been able to hold their mighty Friend; that from His arms He had flung the cold fetters of death; that forth from His prison-house He had emerged in glory, a King of life and death, a Lord of heaven and earth. Let this Passover be the gloomiest the Church has yet kept since Pentecost—days when the unleavened bread must be soaked with the tears of saints who weep over one pastor slain and fear for another in peril; who, if the pastors are one by one removed, must flee again as scattered sheep before the sword—yet no Passover can be like that one when the sword of Jehovah awoke against His fellow, and the chief good Shepherd was laid a dead man in His grave.

After that Passover there came an Easter. Joy, deliverance, victory, life, all things, came with the morning in which Jesus rose. Could they forget, these women who had been to His vacant tomb—these men who had met Him in the upper room, how He had risen? how strong He was, how serene and radiant! how full of the old love, but of new power! how the kings of earth and the angels of heaven were His, for their sakes, who were His early, dear, and chosen friends. Not despairingly, but with the light of hope amid their tears, they gathered round His royal footstool. From Him, not from Herod, did they beg their pastor's life. His feet they held with hands of prayer, to His face they turned their eyes, and would not let Him go.

If it was into the midst of such a Church Saul and Barnabas came, it must have been to join their tears and prayers with those of the brethren. No moment that to speak of presents from dear saints at Antioch: a moment rather for the clinging together of Christian hearts in presence of a common peril, and staying one another's faith in their common Helper. Not money first, but sympathy and prayers, would these Antiochian brethren bring. The Apostle of the Gentiles joined, in his Gentile converts' name, to ask for the life of the Apostle of the Jews. The one Lord, "Who is rich unto all that call upon Him," heard that common cry from the two halves of His beloved Church. It is at the darkest hour of night that the angels of God begin to draw near. Before the earliest dawn Peter stood a free man at Mary's door. Next day came the cessation of the storm, confusion to the adversaries, the departure of the mortified prince to Cæsarea, and leave for the saints to draw safe breath again. Then, at ample leisure, would be laid upon the heart of the delivered Church the sweet love-offering of her far-off brethren, a cordial sent for this time of faintness and distress. A few months later, and even her last fear of further violence was taken away. God smote the evil king that he died, and "the word of God," unbound again, to be spoken by glad delivered lips, "grew and multiplied."

XXII.
Peter and Agrippa.
LOOK HERE UPON THIS PICTURE AND ON THIS.

Acts xii. 5-25.

Revised Version.

So then Peter was being kept in the prison; but earnest prayer was being made by the Church to God for him. But when Herod was about to bring him forth, that very night was Peter sleeping between two soldiers bound with two chains, and guards before the door were keeping the prison. And behold, an angel of the Lord stood by, and a light shone in the apartment; and having struck the side of Peter, he raised him, saying: "Rise up quickly." And his chains fell off from his hands; and the angel said to him: "Gird thyself and bind on thy sandals;" and he did so. And he said to him: "Cast thy robe about thee and follow me." And going out, he followed, and did not know that what was done by the angel was true, but thought he saw a vision. So having passed by the first guard and the second, they came upon the iron gate which leads into the city, which of its own accord opened to them, and when they had gone out they passed along one lane, and immediately the angel was away from him. And Peter coming to himself, said:

"Now I know of a surety that the Lord sent His angel and delivered me out of Herod's hand, and all the expectation of the people of the Jews."

And when he became aware [of it], he went to the house of Mary the mother of John, who is surnamed Mark, where were a good many gathered together and praying. But as he was knocking on the door of the gate, a damsel came close to hearken, Rhoda by name, and when she recognised the voice of Peter, for [very] joy she did not open the gate, but ran in and told that Peter was standing before the gate. But they said to her: "Thou art mad." She however kept stoutly affirming that it was so, while they were saying: "It is his angel." But Peter was going on knocking; and when they had opened they saw him, and were amazed. But beckoning to them with the hand to be silent, he related how the Lord had brought him forth out of the prison, and said: "Tell these things to James and to the brethren." And he went out and departed to another place.

Now, when it was day, there was no small commotion among the soldiers, what was become of Peter. But when Herod had searched for him and not found [him], after examining the guards, he ordered [them] to be executed; and having gone down from Judæa to Cæsarea, he stayed [there]. Now he was in a hostile mood against Tyrians and Sidonians; but with one accord they came to him, and having persuaded Blastos who was over the bedchamber of the king, they were asking peace on account of their country being nourished by the king's. And on a set day, Herod, having put on royal apparel and sat down on the tribune, was making a public oration to them; and the people gave a shout: "God's voice and not man's!" But instantly there smote him an angel of the Lord, in return for his not having given the glory to God; and becoming worm-eaten, he expired.

But the word of God went on growing and multiplying. But Barnabas and Saul returned from Jerusalem when they had completed the ministry, taking along with them also John who was surnamed Mark.

XXII.

ST. LUKE'S very vivid description of the apostle's deliverance and the monarch's death is like a pair of careful historical pictures set in instructive contrast, or like a drama with two scenes and a moral.

When the first half of the narrative opens, Peter's prospects are at their darkest. For some days he has been lying in gaol, in apprehension of sharing the fate of his fellow-apostle St. James, and now it is actually the eve of his execution. The closing day of the sacred festival is past. To-morrow he is to be led forth before the people, to be made, like his Master, first their butt and then their victim. The king has arranged it so, and all the bigoted in Jerusalem who hate the Jesus-party, and all the idle vulgar who only love a scene, expect it. The night wears on to dawn. It is already the fourth watch.[1] Twice has the watch been changed since it was first set at sunset, four Roman soldiers retiring and a fresh quaternion succeeding each time. This was done last at three o'clock, and it is now some time past three, for both Peter and his guards have fallen fast asleep. They are lying in that deep sleep which, during the latest hours of night, comes on men whose rest has been broken in the earlier part of it. The month is April, at the equinox,

[1] This is fixed by the fact that Peter was not missed by the guards till sunrise (six o'clock). See ver. 18, γενομένης δὲ ἡμέρας.

when there is very little light till close on six o'clock: all is still dark therefore in the dungeon. The whole night through the Church has been praying outside, while Peter within has snatched his broken hours of sleep between the relievings of the guard, as a calm-souled martyr may well do who needs to be strong for confession and for death when daylight comes. Soon daylight will come. One hour, at most two hours more;[1] and how shall their prayers be answered? Of help there seems slender hope now, or none. Look at the man. He lies between the two slumbering Romans, uneasily, on one side. On each wrist there is a fetter, attached to a chain which links him to the fettered arm of a soldier—to this one on this side, to that one on that. The least movement, a turning only in his sleep, and his keepers will be instantly startled. Outside the bolted door can be heard the heavy breathing of a third soldier who keeps guard without. A little further along the corridor the fourth is posted. With such precautions, what hope is there of escape?

But God's help comes silently; it comes like the light. His messengers of spiritual aid are everywhere. At all hours, by day or night, they stand beside us, looking upon us in their love. As God bids them they minister to us. It is only our eyes which are holden that we should not see them. This gracious and kindly ministry of strong pure creatures, who are as strong and pure as we should be if we were good, and as we shall be when we grow like them in the resurrection;[2] this blessed companionship, out of vision, of God's perfected servants with His still imperfect saints; this heavenly tutelage

---

[1] The circumstances seem to confine us to somewhere between four and five a.m.   [2] Cf. Luke xx. 36.

and guardianship of each one who loves the Lord by messengers of light from the land of the holy,[1] has been so clearly revealed to faith that it is surprising, even in our sceptical age, that Christians are not more generally won by the sweetness and the fitness of it to believe it. For that Christians of the present day as a rule do actually believe it, or do in practice hold it for a simple daily fact, is more than questionable.

Was it not that angel who through the darkness had been watching over Peter's sleep, who then, somewhere betwixt three and six on that spring morning, became suddenly revealed in light—a form made visible in the dark through its own light, brilliant enough to make beautiful even the condemned cell? The sudden silent light awoke none of the sleepers; but at a blow on the side and a voice in his ear which was for his ear alone,[2] Peter had started to his feet before he noticed that the iron fetters which would have hindered such a movement had been already snapped by a divine touch, and were lying empty on the floor. The sudden awaking and the

[1] In the sense of Matt. xviii. 10, and perhaps in that of this passage, ver. 15, this might be called probably "*Peter's* angel." The author of the art. "Angel," in *Herzog* (iv. 25), quotes Schelling's view that a man's angel represents his own *ideal*. The brethren must have at least supposed Peter's angel to borrow his voice, unless they took the apparition for a "wraith," or double self, appearing before or after death, as a warning. But I am not aware of any trace of such a notion among the Hebrews.

[2] It is a happy fancy of Keble that the touch and the voice, mingling with the prisoner's dreams, seemed to him as the expected summons to execution:—

"His dream is changed—the tyrant's voice
  Calls to that last of glorious deeds;
But as he rises to rejoice,
  Not Herod, but an angel leads."

Christian Year: St. Peter's Day.

dazzling splendour seem to have dazed the apostle, for he had to be told to perform each needful act, and obeyed mechanically. To tighten the girdle which confined his tunic, to strap on the light sandals he had laid aside for ease in sleep, to resume his heavy upper cloak as a defence against the keen morning air outside—these were just what any man fully awake to what was passing, and ready for what was coming, would have done. Peter was neither ready nor quite awake. Only he did what he was bid, and being bidden to follow, he followed. Silently, that light before and the apostle after, they two traversed the galleries of the castle, past the first sleeping guard and past the second, and at last through the great leaves of the outer gate communicating with the street, which swung silently back at their approach; and still, with not a word spoken, the heavenly guide led along one street only, out of sight or risk of immediate pursuit, then became as suddenly invisible again, passing back into the unseen. How slender, yet how firm, must be the partition which keeps this world we know by our senses from that other hidden world which fills, as it were, the same room, yet makes upon our senses no mark of its existence! How closely must the spiritual press upon the material! It even penetrates us at every point. Yet in vain do we beat against the stubborn barrier of sense. In vain do we call with tears and passionate entreaty for some word, or flash, or token, some sensible sign of a spiritual presence with us, here and now "where the night and morning meet." Our loves go from our fingers into the unknown, and for all our yearnings to follow them, follow we cannot, nor will they by so much as a whisper or a gleam send back one hint that still they live and still they love. Nay, God Himself must dwell thus close beside us, yet seems to be so infinitely far off, because He is not touched by any sense. And we, whose faith is weaker than can be told, who, when filled with the darkness of distrust, would give worlds for the reassurances of sense, shall never know by any earthly sign that we have a God. Mute, dark, impalpable spirit-land! wilt thou never more send forth thine angels to shine in mortal eyes?

The disappearance of his guide brought the apostle to a standstill. He had been, naturally enough, following like one in a dream,[1] who is not sure whether the strange things which seem to happen will not melt into air when he awakes. Now he roused himself to think. With perfect consciousness came the certainty that he was free, that the unearthly visitor had been real, that Jesus the Lord had sent him, and that the dreadful to-morrow (it was already a *to-day* about to dawn) would bring to him no horrors of execution, but to his persecutors disappointment. What to do was clear. To advertise the brethren of his liberation and to flee were obvious duties, and to do both with haste, since already the air was quick with the breath of morning. For this reason, when he at last gained admittance at Mary's gate, he stilled his astonished friends with an impatient wave of the hand,[2] and leaving only a hurried message for the head of the Church, hastened into hiding. This woman to whose residence he repaired was probably one of the wealthier disciples. Her brother[3] Barnabas had been originally a man of substance, and her dwelling was commodious enough to form

[1] Cf. Psa. cxxvi. 1.
[2] κατασείσας, "waving up and down," ver. 17.
[3] Col. iv. 10. But Alford (*in loc.*) takes ἀνεψιὸς = cousin; so that Mary would be *aunt* to Barnabas.

a rendezvous for at least one circle of the faithful. Since the family were Cypriotes, it was likely to be the freer Hellenistic side of the Church which chiefly drew around it. James at least was evidently not present at that prayer-meeting. No doubt similar gatherings were being held in other quarters of the city. To Mary's house it was natural for Peter to betake himself, for between him and this whole family there existed some close tie. Mary's son, John Mark (whom his uncle was in a few days to take back with him to Antioch), is, in a letter written from Babylon long after, spoken of affectionately by St. Peter as "my son."[1] The words of course cannot be taken literally, since in that case Mary's house would have been simply Peter's own house, and would have been called so: still they indicate some long-standing and peculiarly tender intimacy between the families. Now if, as was shown in last chapter to be very probable, Saul and Barnabas had already arrived in Jerusalem, it becomes next to certain that Barnabas at least would form one of the party met under his sister's roof; and in that case it is sufficiently probable that his fellow-commissioner might also be present.[2] It is a strangely interesting group which is thus offered to the imagination. In a widow's home at Jerusalem are gathered the men who had already done most and were soon to do much more to spread to the great cultured world the gospel whose birthplace was Jerusalem. In the prayers of that solemn night they join to ask their uplifted King to rescue the famous Jewish

---

[1] 1 Pet. v. 13.

[2] The relationship of Barnabas to Mary and her son, who were such close friends of Peter, helps us to understand the position of the Cypriote Levite as a natural link betwixt Paul and Peter, the apostle of the Gentiles and the apostle of the circumcision.

apostle, still the undisputed first among his fellows,[1] out of the jaws of death. And while Saul and Barnabas and Mark and Mary, with their friends, plead in the inner room beneath the lamplight—unweariedly plead and pray through the last watch—a few streets off, within the gaol, the King's bright messenger has undone the locks of Herod's prison-house, and the captive stands a free man at the gate. Peter's knock—sounding strange, unwelcome, even harsh, in the still night, since it awakened fears of further arrests and violence—Peter's own impatient and repeated knocking breaks through the low voice of prayer in the inner chamber. A few hurried words spoken in the courtyard,[2] broken greetings, brief explanations, counsels, adieus, and they who had met to pray returned with tearful joy to give thanks and praise.

It was a great deliverance. Peter's death at that early date would have been to all human conjecture the sorest blow which could have fallen on the cause of Christ. It was also a signal reply to the prayers of saints—very comforting as a token that the King on high could hear and pity and help, that He was still, as He used to be, accessible to the voice of friends. But by far the chief significance of the wonder for all after time lay here, that above the most powerful forces of earthly kingdoms there is a spiritual King Whose hand is on all His adversaries, Whose eye is upon all His friends, Who will never desert those who are loyal to Him, and Who knows how to

---

[1] The very importance attached by the Church to his arrest shows this, as well as the place he fills throughout the first twelve chapters of the Acts.

[2] It is impossible to decide whether Peter entered the house itself or not. This depends on the meaning of ἐξελθών, in ver. 17, "out of the house," or "out of the city."

deliver them out of the worst trials. If in other cases no such help is sent as was sent in this case; if James is beheaded though Peter escapes; if neither through visible shining executants of the celestial will, nor through the humbler but no less real ministry of natural providences, there should come to the faithful soul any deliverance when strong world-powers threaten to overwhelm; it is not because the unseen King cannot, nor yet because He will not, grant salvation. It can only be because it is kept for a later stage, granted not before but after earthly foes have done their worst; a salvation (it may even chance) on the further, not on the hither side of death, before the eyes not of mortal men but of glorified immortals. Yet come it always must. To serve God and His Son Jesus is sure to mean in the end deliverance, welfare, and success, however it may within the narrow horizon of our darkened time appear to mean nothing else but oppression, disaster, or failure. This is the faith of all the martyrs, and without some martyr-like faith of this sort who of us could live loyal lives for Christ at all?

The lesson has its counterpart, however.

Herod Agrippa I. was at his highest state when the second half of the story opens. He too had been a chained prisoner in his day,[1] but after many vicissitudes his fortune was now in the ascendant. The emperor's favourite, ruling a realm as wide as that of his famous grandfather, he was still comparatively a young man in the August of the year 44.[2] Many years of prosperous and splendid life might be before him. Months had

[1] See Josephus, *Antiq.* xviii. 6. 7.
[2] He died in the fifty-fourth year of his age. See Josephus, *Antiq.* xix. 8. 2.

passed since that spring morning when Peter escaped, and the irritation of a public discomfiture was by this time forgotten. The festival week which his grandfather had established half a century before, to celebrate the honour of the Roman Cæsar by games and banquets, a festival observed only once in five years, had come round again;[1] and the very day on which it opened, the first of August, chanced to be also the birthday of his imperial friend and patron, the reigning Augustus. Everything conspired to crowd his new and splendid sea-coast capital with the fashion and gaiety of Syria. For the second day of the fête and of the month, the king had arranged a state ceremonial at which his own magnificence should be specially displayed before the eyes of the populace.[2] The occasion was this. Some political difficulty had arisen between the Court of Palestine and the rich trading towns which lay along the Mediterranean coast at the base of Lebanon, and ambassadors were at that moment in Cæsarea seeking to propitiate the king and avert a rupture of commercial relations. Tyre and Sidon having next to no back country between them and the mountains, had from remote times been large customers of Palestine for her staple products of wheat and olive oil.[3] In return for these imports, the Tyrian merchants supplied the whole of Palestine, through the old port of Joppa and the new one at Cæsarea, not only with timber from Lebanon, but also with spices and other luxuries of far-off climes, the

---

[1] I follow Wieseler's (pp. 132-6) view, that the Quinquennalia are meant (cf. *Bell. Jud.* i. 21. 8).

[2] For the scene that follows, Josephus is the best commentator on St. Luke. See *Antiq.* xix. 8. 2, and xix. 9. 1.

[3] Cf. the evidences of this trade in Solomon's time, 1 Kings v. 11; at the Captivity, Ezek. xxvii. 17; and after it, Ezra iii. 7.

trade of which was largely in their hands. Hence arose their anxiety to be on friendly terms with the king. Herod, on his part, designed a public reception and reply to the embassy, such as might add to his own credit among his subjects. At an early hour on that second of August the new and spacious theatre was full. Its tiers of marble benches, gleaming white against the blue sky, and sweeping round in lovely curves, overflowed with spectators. Accompanied by his suite, the king entered by the western approach in a robe woven of silver thread, and when the level rays of the early sun fell aslant across the theatre on the glittering tissue, they were reflected into the faces of the audience, so that the monarch seemed for the moment to be "clothed with light as with a garment." He spoke; and when he ceased, amid the plaudits of the people, here one and there another of his courtiers ventured to raise the cry of adulation: "A god, a god! be gracious unto us, O divine lord Herod!" The flattery was too paganish and blasphemous for his Jewish subjects, but not for the prince's taste. Presently—even as his ears drank in, well pleased, the impious homage—he was struck where he sat with sudden illness. An angel from God smote him, says St. Luke. In a state of violent pain he had to be carried from the theatre to his palace, a dying man. After this shocking interruption to the ceremony the crowd broke up in consternation. The town went into mourning. For five days long the king lay in the grip of his horrible and excruciating malady. On the sixth of August the king was dead. Then the false and heartless mob, that had been ready to worship the sovereign while he lived, and had filled the streets with pretended lamentations for his seizure, gave themselves up, troops and populace together, to the most indecent and open rejoicing over his decease, toasting the tyrant's end in public banquets, and heaping cowardly and brutal insults on the royal princesses.[1] So amid lies and shame and execration there passed away into corruption and the grave the godlike Herod.

Why should this old-world story be rehearsed in Sacred Writ? Is it that there was anything miraculous in this man's illness? or that putrid internal ulcers, of which Antiochus Epiphanes[2] and Herod the Great[3] had both died before him, is a disease specially fit to scourge the royal persecutors of the faith? or that the sudden death of wicked men is always to be looked for and accepted as a special judgment from Almighty God?[4] No; but to teach us that God the Avenger, with His spiritual ministers of judgment, stands as close beside wicked and impious sinners, even in the hour of their proudest success, as, in the night of a saint's trial, there stands by him the angel of deliverance. When vice is most flattered, when ambition, pride, lust, and cruelty are seated on their highest or securest seat, and before them the crowd kneels with most abject obeisance, then is insulted and indignant God not far off but nigh at hand. God's angels can touch men to consume as well as to save. The hand of Him in Whom we live can reach up to the loftiest, to pluck down from their seats, as well as down to the lowliest, to uplift. If, here again, we are not often

[1] Josephus says on their "statues;" but Photius (see note to Whiston's *Josephus*) says on themselves.

[2] For the case of Antiochus, see 2 Macc. ix. 5.

[3] See Josephus, *Antiq.* xvii. 6. 5. In this case complicated apparently by syphilitic disease (cf. *Sir.* xix. 8).

[4] So some have understood Isa. li. 8. (See article *Krankheit* in Herzog.)

suffered to see the end as it was seen in the case of Herod Agrippa, if no such dramatic *dénoûment* should point the moral of a selfish life, nor loathsome death follow always like a satire on the heels of pride, it is not because God's angel of wrath has not been standing all the while beside the chair of state or at the board of luxury; it is only that the wicked are kept a little longer for the day of their judgment.

The lesson is precisely the same as the rescued Apostle Peter has deduced, in his second catholic epistle, from the ancient examples of Noah and of Lot—namely, that "the Lord knoweth how to deliver the godly out of temptations—out of a trial [1]—but to reserve the unjust to a day of judgment to be punished." Among the crowd of historical instances by which God has at various times enforced on the world this double lesson, that He can deliver the godly when their peril is greatest and in His set day can overthrow the wicked in the fulness of their pride, this example from Peter's own life holds a prominent place. The lesson is one which men need to be always learning. In that unending contest betwixt good and evil, betwixt men who serve God and men who please themselves, which fills history, we continually find the world's power and prestige on the ungodly side. The relations between David and King Saul, between Elijah and Ahab, between Hezekiah and Sennacherib, between Jeremiah and Zedekiah, between Daniel and Darius, between Mordecai and Haman, between the babe Jesus and Herod the Great, between John Baptist and Herod Antipas, between Peter and Herod Agrippa, between Paul and Nero, are all so many repetitions, age after age, of a

[1] 2 Pet. ii. 9. ἐκ πειρασμοῦ is Tischendorf's reading.

fundamental contrast which is as truly to be found in our modern English life to-day, if we had only eyes to see it, as in Bible story. Still, as ever, the obscure and lonely servant of God finds that faithfulness to truth and right means for him antagonism to the great strong world which has fortune and honour and success and wealth to bestow. Still, as ever, it means an unappreciated, unrewarded wrestle against what is most tempting in life, often with actual overthrow in the wrestle. And still, as ever, he needs to be borne up under real disaster and apparent defeat by the profound spiritual conviction that things are not in this life what they seem to be; that what looks like defeat is not always defeat, and what is at present called success may be no success.

Very helpful to faith are those few recorded instances in which God has made this palpable by working unexpected relief for His oppressed saints, and sending patent discomfiture upon their prosperous persecutors. Miriam sings praise on the shore of a sea which has engulfed the hosts of Egypt. Hymns rise from the temple courts when Sennacherib's troops lie in the sleep of death. An angel breaks Peter's fetters, and an angel smites to death the impious Agrippa. But these things are not in the usual order of present providence. If they were, we should be able to walk by sight instead of having to walk by faith. For the most part we see the good man go down before the prosperity of the wicked, and we do not see that prosperity dashed with everlasting overthrow. It is an old, old complaint:—

> "As for me, my feet were almost gone;
> My steps had well nigh slipped;
> For I was envious at the foolish:
> I saw the prosperity of the wicked.
> * * ▪ * * *

"Their eyes stand out with fatness;
They have more than heart could wish.

* * * * * * *

"Behold these ungodly ones, who prosper in the world;
They increase in riches!
Verily, I have cleansed my heart in vain,
And washed my hands in innocency!"

Let the man who is vexed with this temptation enter into the sanctuary of God; then he shall understand the end of the ungodly :—

"Surely, Thou didst set them in slippery places!
Thou castedst them down into destruction!
How are they brought to desolation as in a moment!
They are utterly consumed with terrors.
As a dream when one awaketh—
O Lord! when Thou awakest, Thou shalt despise their image!"[1]

[1] Psa. lxxiii. 2-20.

XXIII.
Conclusions.

THESE THINGS ARE WRITTEN FOR OUR ADMONITION, UPON WHOM THE ENDS OF THE WORLD ARE COME.

XXIII.

THE task I prescribed for myself at the outset of this volume has now been completed. That task was to trace, under St. Luke's inspired guidance, the course of events from the Lord's ascension down to the commencement of formal missionary enterprise among the Gentiles by the Church of Antioch. Throughout this portion of the earliest Church history the sacred writer has kept in view one definite design, to show how, under the oversight and by the leading of the absent Master Himself, Christ's Church developed from a small and unorganised band of Hebrew sectaries into a free, catholic, self-acting and self-propagating Church for both Jew and Gentile.

Before dismissing the subject, it may serve a useful purpose to gather up briefly some leading conclusions respecting the origin and nature of the Church of Christ which such a study has yielded.

The main outstanding fact about the Church, which lies on the opening page of her history, which is assumed throughout every page, and without which the narrative becomes utterly inexplicable, is this:—That the Church is the product and prolongation among men of a certain spiritual and supernatural force which entered mankind at the birth of Jesus. There are at bottom but two consistent theories to account for Christianity, of which one must be true and the other false. The one is the theory into which all infidel systems resolve themselves in the long run, and to which a rationalistic treatment of the New Testament logically conducts, namely—that Jesus was a wise and great Teacher Whose lessons founded a faith or religion among His fellow-men, which, in virtue of its inherent force of truth, made way after His death and survived all resistance till it became the religion of civilised mankind. The other is the next to universal view of Christians themselves—that Jesus was and is the Son of God, supernaturally incarnate in our nature, Who by His atonement has become the source of superhuman life and virtue to individual men, and Who now creates, inspires, and rules the society of the saved as its living Head, by a divine force continually exerted upon believers. It needs no proof to show that this latter is the view taken by the author of the Book of Acts. Here plainly the life of the Church is represented as a continuation of the life of Jesus. It is put before us as a perpetuation of that supernatural activity of God in history which began when He was born at Bethlehem. The advent of God in the person of Mary's Son introduced into the human race a divine Helper, Who, though put to death for our sins according to a divine purpose, revived through the divine power, and Whose immediate personal connection with His fellow-men by no means ceased when He ceased to be visible upon earth. He is the person uniformly styled in Luke's pages "the Lord." He it is to Whom the disciples pray, as if He were still beside them, or at least could still hear them as He used to do. He it is Who sends into their hearts a superhuman influence which they recognise as a personal Spirit meant to animate their spirits, filling them with light and power. He it is moreover who draws new members into the fellowship of the believing; He Who enables them to work wonders just as He Himself had been wont to work them; He Who by His messengers opens their prison doors, and restrains the hostility or defeats the plans of their enemies. He directs their movements. He shows Himself to their chief leaders. He reveals His will at new crises of the history. He is from first to last the moving mainspring and director of the whole enterprise, the heart and head of the whole body. To attempt to subtract the continued action of Jesus from the narrative of Luke would not be to mutilate, it would be to destroy it. This fact is so plain that every one admits it, and of course for such as pay any respect to the document as inspired of God, this fact is simply conclusive. But even non-Christian readers, who read the history with no religious faith but merely with historical criticism, may convince themselves that the events which are said to have followed Pentecost never could have happened if Pentecost had not happened. In other words, take away from the forefront of this history the coming to life again of the crucified Jesus, His departure visibly towards heaven, and the real inspiration of His Church by a supernatural afflatus from heaven— that is, take away the three connected miracles of Easter, Ascension-Day, and Pentecost, and the after history of His followers becomes a riddle. It is simply impossible on that supposition to explain how the little company of dispirited and disappointed men who survived their Leader's death attempted anything beyond nourishing, through hidden meetings among themselves, what could only be at best a feeble and flickering faith in the Cru-

cified; how they had the heart to do more than cling to
a dear but vanishing memory during the first generation;
or how both the faith and the memory of the dead Teacher
escaped being trampled out in the second or lingering to
death in the third generation. So true is this, that if no
Easter or Pentecost had been recorded, we should have
had to imagine both. Some facts corresponding to Easter
and to Pentecost, some resuscitation of the marvellous
Life which seemed to end at Calvary, some reinvigora-
tion of the spiritual life which He had kindled indeed in
His followers, but which burned in them so feebly, the
philosophical historian must have postulated, had he been
called upon to explain without assistance the first forty
years of Christian Church history.

If the Church is thus a supernatural product, and its
life the life of Jesus under another form, it will follow that
the Church itself ought to be the best possible demonstration that in Jesus God appeared on earth. To persons
who look at the Church from the outside or possess only a
nominal attachment to it, it is not strange that it should
seem to be anything rather than that. About the mere
framework of Church order, and in the lives of its average
members, there is so much which is most commonplace,
weak, vulgar, unspiritual and undivine, that few spectators might take it for a superhuman thing bearing within
it a celestial life. Yet I do think that any man who will
take the Christian gospel into his heart, and let the
Christian faith become his own faith, so as to get into the
penetralia of church-life and learn to know it from within,
will find in it sufficient evidence of its superhuman origin
and of the divineness of Him Who is its Head. This
species of evidence it is impossible to analyse; yet all

genuine Christians are aware of it. They know [1] that they have in Christ touched God our Father, that the new life they share in common with their fellow-churchmen is God's life, that they are become free of a commonwealth, parts of a body, the animating Spirit of which is from above. Nor do I know what else can be done by those who have received this interior and immediate certainty, reposing upon their deepest experience, than continue quietly and steadily to bear witness to it. Such a witness, drawn from men of the most varied types of Christian opinion and modes of Christian worship, as well as continued unbroken along the line of Christian history, ought in the judgment of a sober science to reckon for something.

The ministry of Jesus of Nazareth was a constant protest against two evil tendencies, which are not confined to His day or to the corner of Syria where He lived. The one, which is only clumsily described by the term "rationalism," is the tendency to doubt the supernatural and believe only in what can be discerned by the physical senses. He was from above, from a spirit home, an Eternal Being, and during His short mortal life here He kept Himself linked still to the immaterial or unseen spirit-land from which He had come. Visitors from it visited Him, and forces which were more than earthly worked at His call. Jesus is the great fact in history which rationalism or naturalism fails to explain. He was nothing if not supersensuous, spiritual. The other falsehood with which He warred may be termed hierarchism

[1] Compare one of the very earliest and most explicit statements of this interior certainty, in 1 John v. 18–20.

or priestcraft or superstition or Pharisaism—for its names are many. It is the inveterate tendency to dissociate devotion from morality, so that religion degenerates into a system of forms and names and offices, a thing which a man may be perfect at, yet have no spirit of God within him. Against this false caricature Jesus uttered His most fearful invectives. With Him religion meant to be one in life with the Father in heaven. Worship was in spirit and in truth. The test of piety was practical righteousness; not to wash hands, or wear phylacteries, or recite long prayers, or be of a chosen race or of a sacred order.

Now it belongs to the Church to continue this two-faced fight. Born of a miracle, maintained by a superhuman Presence, leaning always on the invisible, the Church of Christ is nothing if not super-rational. It must protest on behalf of a spiritual world, near and accessible to mortals, in which dwell God and His Christ, and from which proceeds the Spirit of its own life. On the other hand, it began by being inward, free, a thing of moral and spiritual life, and not of forms. Against all narrowing and trammelling of itself through external ritual or arrangement, therefore, it must for ever protest. In its earliest shape, while still enclosed within its Hebrew cradle, it was simply a brotherhood who clung to the genuine faith of their fathers, protesting only against Pharisaic accretions, and preached a gospel of penitence and faith in the Messiah. It possessed at first no organisation. It aimed at no separate existence. It had but its twelve witnesses whom Jesus trained. Hierarchy, ritual, liturgy, holy places of its own, it had none. A mere temporary difficulty suggested the creation of its first office-bearers. How other orders arose we do not even know. Nor would it ever have sought, apparently, to detach itself entirely from Hebrew worship or to consolidate the framework of an independent Society, had not Judaism with a murderous hand pushed it from its bosom. So far from being hierarchical or bound by official rules, its chief progress was made through unlicensed preaching. Everybody preached. Its scattered adherents became volunteer missionaries. The man who evangelised Samaria was only a deacon; the men who founded the Gentile Church at Antioch were laymen. Barnabas himself, so far as we hear, was a layman; so was Saul, till Christ made him an apostle. It was only by degrees and under the pressure of circumstances that even the rudiments of a Church system showed themselves. At first there was simply life—hardly more than life. The spirit was everything, the form nothing. The fact is, that the earliest work Christ's Church found to do, once it came to be full-grown, was to overthrow an ancient and venerable system of stereotyped usage and ritual. Its earliest martyr died because he taught that Jesus would abolish the temple and the customs of Moses. Its foremost chief was the man who set aside at his Master's bidding, along with the distinction of clean and unclean food, the deeper distinction between clean and unclean men. Its greatest convert spent his life in fighting for freedom from everything Jewish, even from circumcision. In the room of the stiffened prescriptions which it thus laboured to destroy, the Church set up no hard and fast system. Wherever disciples were, there was the Church. Each Christian's house constituted a place of worship. The most stereotyped or ritualistic act which it performed was the holding of a family meal with bread and wine. It is true that from the first there was order, for order is necessary to healthful life. Without order of some sort there could have been no discipline, and Ananias and Simon show that from the first discipline was indispensable. It is no less true that as the Church grew more independent of the synagogue and realised better its corporate unity, officers were multiplied, regulations were laid down, and a polity and an order of worship became inevitable. But the important point to note is this, that life came first, and forms only second. Life shaped forms for itself as it wanted them. The Church took its external mould under the slow pressure of providence. Through the inward impulse of Christ's Spirit it grew, as living things grow, freely, variously, everywhere. It did not come full-fledged, officered, accoutred, or organised, into the world.

So far indeed was the Church from being launched in its final or perfect shape, that it is extremely difficult to say at what point of its slow development it really became the Church at all. The *personnel* of a Church met in Jerusalem before Pentecost, but these hundred and twenty formed only the materials for a society—the Spirit had to enter the body. At Pentecost the new brotherhood received its Spirit, and it may be said the Church was born; yet it continued to worship in the temple and form an integral part of Judaism for years. The death of Stephen broke that spell and cut that bond, yet the scattered Hebrew believers remained as Hebrew as ever. A society from which every one but a Jew was shut out hardly deserved to be called in strict sense the Church of Christ. The reception of Cornelius settled the wide spiritual basis of the Church in principle indeed, yet it was not at once followed up by the apostles. In fact, it might be said that

CONCLUSIONS.

not till Jerusalem had welcomed Antioch, and Antioch greeted Jerusalem, was there really and truly a Church free of Mosaism or catholic for all men. Even after this point was reached, questions of organisation and legislation, about office-bearers, liturgy, discipline, and the like points of controversy, still slumbered among the unstirred difficulties of the future. So gradually did the Church become the Church.

There is nothing to be gained by childishly striving to mimic, even if we knew them, the earliest forms (or rather formlessness) of the Christian brotherhood in its inceptive and infantile period. Well-meaning but not over-wise enthusiasts for simplicity are every now and again striving to hark back upon what they call primitive models, and object to everything for which there is no written precedent in these scanty records of the primitive age. They do not appear to see that this is to fly in the face of the primitive spirit. The characteristic of the earliest believers was that they had no model, worked without precedent, and let rules arise as they were required. To make their ways therefore a rule or a precedent or a model for ourselves, is to do them the poor compliment of aping their acts in defiance of their spirit. Rash change of usages which are harmless, or an abandonment of those legitimate means for securing order and edification which the experience of the past has suggested, merely in the interests of what is termed "primitive simplicity," is not a course which commends itself to sober Christian wisdom. On the other hand, it must ever be maintained that the living Church of the present is not the slave of her own past. Where there is life, there must be movement and freedom. To bind upon the Christian Church an inelastic, immovable code of arrangements or formula of belief contrived by the Christians of some long past century, to forbid her to touch one of the traditions of the fathers, to legislate for every utterance, robe, and posture of her ministers by minute and express enactment, to tremble when Christian faith asks leave to utter itself to God through a new channel—in short, to confer upon each man-invented, man-imposed detail of worship, government, or usage, the consecration and the indestructible authority of a divine law, certainly seems to be a procedure out of all harmony with the opening pages of Christian history. It is to undo, as I conceive, what the infant Church did when it cast off the sheath of Mosaism. It is to put form above life, and law above spirit. It is to go back again to be in bondage to what Paul's robust, incisive, and masculine intellect, liberated by the Spirit of God, long ago branded as "beggarly elements."

The characteristic of the earliest Church, as we see it in these chapters, was life, fresh, intense, overflowing spiritual life. It was a sudden breath from heaven. The means by which so many human souls were unexpectedly and simultaneously moved was the most elementary gospel truth. It was only elementary truth which people seemed as yet to care for or need—the truth of God's mercy newly granted to men in the conscious forgiveness of sins through His slain but revived Son. This one truth, seizing candid hearts, inspired them. But the power which used this truth, bore it home to the conscience and affections, roused the dormant nature to recognise it, flooded the receptive soul with swift clear joy over it, and with a burning affection for its Saviour: this power was a personal one, a divine messenger, God the Holy Ghost. These were eminently days of the Spirit. Men lived intensely, because a Spirit worked in them mightily. His breath both set hearts on fire and kept them burning. The serene, confident courage of the first confessors, their insight into truth, their hopefulness, their close cleaving to one another, their superiority to fear or peril, their tender charity, their strong appeals to heaven and their certainty that God was with them, are all marks of a Spirit within man Who lifteth up man's fearful, craven, selfish spirit above itself, and inflameth him with a celestial fire. This Spirit disclosed no doubt within the secret haunts of the disciplehood endless tokens, sweet and memorable, of warm brother-love, of generosity, of mutual forgiveness, and of that self-forgetfulness in ministering to each other's wants which promised at one time actually to realise prematurely a voluntary Christian communism. To the outside world, however, the most striking feature about the new life in the Spirit was its contagious and aggressive enthusiasm. The brethren were like men who, in the first intoxication of a glorious discovery, ran telling it to all around. They were so sure of life and peace in Jesus that they bubbled over with it. To each one of them the message was so real, that, when they told it, they made men listen. It sounded like a true thing, it evidently was a great thing. The propulsive force of such enthusiasm carried Christ's mighty fame from man to man, from land to land. How else can we explain that, with absolutely no formal propagandism, within fourteen years from His death His worshippers were to be found from Cyprus to Damascus and from Abyssinia to the Orontes? If we may judge by the fragments of Peter's sermons preserved in Luke's narrative, the gospel preached during this period (as indeed for long after) was a very simple and naked message. No theological divergence could as yet appear in the Church, for as yet there was no theology. A theology arises after men have had time to reflect on their religious faith and to formulate it. The time for such reflection had not yet arrived. Preaching was, what it always is at its essence, a personal witness to facts connected with life in Jesus Christ. That He was sent of God, that He had died and was now alive, that He gave the Holy Ghost, that some men had been forgiven and saved by Him, that all men might be—this was the whole. The proof? It lived and spoke before you. Apostles and first disciples could speak to outward facts of Jesus' history; each believer could attest the inner fact of his own change. Indeed, such attestation was hardly needful. Men's altered lives, their new virtues, their beaming faces, their happy hymns—these spoke for them. It was a revival. That is to say, it was a wide-spread, sympathetic quickening of many men under a swift and pronounced movement of God upon their souls. Of all revivals, it was the first, the greatest, and the most typical. And this is the characteristic of all revivals—that the visible change effected, together with the spontaneous testimony of each changed soul, touches neighbour souls, and carries on the work of quickening as by a spiritual contagion.

Two leading elements blend in this enthusiasm of aggression—the one a faith in the living Saviour as having saved us, so vivid that it is usually joyful and sometimes jubilant; the other a godlike love for others who are yet unsaved, so overpowering that it compels the convert to

CONCLUSIONS.

speak. Search the popular literature of any genuine revival—say its hymn literature—and it will be found how prominent are these two moods, the joy of assured personal possession of Christ, and the burning insistence that others shall get it too. Both of these we find in the early records of the first age—the expulsive, self-expanding age—of the Church. They are genuinely apostolic. It is true that after such a time of rapid development there must follow, by spiritual laws, one of slow consolidation, the marks of which are theological reflection and practical upbuilding. It is also true that after both these stages there is ready to follow, by the laws of a *fallen* nature, a period of stagnation, formalism, and decadence, which may last longer than both the others put together. Still, whenever the Church is to be mightily and widely aggressive, her life must revert to the primitive type. These elementary graces of joyful assurance and passionate pity for sinners must be anew developed; her old style of personal testimony must be resumed; and quite as certainly, something of her early freedom, informality, directness, and unofficial activity will also reappear.

www.ingramcontent.com/pod-product-compliance
Lightning Source LLC
Chambersburg PA
CBHW051900300426
44117CB00006B/470